CHURCHES AND CATHEDRALS

Published
by
Moonrise Press, Ludlow 2014

All rights reserved
Copyright © David Phillips 2014

ISBN 978-1-910169-01-8

Printed in Great Britain

CHURCHES AND CATHEDRALS

David Phillips

ACKNOWLEDGEMENTS

I should like to thank most gratefully these people and institutions who have helped me with information and advice:

Beverley Minster (Christine Bull, parish secretary, and Neil Pickford, duty virger)
The British Horological Institute
Peter Collins, of Peter Collins Ltd
Michael Counahan
Dromore Cathedral, Co Down (the Dean)
Ironbridge Gorge Museums (John Powell, Librarian and Information Officer)
Lichfield Cathedral (Sue Johnson, receptionist, Chris Craddock, head verger, and Simon Ferguson, verger)
Jamie Bruce Lockhart
Andrew Mottram
Northamptonshire Records Society
Peel Cathedral (Val Garrett, PA to the Dean)
St Margaret's Cathedral, Ayr (Frances Campbell, Admin Assistant to the Diocese of Galloway)
St Mary's, Ilminster, Som (Lesley Lusby, Secretary)
St Mary's, Painswick, Glos (Revd John Longuet-Higgins, vicar, David Bishop, churchwarden, and Douglas Robinson, clock keeper)
Jerry Sampson
Southwell Minster, Notts (Caroline Jarvis, chapter clerk, and David Turner, head steward)
Catherine Ware
Jane Wood
Worcester Porcelain Museum (Wendy Cook, Curator).

Many thanks to Sally Bruce-Lockhart, Mary Phillips, Stephen Porter, Jerry Sampson, and Alma and John Siret who took some of the photographs for me, and to the Dean and Chapter of Canterbury Cathedral, and the Vicar and Churchwardens of Beverley Minster, who kindly gave me permission to use my photographs of the Cathedral and of the Minster respectively in this book.

CONTENTS

The rise and fall of church buildings	1
The church hierarchy	6
Laymen and laywomen	11
The cathedrals	13
Church buildings	20
Other religious buildings	50
Architects and master craftsmen	53
Church furnishings	85
Stained glass	112
Floor tiles	131
Church plate	136
Scratchdials and sundials	139
Clocks	142
Churchyards	149
Music and singing	161
The organ	165
Libraries	175
Bells	179
Symbols of the apostles	185
Calendar and colours	186
Crosses	188
Five pagan symbols?	189
Largest, smallest, tallest, shortest	193
County abbreviations	196
Styles and periods	197
Short bibliography	198
Main index	201
Index of personal names	211
Index of churches	219

THE RISE AND FALL OF CHURCH BUILDINGS

Christianity arrived in Britain sometime in the second century, during the Roman occupation (43–406). The earliest written evidence is a passage in Tertullian (c.160–c.220), himself a Carthaginian Christian, in which he refers to the Britons as 'subjugated to Christ' (c.200, chapter 7 of *Adversus Judeos*). The earliest archaeological evidence is around a hundred years later, in the form of the remains of timber churches at Lincoln and Silchester, Hants, and fonts at Icklingham, Suffolk and Richborough, Kent. In Wales, Christianity arrived around 350; later in Ireland (traditionally brought by St Patrick in 461); and in Scotland in the fifth century. At the Council of Arles in 314 there were already three dioceses in Britain, at York, London, and Lincoln. There may have also been one at Cirencester, dating from slightly later.

In 406, Rome abandoned Britain. The Angles, Saxons and Jutes invaded, heathen kingdoms rose and fell, the Vikings raided and colonised, but Christianity continued, especially in Northumberland, Ireland, Wales and Scotland. In 597, St Augustine's mission arrived in Kent, and by the seventh century Britain was mostly Christian. Benedictine monasteries began to be established in the sixth century, Cluniac in the eleventh, and Carthusian and Cistercian in the twelfth.

The oldest churches still in use in England are: St Martin's, Canterbury, Kent (597); All Saints', Brixworth, Northants (650); St-Peter-on-the-Wall, Bradwell-on-Sea, Essex (654); St John's, Escomb, Durham (670); and St Laurence's, Bradford-on-Avon, Wilts (seventh century). Llanrhychwyn Church, Trefriw, Conwy, claims to be the oldest in Wales (sixth century); in Ireland, St Brendan's Cathedral, Clonfert, South Galway (sixth century), and the oldest in Scotland may be St Margaret's Chapel, Edinburgh Castle (c.1120).

Most churches were built, and are still built, with the altar at the east end and the entrance at the southwest corner. But some were not, because the site was constricted or for some other reason. The altar ('liturgical east') is at the south at, for example, St Mary Magdalene's, Bridgnorth, Salop, and at the north at St Michael's, Bath, Som, St Martin's, Brighton, Sussex, Coventry Cathedral, W Mid, and Salford Cathedral, Manchester.

Some ten thousand mediaeval churches still survive. But in the fourteenth century a series of disasters occurred, ending the unprecedented period of growth that had started around 1050. The weather changed: the Mediaeval Warm Period was succeeded by the Little Ice Age. Between 1310 and 1330 northern Europe saw the worst period of bad weather in the Middle

Ages. Bad weather and crop failures brought about the Great Famine (1315–17) over the whole of northern Europe, killing perhaps 10% of the population. Just over thirty years later, the Black Death (1348–50) is estimated to have killed an additional 1.3 million in Britain and 25 million in Europe.

Together, famine and disease reduced the population of the British Isles by 50% to about three million. Many towns and villages were abandoned, never to be reoccupied, and it took over three hundred years for the population to return to its previous level.

The impact of this decrease in population on church building was odd. On the one hand, constant preoccupation with death resulted in a compulsion for building new churches and improving old ones, and some of the finest churches in the United Kingdom were the result. On the other hand, religion as it was practised had conspicuously failed to avert these crises, and this led to the feeling that something must be wrong.

By the beginning of the sixteenth century, in the eyes of many, especially in northern Europe, the church was seen as corrupt, self-indulgent and materialistic, and desperately in need of reform. In 1517 Luther nailed his ninety-five theses to the door of the Schlosskirche at Wittenberg. It is in this context that Henry VIII's Dissolution of the Monasteries (1536–40) should be seen, although Henry did have strong financial, political and personal reasons too. During these five years, all monasteries in England and Wales were closed and most of their buildings and contents either destroyed or sold off. Nearly ninety of their churches became parish churches and, in five cases, they became cathedrals (Bristol, Chester, Ches, Gloucester, Christ Church, Oxford and Peterborough, Cambs). Westminster

Statues beheaded at Lincoln Cathedral   The ruins of York Abbey

Abbey was also made a cathedral in 1540, but its cathedral status was withdrawn in 1550. Between 1545 and 1547, most collegiate churches and chantries were also closed. In Scotland, largely under the influence of John Knox and his followers, all monasteries were closed by the Act of Annexation in 1587, which handed over to James VI all monastic estates and their contents.

Throughout the sixteenth century, Puritanism steadily gained ground, coming to fruition in the brief period of the Commonwealth (1645–60) when most church buildings and their remaining contents were vandalised. Most (in Scotland, almost all) of the remaining stained glass was smashed, wall paintings were destroyed or whitewashed over, statues were torn down or beheaded, monuments defaced, roods and rood screens were broken down, and bells and organs were removed or destroyed.

Very few churches were built during the Commonwealth. Although the exact number is disputed, there is general agreement about five: Holy Trinity and St Mary's, Berwick upon Tweed, Northumb (1650–2); Holy Trinity, Staunton Harold, Leics (1653); St Matthias Old Church, Tower Hamlets, London (1652–5, made redundant 1977); St Barnabas's, Brampton Bryan, Herefs (1656); and St Ninian's, Ninekirks, Cumbria (1659). Other contenders are Bramhope Chapel, W Yorks (1649, now redundant); Plaxtol Parish Church, Kent (1649); St Michael and All Angels, Great Houghton, S Yorks (about 1650, originally a chapel); St John's, Stokesay, Salop (1654); and Charles Church, Plymouth, Devon (1657). They had no chancels, altars, towers, organs or bells.

Within six years of the Restoration of Charles II, the Great Fire of London (1666) destroyed St Paul's Cathedral and eighty-seven parish churches, as well as 13,500 houses, forty-four Company halls, the Royal Exchange, the Custom House, the General Letter Office, several prisons, and the three western city gates, Ludgate, Newgate and Aldersgate. It was a disaster, but it also presented an opportunity, which was in some ways not taken advantage of. Despite plans for rebuilding submitted by, among others, Sir Christopher Wren and John Evelyn, the City was laid out on much the same lines as before the fire. All new buildings, however, had to be built of brick or stone, there were to be no projections over the streets, and minimum street widths were specified. By 1672, nearly all the rebuilding of houses and the Company halls was finished. St Paul's Cathedral and fifty-one churches replaced the eighty-seven lost, and Sir Christopher Wren was commissioned to design all of them. Only twenty-four now survive, due to the combined effect of the Union of Benefices Act of 1860, which reduced the number of parish churches in the City of London as the residential population declined (ten of Wren's churches were demolished between 1868 and 1897), road improvements (eight demolished between 1781 and 1904), bombing in the Second World War (seven lost in 1940), and relocation (one in 1937 to Twickenham and one in 1966 to Westminster College, Fulton, Missouri).

Three years after the consecration of St Paul's Cathedral, the New Churches in London and Westminster Act was passed (1711). This was intended to provide London, which was continuing to expand, with more churches, and to counteract nonconformism. The Act funded the construction of twelve churches: Christ Church, Spitalfields (1729); St Alfege's, Greenwich (1718); St Anne's, Limehouse (1730); St George's, Bloomsbury (1731); and St George's in the East (1729), all by

Hawksmoor; St John Horsleydown (1733); St Luke's, Old Street (1733), both by Hawksmoor and John James; St George's, Hanover Square (1725) by James; St John's, Smith Square (1728); St Paul's, Deptford (1730), both by Archer; St Mary-le-Strand (1717) by James Gibbs. A further five were part-funded (St George's, Gravesend, Kent; St George the Martyr, Southwark; St Giles in the Fields; St Mary Magdalene's, Woolwich; and St Michael, Cornhill) and two were purchased (St George the Martyr, Holborn, and St John's, Clerkenwell).

The closing years of the eighteenth century and especially the nineteenth saw the most explosive period of church and chapel building since the Middle Ages. During this century there was a massive increase in population and, simultaneously, a radical shift from country-dwelling to town-dwelling. From 1800 to 1900 the population grew fivefold, from eight million to forty million. In 1750 about 15% of the population lived in towns, by 1850 it was around 50%, and by 1880 it had risen to 80%. Churches in the country were increasingly semi-deserted and there were hardly any churches in the new towns.

To counteract this, the Church Building Acts (1818 and 1824) established the Church Building Commission (which was absorbed within the Ecclesiastical Commission in 1857) and provided one million pounds to build churches in areas without them. Six hundred churches were built. These were known as Commissioners' churches, or Waterloo churches (after the recent victory), or Million Act churches, after the initial grant.

The Incorporated Church Building Society (ICBS) was founded in 1818 to provide funds for the building and enlargement of Anglican churches throughout England and Wales. By 1845, it was helping with the building of fifty churches a year. In 1982 the administration of ICBS was transferred to the Historic Churches Preservation Trust, which still gives grants for church buildings. The archives of the ICBS, running from 1818 to 1982, was deposited in Lambeth Palace Library. It contains over 12,500 church plans and is accessible on-line.

In Scotland, a commission was set up in 1823 which recommended the construction of forty-three churches – the Parliamentary Churches – with a manse for each, in the Highlands and Islands in communities without any church buildings. The total cost was not to exceed £1,500 on any site. Thomas Telford was commissioned to undertake the design. Thirty-two churches were eventually built, nineteen in the Highlands, of which sixteen survive, and thirteen in the Islands. Eleven existing churches were renovated.

There were no Church of England cathedrals created between the 1540s, when Henry VIII turned five abbey churches into cathedrals, and 1836, when Ripon was made a cathedral. But in the rest of the nineteenth century seven cathedrals were created, and, between 1900 and 1914, seven more.

Nonconformism continued to spread. The United Kingdom census of 1851 revealed that there were almost as many nonconformists as Anglicans. It is impossible even to guess how many new and converted (from other uses) chapels and meeting houses were built between 1800 and 1900.

The Roman Catholic Relief Act was passed in 1829, which gave emancipation to all Catholics in Britain. This did not in itself lead to great numbers of new Catholic churches being built, but the Great Famine in Ireland (1845–9) did. Large numbers of impoverished Irish emigrants landed in south Wales, Liverpool and

Glasgow, perhaps more than emigrated to the New World. In 1850 Pope Pius IX established Catholic hierarchies in England and Wales to provide spiritual leadership to the hundreds of thousands of newcomers. In 1878 Pope Leo XIII did the same for Scotland. Between 1850 and 1900, approximately 3,000 Catholic churches were built. The first Catholic cathedral (St Chad's in Birmingham, W Mid) was built by A W N Pugin in 1839.

It couldn't last. Since the First World War, the tide has turned increasingly and inexorably in the other direction. The accelerating decline in church going has inevitably led to mass closures of places of worship. The number of Methodist chapels, for example, has decreased from about 14,000 in the second half of the nineteenth century to 6,000 today. Currently, about 150 places of worship close each year. Hence arises the closure of churches and chapels which are near together, the amalgamation of parishes, the formation of team ministries, and the general half-emptiness of churches. At present, for example, Dudley, W Mid, has accommodation for 5,000 people in its seven Anglican churches, none of which is financially viable, but on an average Sunday is lucky to see a total of 300 churchgoers.

The Anglican church closes some fifty or sixty churches a year. Closures are looked after by the Closed Churches Division in the Church of England, the Representative Body in the Church in Wales, the General Trustees in the Church of Scotland and the Legal Department in the Church of Ireland. In the Roman Catholic Church, closing a church is the responsibility of the bishop. In the nonconformist movement, about a hundred churches and chapels close a year: responsibility for closures varies with the church.

For all those responsible for closed churches and chapels, demolition is the last resort. Some, but very few (most of them listed), are handed to trusts to look after. At present, the Churches Conservation Trust looks after some 340 churches in England; the Friends of Friendless Churches owns some forty-five in England and Wales; the Scottish Redundant Churches Trust, five; the Welsh Religious Buildings Trust, three; and the Historic Chapels Trust, twenty in England. There appears to be no similar trust for redundant churches and chapels in Northern Ireland.

For the rest, some are ultimately demolished, and some bought by other religious faiths. Many are sold for residential accommodation or converted for use as stores, or as community, education, festival or heritage centres, or as art galleries, coffee shops, or clubs.

THE CHURCH HIERARCHY

The Anglican Church

Structure
In the Church of England, the hierarchy consists of:
  Archbishop of Canterbury: Primate of All England and responsible for the Province of Canterbury
  Archbishop of York: Primate of England and responsible for the Province of York
  Bishop, responsible for a diocese
  Suffragan or Assistant Bishop, assistant to the bishop
  Archdeacon, responsible for an archdeaconry
  Rural Dean, responsible for a deanery
  Rector, vicar or priest in charge, responsible for a parish
  Curate, assistant to the rector

These are all stipendiary posts: the holders receive payment – a stipend – for their work. There are also members of the non-stipendiary ministry who are ordained priests, but do not receive any payment for their services. They usually have secular jobs or pensions.

The structure of the Church in Wales, the Scottish Episcopal Church and the Church of Ireland is the same, except that the Church in Wales and the Scottish Episcopal Church have only one archbishop, and so the distinction between primacies does not exist. In the Church of Ireland, which covers the whole island, the Archbishop of Armagh is Primate of All Ireland and the Archbishop of Dublin Primate of Ireland.

Archbishops. In the Church of England, archbishops are appointed by the Prime Minister; in the Church in Wales and in the Scottish Episcopal Church by the bishops. In the Church of Ireland the Archbishop of Armagh is appointed by the House of Bishops, and the Archbishop of Dublin is appointed by an elected Episcopal Electoral College consisting of clerical and lay members.

The Anglican archbishops in the United Kingdom and Ireland are Canterbury, York, Wales, the Primus of the Scottish Episcopal Church, Armagh, and Dublin.

Bishops. In the Church of England, bishops are effectively appointed by the Prime Minister, following the recommendations of the Crown Nominations Commission. In the Church in Wales, they are elected by an electoral college consisting of representatives of the diocese in which the vacancy occurs, representatives of the other dioceses in Wales, and all bishops of the Church in Wales. In the Scottish Episcopal Church, they are appointed by an electoral synod of the vacant bishopric with clerical and lay members. In the Church of Ireland they are appointed by an elected

Episcopal Electoral College with clerical and lay members.

The dioceses in the United Kingdom and Ireland are:

Province of Canterbury: Bath and Wells; Birmingham; Chelmsford; Chichester; Coventry; Derby; Ely; Exeter; Gibraltar in Europe (the cathedral is in Gibraltar); Gloucester; Guildford; Hereford; Leicester; Lichfield; Lincoln; London; Norwich; Oxford; Peterborough; Portsmouth; Rochester; Salisbury; Southwark; St Albans; St Edmundsbury and Ipswich; Truro; Winchester; Worcester.

Province of York: Blackburn; Carlisle; Chester; Durham; Liverpool; Manchester; Newcastle; Sheffield; Sodor and Man; Southwell and Nottingham; West Yorkshire and the Dales.

Church in Wales: Bangor; Llandaff; Monmouth; St Asaph; St Davids; Swansea and Brecon.

Scottish Episcopal Church: Aberdeen and Orkney; Argyll and the Isles; Brechin; Edinburgh; Glasgow and Galloway; Moray; Ross and Caithness; St Andrews, Dunkeld and Dunblane.

Province of Armagh: Clogher; Connor; Derry and Raphoe; Down and Dromore; Kilmore, Elphin and Ardagh; Tuam, Killala and Achonry.

Province of Dublin: Cashel and Ossory; Cork, Cloyne and Ross; Dublin and Glendalough; Limerick, Killaloe and Ardfert; Meath and Kildare.

Suffragan or assistant bishop. An assistant to the diocesan bishop, sometimes named after the area he is responsible for. The Scottish Episcopal Church has no suffragan bishops at present. The Church of Ireland has no suffragan bishops.

Archdeacon. The archdeaconry is the largest subdivision of the diocese and the archdeacon is appointed by the bishop. Archdeacons do not exist in the Scottish Episcopal Church.

Rural dean, area dean, regional dean. An archdeaconry is made up of several deaneries. A rural dean is appointed by the bishop and is responsible for each deanery, consisting of several parishes, and normally the incumbent of one of them. He is assisted by the deanery synod, a lay body the members of which are elected by the parishes.

Rector, vicar. The priest responsible for a parish, appointed as a cooperative exercise by the patron (who may be an individual or an institution), the Parochial Church Council and the bishop. Strictly, a rector is an incumbent who used to receive both Greater Tithes (levied on harvests and stock) and Lesser Tithes (levied on labour and minor produce), until they were abolished in 1936, and in return was responsible for the upkeep of the chancel and providing the service books and vestments. A vicar only received the Lesser Tithes. Today, the terms are sometimes a matter of custom. In the Church of Ireland and the Scottish Episcopal Church, most parish priests are rectors. In England, sometimes 'rector' refers to the leader of a team ministry (an amalgamation of parishes with more than one church which is run by a team of clergy) and 'vicar' refers to a member of his team.

Priest in charge. A priest in charge of a parish is not nominated by a patron but appointed by the bishop, and holds a licence rather than the freehold of the church. (Having freehold means that the priest cannot be removed from office except in extreme circumstances). Priests in charge give bishops greater control over the disposition of clergy and so are increasingly used. Legally, priests in charge are temporary curates, though they receive the same stipend as vicars. In the Church of Ireland, priests in charge are called bishop's curates.

Curate. Assistant to the parish priest and appointed by him or her, unless the parish priest is a priest in charge, in which case the curate is appointed by the bishop.

Perpetual Curate. A priest nominated by a lay rector (lay rectors have a legal responsibility for meeting the cost of repairs to the chancel) and licensed by the bishop to serve a parish that has no vicar or rector.

Deacon, deaconess. A person generally serves for a year as a deacon or deaconess before becoming a priest, during which time he or she assists the curate.

Cathedrals

Cathedrals have their own hierarchies, independent of the 'mainstream' structure.

The Dean is the chief residential cleric of a cathedral. Deans are appointed by the Prime Minister in the Church of England. In the Church in Wales, the Scottish Episcopal Church (where deans are called provosts) and the Church of Ireland, deans are appointed by the bishop, or in some cases by the archbishop. The Sub-dean (Church of England and Church of Ireland only) is deputy to the dean and appointed by him.

The Dean is also the head of the cathedral chapter, the governing body of the cathedral. The chapter consists of the Dean, usually the archdeacon of the 'home' archdeaconry, and a number of canons, both clergy and lay, appointed by the Queen, following the recommendations of the Crown Nominations Commission, or by the Bishop. In some cathedrals, canons are called prebendaries; in others, a prebendary is a lay canon; in still others, a prebendary is a retired canon. Minor canons are junior clergy who are on the cathedral staff but are not members of chapter, and are appointed by the chapter. One of the canons (or minor canons, as at Canterbury Cathedral) may be the precentor (in charge of liturgy and worship) and he may have a second-in-command, as at St Paul's Cathedral and Durham Cathedral, called a succentor. The succentor is usually a minor canon.

The Roman Catholic Church

The hierarchy of the Roman Catholic church is very similar to the Anglican hierarchy, which is not surprising since the Anglican hierarchy derived directly from the Roman Catholic, but more complicated, since the Roman Catholic church has been around much longer. The Catholic church, like the Church in Ireland, treats Ireland as a whole. Only one of the four provinces, Armagh, is mostly in Northern Ireland. (The others are Cashel, Dublin and Tuam).

There are seven Roman Catholic provinces and archbishops in mainland Britain: Birmingham, Cardiff, Glasgow, Liverpool, Saint Andrews and Edinburgh, Southwark, and Westminster. The Archbishop of Westminster is the *de facto* Primate of England and Wales. There is one archbishop in Northern Ireland, Armagh. Archbishops are appointed by the Vatican.

Bishops and dioceses

There are nineteen dioceses in England, three in Wales, eight in Scotland and eight in Northern Ireland, five of them straddling the Republic/Northern Ireland border. In addition there is the Bishopric of the Forces, The Personal Ordinariate of Our Lady of Walsingham, and the Apostolic Exarchate for Ukrainians: these three come directly under the Holy See.

Bishops are appointed by the Congregation of Bishops in the Vatican, which takes local soundings, e.g. from the Irish Episcopal Conference (a standing committee of archbishops and bishops in Ireland and Northern Ireland).

Dioceses in England: Arundel and Brighton, Birmingham, Brentwood, Clifton, East Anglia, Hallam, Hexham and Newcastle, Lancaster, Leeds, Liverpool, Middlesbrough, Northampton, Nottingham, Plymouth, Portsmouth, Salford, Shrewsbury, Southwark, Westminster. In Wales: Cardiff, Menevia, Wrexham. In Scotland: Aberdeen, Argyll and the Isles, Dunkeld, Galloway, Glasgow, Motherwell, Paisley, St Andrews and Edinburgh. In Northern Ireland: Armagh, Clogher, Derry, Down and Connor, Dromore, Kilmore. (The other dioceses of the province of Armagh – Ardagh and Clonmacnoise, Meath, Raphoe – are wholly within the Republic).

The diocesan bishop may be assisted by a titular bishop who might be a coadjutor bishop, auxiliary bishop, emeritus bishop (and there are several more titles), who equates roughly with a suffragan or assistant bishop in the Anglican church.

The bishop is also assisted by a College of Consultors or Chapter. Unlike the Anglican chapter, the Roman Catholic chapter is not a cathedral body, but a diocesan one.

There are no archdeacons or archdeaconries in the Roman Catholic church. The administrative duties are mostly carried out by the Vicar-general, the bishop's chief assistant, whom the bishop himself appoints.

Parishes are grouped into deaneries, supervised by a dean or vicar forane, who is normally the most senior parish priest. The parish is led by a pastor or parish priest. The archbishop or bishop appoints the vicar forane and the parish priests.

A transitional deacon is a man who (usually) has completed his third year at a seminary and intends to become ordained as a priest, normally about six months after being ordained deacon. A permanent deacon is a man who does not intend to become a priest and therefore may be married. Deacons can preach, perform baptisms and witness marriages. They can assist at Mass but cannot celebrate it. All deacons are appointed by the bishop.

A cathedral is led by an administrator or cathedral dean, appointed by the archbishop or bishop in whose diocese it lies. The administrator is sometimes supported by a sub-dean.

Other Denominations

Most other churches were started in order to purify worship, so it is not surprising that few, if any, have elaborate hierarchies.

Quakers have no hierarchy at all. They have no ministers, but only elders elected by each congregation for three years.

For Baptists, each church is self-governing, and those that have been baptised appoint their own minister, elders and deacons, agree financial policy and determine mission strategy. Most Baptist churches belong to the Baptist Union, which is not a governing body, but simply a resource for assisting churches.

In Presbyterianism, each congregation is governed by elected elders sitting in 'session' (sometimes called a consistory or church board). The elders are of two kinds: the teaching elder (or pastor, or minister), responsible for worship and preaching, and the ruling elders, responsible for governance. The teaching elder normally presides over session meetings, but often has no vote other than a casting vote. The next level up is the presbytery, which meets sometimes monthly, sometimes quarterly, sometimes half-yearly. Presbyteries are made up of the minister and an elder chosen from each parish, and other clergy such as theological college professors, chaplains, and retired ministers. The presbytery is presided over by an elected moderator, who also has no vote other than a casting vote. At the highest level, each presbytery is represented on the General Assembly, which meets usually once a year, and once again has an elected moderator. Synods, which used to be an intermediary stage between presbytery and General Assembly, were abolished in the 1990s.

The United Reformed Church (a union of English Presbyterian and English and Scottish Congregationalist churches) has, as one might expect, similarities with Presbyterianism. Each church has a group of elected elders having day-to-day responsibility for the church's affairs. Each church is represented in synod, of which there are thirteen (one each for Scotland and Wales and eleven for England). Each synod has its own synod moderators and staff. A General Assembly meets twice a year and makes policy decisions. The Assembly is led by two moderators (one minister, one layman), elected by the Assembly and serving for two years. A permanent staff, led by the General Secretary, services the Assembly.

Methodism is the closest to Anglicanism. John Wesley was a Church of England clergyman, and he himself said 'I live and die a member of the Church of England'. Each church has its minister (though ministers are appointed to the circuit, not the individual church) and its church council. Groups of churches in the same area form a circuit (there are over 600 circuits in the United Kingdom), each of which has a superintendent minister. Groups of circuits form a district, each of which has a chairman and a district synod. There are thirty-three districts in Britain. The Church is governed by the Methodist Conference which meets once a year. The Conference is presided over by a President, a Methodist minister, and a Vice President, who may be a layman. Both of these appointments are made annually.

The sole remaining consistory courtroom, ? fifteenth century, in Chester Cathedral, Ches. The furniture is c.1630, though the table may be older

LAYMEN AND LAYWOMEN

These posts relate to the Anglican church, though some exist in other denominations too.

Canon chancellor. In Anglican cathedrals, the Canon Chancellor, who may be be a lay person, looks after education and sometimes the library. In the Roman Catholic church, he is the diocesan archivist, notary and manager of administration (and sometimes finances and personnel). Not be confused with the Diocesan Chancellor.

Chancellor, Diocesan Chancellor. The judge in a diocesan church court (see Consistory court) and the lawyer who represents the diocese in legal matters. He must be a barrister of seven years standing and is appointed by the crown.

Churchwarden. Each church has two lay churchwardens, elected, usually annually, by the Parochial Church Council and serving voluntarily. Their duties vary from parish to parish, but usually they are responsible for keeping good order in the church and the churchyard, for looking after the fabric of the church, and keeping an inventory of the church's valuables. The bishop tends to consult them before appointing a new incumbent.

Consistory court. The ecclesiastical court presided over by the chancellor of the diocese. Its powers were once considerable, but nowadays it only meets to give faculties (permissions) dealing with church property and churchyards; and, rarely, to hear the trial of clergy below the rank of bishop accused of immoral acts or misconduct. The court can meet wherever is most convenient, though once every cathedral had a courtroom. The courtroom at Chester Cathedral still survives.

Diocesan Advisory Committee for the care of churches (DAC). The committee of clerical and lay experts which advises parishes on church buildings and furnishings. The members are in theory appointed by the bishop, but in effect are appointed by co-option, with the bishop rubber-stamping the appointment.

Electors, electoral roll. The parish church's register of electors. They are qualified to attend the annual Parochial Church Meeting and elect the Parochial Church Council and the parish's representatives on the deanery synod. The electoral roll is renewed every six years: all members must make a new application.

Lay rector. With the Dissolution of the Monasteries (1536–40), most monastic estates were sold. If the estate had a rectorial benefice (i.e. the right to appoint vicars), the new owner, the lay rector, acquired the right to appoint vicars to the parish with the approval of the bishop, to receive rectorial tithes, and had the responsibility for meeting the cost of maintaining the church chancel. (Maintaining the nave was the responsibility of the laity). Although tithes were abolished in 1936, many old ex-church buildings still carry with them the duty of maintaining the chancel.

Parish Clerk. In the past, an office of considerable power. He was appointed by the incumbent and was his second in command, assisting in the services, leading the singing and responses, and writing up the parish registers. Acts of Parliament of 1844 and 1894 left them with no responsibilities.

Parochial Church Council (PCC). Consists of the parish priest as chairman, the two churchwardens, and members elected by the members of the church electoral roll. A lay member is vice-chairman. The PCC works with the incumbent to run the parish and is responsible for the church finances, the fabric of the church and the appointment to several posts (such as treasurer and sidepersons).

Patron. The person or institution who has the right of nomination to a benefice.

Reader. A lay person, usually a volunteer, who is trained and licensed to take services, preach and generally assist in the work of the parish.

Registrar, diocesan registrar. A solicitor, usually in private practice, who acts as the bishop's legal secretary and the consistory court's registrar. He is appointed by the bishop.

Sacristan. The person who used to be responsible for the security of the sacristy or vestry and the valuables and vestments it contained.

Server. Assistant to the priest during services, especially Holy Communion.

Sexton. The sexton used to be a salaried assistant to the parish clerk who carried out duties around the church and churchyard such as bell ringing and grave digging. Nowadays, the sexton is appointed by the incumbent and the Parochial Church Council, who also set his terms of appointment.

Sidesmen, sidesperson, usher. Generally responsible for greeting the congregation, overseeing seating in church and for taking the collection. They are usually appointed by the Parochial Church Council and receive guidance in their duties from the churchwardens.

Synod. An ecclesiastical governing assembly which generally has clerical and lay members. The Church of England has three, apart from the parochial church councils: the deanery synod, consisting of all the clergy within a deanery, and lay members elected by the parochial church councils; the diocesan synod, consisting of the bishop, the suffragan and area bishops, and clergy and lay members elected by the deanery synods; and the General Synod. The General Synod has 467 members at present and comprises three Houses: the House of Bishops (forty-four bishops (including the Bishop of Europe), the Bishop of Dover, who is the suffragan bishop of the diocese of Canterbury, and seven other suffragan bishops elected by the suffragan bishops themselves); the House of Clergy (excluding bishops, and with its members elected, appointed and co-opted); and the House of Laity (elected by the deanery synods).

Verger. Layman who is, in effect, the caretaker of a church. He also precedes the clergy in processing in and out of the church.

Vestry clerk. Officer who used to be responsible for organising vestry meetings and keeping the minutes.

THE CATHEDRALS

Anglican and Roman Catholic cathedrals in the United Kingdom are listed here. There are more; England has at least twenty cathedrals of other persuasions, mostly in London, and Scotland one. Wales and Northern Ireland have only Anglican and Roman Catholic cathedrals.

The older cathedrals are often the third, fourth or fifth building on the site. The date given as the foundation date is the date, sometimes approximate, when the present building was begun.

The architects are the architects most significantly connected with building or altering the cathedrals. In many cases, usually with the mediaeval buildings, details are sparse, if not non-existent. For example, for Leicester Cathedral, built 1086, and Chelmsford Cathedral, built c.1400, we have no records of master craftsmen or architects until Raphael Brandon (1817–77) and John Johnson (1732–1814) respectively, both took a hand in the nineteenth century. The architects named here are all mentioned in the Architects and master craftsmen section except where their names appear in italics. A question mark next to a name means that the architect probably contributed to the building, but not certainly.

Anglican Cathedrals

England: the Church of England			
Province of Canterbury			
Location	Dedication	Date present building founded and architect(s), if known	Made a cathedral
Birmingham	St Philip	1715. Thomas Archer	1905
Bristol	Holy and Undivided Trinity	1220. Adam Lock? G E Street, J L Pearson	1542
Bury St Edmunds	St James	1503. Thomas Mapilton, John Wastell, Sir Gilbert Scott, Stephen Dykes Bower	1914

CHURCHES AND CATHEDRALS

Canterbury	Metropolitan Church of Christ	1070. William of Sens, William the Englishman, Michael of Canterbury, Richard Beke, Henry Yevele, Thomas Mapilton, John Wastell, Sir Gilbert Scott	built as a cathedral
Chelmsford	St Mary the Virgin, St Peter (1954) and St Cedd (1954)	c.1400. *John Johnson,* Stephen Dykes Bower	1913
Chichester	Holy Trinity	1075. William the Englishman? William Wynford, Sir Gilbert Scott	built as a cathedral
Coventry	St Michael	1956. Sir Basil Spence	built as a cathedral
Derby	All Saints	1725. James Gibbs	1927
Ely	Holy and Undivided Trinity	1083. Alan of Walsingham, William Hurley, Sir Gilbert Scott	built as a cathedral
Exeter	St Peter	1133. Thomas of Witney, William Joy, Richard of Farleigh, Sir Gilbert Scott, J L Pearson	built as a cathedral
Gloucester	St Peter and the Holy and Indivisible Trinity	1089. Thomas de Cambridge? Sir Robert Smirke, Sir Gilbert Scott	1541
Guildford	Holy Spirit	1936. Sir Edward Maufe	built as a cathedral
Hereford	Blessed Virgin Mary and St Ethelbert	1110. Thomas de Cambridge, James Wyatt, Lewis Nockalls Cottingham, Sir Gilbert Scott, Oldrid Scott	built as a cathedral
Leicester	St Martin	1086. *Raphael Brandon*, G E Street, J L Pearson	1927
Lichfield	Blessed Virgin Mary and St Chad	1195. Henry Yevele? James Wyatt, Sir Gilbert Scott	built as a cathedral
Lincoln	Blessed Virgin Mary	1185. Alexander the Mason, Ivo de Raghton? Sir Christopher Wren, James Gibbs	built as a cathedral
London	St Paul	1675-1708. Sir Christopher Wren	built as a cathedral
Norwich	Holy and Undivided Trinity	1096. William de Ramsey, Robert Everard, Anthony Salvin	built as a cathedral
Oxford	Christ Church	1160. William Orchard, Sir Gilbert Scott	1546
Peterborough	St Peter, St Paul, St Andrew	1118. John Wastell, Sir Gilbert Scott, J L Pearson	1541
Portsmouth	St Thomas of Canterbury	1180	1927
Rochester	Christ and the Blessed Virgin Mary	1080. Lewis Nockalls Cottingham, Sir Gilbert Scott, J L Pearson	built as a cathedral

Lincoln Cathedral

York Minster

St Davids Cathedral, Pembs

St Albans	St Alban	1077. Robert the Mason, Henry Yevele? Lewis Nockalls Cottingham, Sir Gilbert Scott, Lord Grimthorpe, Oldrid Scott	1877
Salisbury	Blessed Virgin Mary	1220. *Elias of Dereham*, Richard of Farleigh, Sir Christopher Wren, James Wyatt, Sir Gilbert Scott	built as a cathedral
Southwark	St Saviour and St Mary Overie	1220. George Gwilt, Sir Arthur Blomfield,	1905
Truro	Blessed Virgin Mary	1880. J L Pearson, Frank Pearson	built as a cathedral
Wells	St Andrew	1175. Adam Lock, *Elias of Dereham*? Thomas Norreys, Thomas of Witney? William Joy, William Wynford, William Smyth, Anthony Salvin	built as a cathedral
Winchester	Holy Trinity, St Peter, St Paul and St Swithun	1079. Thomas of Witney, William Wynford, Sir Gilbert Scott, Sir T G Jackson	built as a cathedral
Worcester	Christ and the Blessed Virgin Mary	1170. John Clyve, Sir Gilbert Scott	built as a cathedral
Province of York			
Blackburn	St Mary the Virgin	1826. John Palmer, Thomas Rickman	1926
Bradford	St Peter	c.1400. Sir Edward Maufe	1919
Carlisle	Holy and Undivided Trinity	1123. Ivo de Raghton? Ewan Christian	1133
Chester	Christ and the Blessed Virgin Mary	1283. Sir Gilbert Scott	1541
Durham	Christ, the Blessed Virgin Mary and St Cuthbert	1093. Henry Yevele? Thomas Mapilton, Christopher Scune, James Wyatt, Sir Gllbert Scott, Anthony Salvin	built as a cathedral
Liverpool	Christ and the Blessed Virgin	1904. Giles Gilbert Scott	built as a cathedral
Manchester	St Mary, St Denys and St George	c.1490. John Wastell? Sir Gilbert Scott, J S Crowther	1847
Newcastle	St Nicholas	1359. Sir Gilbert Scott	1882
Peel	St German	1879-84. *Thomas Barry & Son*	1980
Ripon	St Peter and St Wilfrid	1160. Christopher Scune, Sir Gilbert Scott	1836
Sheffield	St Peter and St Paul	c.1430. Flockton and Gibbs, Ewan Christian, Sir Charles Nicholson, George Pace	1914

Southwell	Blessed Virgin Mary	1108. Ivo de Raghton?, Ewan Christian	1884
Wakefield	All Saints	c.1430. Sir Gilbert Scott, Oldrid Scott, J L Pearson, Frank Pearson	1888
York	Metropolitical Church of St Peter	c.1230. Simon the Mason, Ivo de Raghton	built as a cathedral

Wales: the Church in Wales

Bangor	St Deiniol	c.1250. Sir Gilbert Scott, A D R Caröe	built as a cathedral
Brecon	St John the Evangelist	c.1215. Sir Gilbert Scott	1923
Llandaff	St Peter, St Paul, St Dubricius, St Teilo and St Oudoceous	1193. John Prichard, George Pace	built as a cathedral
Newport	St Woolos	c.1080. W G and M E Habershon, A D R Caröe	1949
St Asaph	St Asaph	1284. Sir Gilbert Scott	built as a cathedral
St Davids	St David and St Andrew	1181. Sir Gilbert Scott, Oldrid Scott, W D Caröe	built as a cathedral

Scotland: the Scottish Episcopal Church

Aberdeen	St Andrew	1817. Archibald Simpson	1914
Dundee	St Paul	1853. Sir Gilbert Scott	1905
Edinburgh	St Mary the Virgin	1874. Sir Gilbert Scott	built as a cathedral
Glasgow	St Mary the Virgin	1871. Sir Gilbert Scott	1908
Inverness	St Andrew	1866. Alexander Ross	built as a cathedral
Millport	Holy Spirit	1851. William Butterfield	1876
Oban	St John the Divine	1864. Charles Wilson, David Thomson, James Chalmers, Ian G Lindsay	1920
Perth	St Ninian	1849. William Butterfield, J L Pearson, Frank Pearson	built as a cathedral

Northern Ireland: the Church of Ireland

Armagh	St Patrick	1834-7. Lewis Nockalls Cottingham	built as a cathedral
Belfast	St Anne	1899-1948. Sir Thomas Drew, Sir Charles Nicholson	built as a cathedral
Clogher	St Macartan	1744. *James Joseph McCarthy, William Hague*	built as a cathedral
Derry	St Columb	1633. *William Parrot(t)*	built as a cathedral
Downpatrick	Holy and Undivided Trinity	1790-1818. *Charles Lilly*	built as a cathedral

Dromore	Christ the Redeemer	1661. Sir Thomas Drew	built as a cathedral
Enniskillen	St Macartin	1842. *Thomas Elliott, William Farrell*	1923
Lisburn	Christ Church	1708	built as a cathedral

Roman Catholic Cathedrals

England			
Province of Westminster			
Aldershot	St Michael and St George	1892. *Pitt and Michie*	1986
Brentwood	St Mary and St Helen	1861. *Quinlan Terry*	1917
Norwich	St John the Baptist	1882. George Gilbert Scott Jr	1976
Northampton	Our Lady and St Thomas of Canterbury	1844. A W N Pugin	1964
Nottingham	St Barnabas	1844. A W N Pugin	1852
Westminster, London	The Most Holy Blood, St Mary, St Joseph and St Peter	1903. J F Bentley	built as a cathedral
Province of Birmingham			
Birmingham	St Chad	1839. A W N Pugin	1850
Clifton	St Peter and St Paul	1970. *Percy Thomas Partnership*	built as a cathedral
Shrewsbury	Our Lady Help of Christians and St Peter Alcantara	1853. E W Pugin	built as a cathedral
Province of Liverpool			
Lancaster	St Peter	1859. E G Paley	1924
Leeds	St Anne	1901. *John Henry Eastwood*	built as a cathedral
Liverpool	Metropolitical Church of Christ the King	1962. *Sir Frederick Gibberd*	built as a cathedral
Middlesbrough	St Mary the Virgin	1985. *Frank Swainston*	built as a cathedral

Newcastle	St Mary	1842. A W N Pugin	built as a cathedral
Salford	St John the Evangelist	1844. M E Hadfield	1852
Sheffield	St Marie	1846. M E Hadfield	1980
Province of Southwark			
Arundel	Our Lady and St Philip Howard	1868. J A Hansom	1965
Plymouth	St Mary and St Boniface	1856. J A Hansom and C F Hansom	built as a cathedral
Portsmouth	St John the Evangelist	1881. J A Hansom	built as a cathedral
Southwark	Metropolitical Church of St George	1846. A W N Pugin	1850

Wales

Cardiff	St David	1887. Peter Paul Pugin	1916
Swansea	St Joseph	1889. Peter Paul Pugin	1987

Scotland

Aberdeen	St Mary	1860. *Alexander Ellis, R G Wilson*	1878
Ayr	St Margaret	1827. *James Dempster*	2007
Oban	St Columba	1932. Sir Giles Gilbert Scott	built as a cathedral
Dundee	St Andrew	1836. *George Mathewson*	1878
Edinburgh	Our Lady of the Assumption	1814. James Gillespie Graham	1886
Glasgow	St Andrew	1814. James Gillespie Graham	1947
Motherwell	Our Lady of Good Aid	1900. Peter Paul Pugin	1948
Paisley	St Mirin	1931. *Thomas Baird*	1948

Northern Ireland

Armagh	St Patrick	1904. *Thomas Duff, J J McCarthy*	built as a cathedral
Newry	St Patrick and St Colman	1825-9. *Thomas Duff, Dr Thomas McGivern, G C Ashlin*	1919
Belfast	St Peter	1860. *Fr Jeremiah McAuley, John O'Neill*	1866

CHURCH BUILDINGS

This section is a glossary of terms used specifically in descriptions of church buildings.

Almery. See Aumbry.
Ambulatory. A covered walkway. In cathedrals and large churches, it is the walkway behind the high altar.
Angel roof. Form of timber roof decoration common in the fourteenth and fifteenth centuries, in which angels were carved on corbels, hammer beams, roof beams etc. Especially common in East Anglia. See also Hammerbeam.

In Norfolk: St Mary's, North Creake; St Mary's, South Creake; All Saints', Necton; St Peter and St Paul's, Swaffham; St Peter Mancroft, Norwich. In Suffolk: Holy Trinity, Blythburgh; St Mary's, Mildenhall; St Mary's, Bury St Edmunds. In Cambs: St Wedreda's, March; St Kyneburgha's, Castor; St Mary's, St Neots. St Nicholas's, Addlethorpe; St Mary and St Nicholas's, Spalding, both in Lincs; All Saints', Leighton Buzzard, Beds; St Ia's, St Ives, Cornwall; St Mary's, Ewelme, Oxon; St Cuthbert's, Wells, Som; All Saints', North Street, York.
Apse. Semicircular or polygonal chapel or other extension to the end of the chancel or a transept.
Arcade. A row of arches.
Arches, doors and windows. Early Saxon windows, from the seventh century to the tenth, were often triangular, consisting of a pair of rectangular slabs joined at the top, but not infrequently had semicircular heads. Doors and arches usually had semicircular heads. Not much Saxon work survives, but see St Peter's, Barton-upon-Humber, Lincs and St Mary's, Deerhurst, Glos. They were mostly supplanted in the tenth century by the semicircular, Norman or Romanesque arch. The lancet arch, steeply pointed, tall in relation to its width and without tracery, often grouped in threes or fives, appeared about 1200. In the late thirteenth century arches became wider in relation to their height and tracery appeared. In the first half of the fourteenth century, the ogee S-shaped or four-centred arch appeared. The perpendicular arch, with its top flattened, giving it an almost rectangular appearance, appeared about 1350. It is peculiar to England and lasted till the early seventeenth century.
Aumbry, almery. Cupboard-shaped opening in the wall near the altar in which the holy vessels were kept. Common, though rarely used these days. Most have had their doors removed.
Axial tower. See Tower.
Baptistery. The area around the font, usually at the west end.
Bar tracery. See Tracery.
Bargeboard. An ornamental flat piece of timber fixed where the roof extends over

Angel roof, c.1400, St Agnes's, Cawston, Norfolk

Norman south door with contemporary ironwork and the figure of a priest above, early twelfth century, St Mary's, Haddiscoe, Norfolk

Early English lancet windows, early thirteenth century, St Mary's, Shrewsbury, Salop

Decorated east window, c.1330, St Mary's, Dennington, Suffolk

Ogee tracery, fifteenth century, St Michael's, Framlingham, Suffolk

Aumbry and sedilia, twelfth century, St Mary's, Shrewsbury, Salop

Roof bosses beneath the rood loft, c.1520, St Margaret's, St Margarets, Herefs

Angle buttresses, thirteenth century, St Andrew's, Shifnal, Salop

Diagonal buttress, 1589, St James's, Shipton, Salop

Clasping buttress, c.1250, St Michael's, Alberbury, Salop

Chapter house with flying buttresses, 1230-50, Lincoln Cathedral

the gable, to hide the ends of the ridge beam and purlins.

Barrel roof. See Wagon roof.

Basilica. A large or important church. 'Basilica' and 'minor basilica' are technical terms of status in the Roman Catholic church. There are only three minor basilicas in England: St Chad's Cathedral, Birmingham, W Mid; Downside Abbey (the Basilica of St Gregory the Great), Stratton-on-the-Fosse, Som; and Corpus Christi Priory (now disused), Manchester.

Bay. The distance between two pillars, columns or pilasters.

Belfry. The place where the bells hang. It may be a room in the tower, a structure on the roof or gable (a bell-cote or bell-gable) or a separate building. See Campanile.

Bell flèche. See Flèche.

Blind. *Blind arcade*: row of unpierced arches.
Blind clerestorey: clerestorey with no windows.
Blind tracery: tracery drawn on a solid wall.
Blind triforium: blank wall above the arcade and below the clerestorey.

Boneyard. See Charnel house.

Boss. Carved ornament placed where two or more ribs in a vault or roof meet. Bosses are often sixty or seventy feet up, so that they are practically invisible, but nonetheless they are often beautifully carved.

Burial vault. Underground burial chamber, sometimes holding a single coffin, sometimes many hundreds. (The Docklands Light Railway website states that there are sixty vaults at St Alfege's, Greenwich, London, containing 1,058 interments). Originally built for the wealthy in monastic and collegiate churches, the Dissolution of the Monasteries transferred the practice to parish churches. Partly due to overcrowding in churchyards, vaults became widespread from the seventeenth century, with family vaults, incumbents' vaults (where the vicar could supplement his stipend by charging for occupation), and community vaults.

See the Harvey vault at St Andrew's, Hempstead, Essex; the Raynor vault at St John's, Thaxted, Essex; the St John vault at St Mary's, Lydiard Tregoze, Wilts; the Sackville chapel and vault, St Michael and All Angels, Withyham, Sussex; the Poulett vault in St George's, Hinton St George, Som; the Ashley-Cooper vault at St Giles's, Wimborne St Giles, Dorset.

Buttress. Brick or stone support to a wall, counteracting its outward thrust.
Angle buttress: two buttresses meeting at the corner of a building, supporting two walls joining each other at right angles.
Clamp or *clasping buttress*: L-shaped buttress wrapping the corner of a building.
Diagonal or *French buttress*: a single buttress at the corner of a building, set at 135 degrees to both walls, especially common in East Anglia.
Flying buttress: an arch from wall to a detached pier, which usually has a pinnacle on top.
Setback buttresses: buttresses at the corner of a building, set back at equal distances from the corner.

Campanile. A bell tower, detached or semi-detached from the church. See the introductory note to the Bells section.

Carrel. A desk or study place. Those in the cloisters at Gloucester Cathedral (late fourteenth to early fifteenth centuries) are the most complete set of mediaeval carrels in existence.

Capital. The top of a column or pilaster, often richly carved.

Caryatid. Pillar in the shape of a woman.

Chancel. Area of the church containing the altar and reserved for the clergy and the choir, often separated from the nave by a screen (the chancel screen, rood screen (see the Church furnishings section) or pulpitum), rails or steps.

Chantry, chantry chapel. Side chapel (usually small, but not always) or side altar at which masses were said for the soul of the person who endowed it. It frequently contains a tomb or memorial.

Chapter house. Meeting house in cathedrals, or nearby, in which the cathedral chapter conducted its business. They are often polygonal or circular. See Wells Cathedral, Som; Ely Cathedral, Cambs; York Minster. The only chapter house in a parish church is in St Mary's, Warwick (fourteenth century).

Charnel house, boneyard, ossuary. Room or building where exhumed bodies were kept when a grave had to be re-used, sometimes in as little as five years. Most were cleared out and sealed, for hygienic reasons, in the nineteenth century, but a few survive.

St Leonard's, Hythe, Kent (where the bones (or some of them) of 4,000 people are kept); Holy Trinity, Rothwell, Northants (only 1,500); St Michael and All Angels, Mitcheldean, Glos; St John the Baptist's, Thaxted, Essex; St Mary's, Mildenhall, Suffolk.

Choir. Part of the church where the clergy and choristers sit. Where there are pews, they usually face north and south, unlike the congregation's pews, which face east.

Church plans. From the twelfth or thirteenth centuries, churches were continually expanded, with chapels, aisles and porches being added.

Round churches: only four mediaeval examples exist (excluding the ruinous chapel at Ludlow Castle, Salop). They are St Sepulchre's, Northampton (c.1100, greatly restored by Sir Gilbert Scott, c.1850), Holy Sepulchre, Cambridge (c.1130), Temple Church, London (1185) and St John the Baptist's, Little Maplestead, Essex (c.1340, largely rebuilt 1849–55). Later ones include All Saints', Newcastle upon Tyne, Tyne & W (1786–9, deconsecrated 1961, now offices and an auditorium) and St Chad's, Shrewsbury, Salop (1792).

Single-cell churches: consisting of a single space. Very early.

St Andrew's, Winterborne Tomson, Dorset (twelfth century).

Two-cell churches: nave and chancel, with chancel either square-ended or apsidal.

Heath Chapel, Heath, Salop (twelfth century, square); St Michael's, Bulley, Glos (twelfth century, apsidal); St Giles's, Pipe Aston, Herefs (twelfth century, square); St Leonard's, South Stoke, Sussex (eleventh century, square).

Three-cell churches: with nave, chancel and sanctuary.

St Mary and St David's, Kilpeck, Herefs (twelfth century); St Michael's, Stewkley, Bucks (twelfth century); St Mary's, Acocks Green, Birmingham, W Mid (1866).

Cruciform churches: with nave, transepts, and chancel or sanctuary.

St Michael and St Mary's, Melbourne, Derbys (twelfth century); St Michael's, Dowdeswell, Glos (fifteenth century); St Andrew's, Great Ryburgh, Norfolk (eleventh to fourteenth centuries).

Clerestorey, clearstory. In larger churches and cathedrals, the upper storey of the nave, mostly with windows set into it.

Cloister. A square or rectangular space (the garth), surrounded by arcades, usually on the south side of a monastic church. It was used for exercise, for study and, where it was permitted, socialising. Most cathedrals have them. Salisbury Cathedral, Wilts, has the largest (thirteenth century), but see also Norwich Cathedral, Norfolk (late thirteenth to early fifteenth centuries); Gloucester Cathedral (late fourteenth century), built to the north of the cathedral because the graveyard was to the south; Lincoln Cathedral, also built to the north; Durham Cathedral (early fifteenth century); and Wells Cathedral, Som (fifteenth century).

Carved capital, man with toothache, c.1200, south transept, Wells Cathedral, Som

Chancel arch, early twelfth century, St Michael's, Upton Cressett, Salop

Boneyard beneath the chancel, thirteenth century, St Leonard's, Hythe, Kent

Cloisters, 1297-1430, Norwich Cathedral, Norfolk

Two-cell church (nave and chancel), c.1140, Heath Chapel, Salop

Consecration cross, late fifteenth century, All Saints, Carleton Rode, Norfolk

Corbels, c.1140, St Mary and St David's, Kilpeck, Herefs

Crockets, c.1477, St Mary's, Shrewsbury, Salop

Devil's door?, early eleventh century, St Gregory's, Heckingham, Norfolk

Easter sepulchre, fourteenth century, St Mary's, Billingsley, Salop

Flying ribs, fourteenth century, St Mary's, Warwick

Gargoyle, 1340, St Peter's, Great Walsingham, Norfolk

Graffiti, undated, on the back of the reredos Beverley Minster, E Yorks

Consecration cross. Mediaeval cross incised or painted on a church wall at the time of its consecration. No church still possesses the full set of twenty-four (twelve inside, twelve outside) but St Mary, St Katherine and All Saints', Edington, Wilts, has twenty-one, eleven inside and ten outside. Others can be seen at St Kentigern's, Crosthwaite, Cumbria (nine inside, twelve outside); St Peter's, Creeting St Peter (five outside), and St Peter's, Great Livermere (two inside), both in Suffolk; All Saints', Carleton Rode (eight inside), Norfolk.

Corbel. Short piece of timber or masonry projecting from a wall to support a beam or arch, often elaborately carved.

Cove. Concave arch at the junction of wall and ceiling.

Cradle roof. See Wagon roof.

Cradle vault. See Vault.

Crocket. Carved projection, in the shape of a flower, foliage, buds etc, placed at regular intervals along the sides of spires, gables, pinnacles or arches.

Cross vaulting. See Vault.

Crossing. The space where the nave, chancel and transepts meet.

Cruciform churches. See Church plans.

Crypt. Cellar or series of underground rooms: the undercroft.

Cylindrical vaulting. See Vault.

Cupola. A small dome on top of a roof or turret.

Detached tower. See Tower.

Devil's door. Mediaeval doorway in the north side of the church, often too small to use, to let bad spirits out during a christening, particularly common in Sussex. Nowadays mostly bricked up. See St Peter and St Paul's, Broadhempston, Devon; and in Sussex, St Nicholas's, Worth; St Helen's, Hangleton; All Saints', Patcham; St Mary's, Sompting.

Diagonal ribbed vaulting. See Vault.

Dog door. Like a cat-flap, but for dogs. It was built into the church door to allow sheepdogs in and out. See St Mellanus's, Mullion, Cornwall; St John's, Paignton, Devon; St Mary's, Brecon, Powys.

Double hammerbeam. See Hammerbeam.

Dovecote. Sometimes built into the fabric of a church, in the tower or above the chancel. See Dovecote in the section on Churchyards.

Dripstone. Moulding on an external wall above a door or window to throw the rain off. Also called a hood moulding or a label.

Easter sepulchre. Recess on the north side of the chancel, like a tomb without an effigy, used to keep the Host from Good Friday (some say Maundy Thursday) to Easter Day. See St Andrew's, Heckington, Lincs; St Mary's, Gillingham, Dorset; St Mary's, Arnold, Notts; Holy Trinity, Long Itchington, Warwicks; St Stephen's, Old Radnor, Powys.

Fan vaulting. See Vault.

Flèche, bell flèche. Very narrow spire, usually made with wood covered with lead, on top of a tower; sometimes called a spirelet. See Coventry Cathedral, W Mid; and in Norfolk, St Peter and St Paul's, Swaffham, All Saints', Shipdham and St Mary's, Diss.

Finial. Decoration at the very top of a tower corner, gable, canopy etc.

Flying rib. A free-standing rib (ie a rib that is not infilled with webbing), which 'flies' from a pier to the ridge rib. Only two exist in the UK, at Bristol Cathedral, and at St Mary's, Warwick, though miniature examples occur on the screens at Southwell Minster, Notts and St Davids Cathedral, Pembs.

Galilee chapel, Galilee porch. Chapel or porch at the west end of a church, where the clergy would pause before entering the church proper. See Durham Cathedral,

Ely Cathedral, Cambs, Lincoln Cathedral, Newport Cathedral, Glam.

Gallery. Upper storey, above the aisle or at the west end. It could be used for additional seating or the church musicians or both. See Music and singing section.

Gargoyle. Stone waterspout, carrying rainwater from a gutter and throwing it clear of the walls. Gargoyles are usually carved with grotesque human or animal faces.

Garth. See Cloisters.

Graffiti. Maybe not strictly part of the church building. Mediaeval graffiti are hard to identify and a relatively new subject of research. They date from the mid-fourteenth century.

St Mary's, Ashwell, Herts; St Nicholas's, Stevenage, Herts; St Andrew's, Burton Overy, Leics (on the organ, nineteenth century and later); St Mary's, Colkirk, Norfolk; St Mary's, Bletchingley, Surrey; St Peter's, Limpsfield, Surrey; St Thomas's, Winchelsea, Sussex.

Groined vaulting. See Vault.

Hagioscope. See Squint.

Hammerbeam. A way of making a wooden framework carry the roof across a much greater span than would otherwise be possible. It evolved towards the end of the fourteenth century, probably in East Anglia, and was perfected in the fifteenth. Hammerbeams project from the wall, supported by curved braces, and carry vertical hammer posts, which in turn are joined to collar beans. The hammer beams sometimes terminate with carved angels (see Angel roof). A double hammerbeam is a roof with two rows of hammer beams, one above the other.

See: in Suffolk St Mary's, Mildenhall; St Andrew's, Cotton; St Mary's, Gislingham; St John the Baptist's, Needham Market (double hammerbeam) and St Mary's, Woolpit (double hammerbeam, angel roof); in Norfolk St Peter Mancroft and St Stephen's, both in Norwich; St Agnes's, Cawston (angel roof), St Peter and St Paul's, Knapton (double hammerbeam and angel roof) and St Peter and St Paul's, Swaffham; St Nicholas's, Blakeney; in Cambs, St Helen and St Mary's, Bourn, and All Saints', Elm; St Mary and St Nicholas's, Spalding, Lincs; St Nicholas's, Castle Hedingham, Essex.

Hexagonal tower. See Tower.

Hood moulding. See Dripstone.

Jesse. See Tree of Jesse.

Jube. The gallery above a Pulpitum, sometimes the pulpitum itself.

Keystone. Central stone of an arch or vault, which holds the whole structure together.

Label. See Dripstone.

Lady chapel. Chapel dedicated to the Virgin Mary. In cathedrals it is usually to the east of the main altar; in churches it may be in one of the side chapels.

Lancet. See Arches, doors and windows.

Lantern tower. A crossing tower with windows or openings at the top. See Ely Cathedral, Cambs (1340); Pershore Abbey, Worcs (fourteenth century); All Saints Pavement, York (about 1400); St Botolph's, Boston, Lincs (about 1520).

Lavatorium. In monasteries, a washing place. A few survive: in Wenlock Priory (c.1220, ruinous), Norwich Cathedral, Norfolk, in the cloisters (fourteenth century), in the north cloister at Gloucester Cathedral (late fourteenth century),

Leper's window. See Squint.

Lesene. In Anglo-Saxon architecture, an ornamental vertical strip on the outside of a rubble wall, resembling a pilaster but with no capital or base. Also known as stripwork.

Lucarne, spire light. A window in a spire, usually unglazed.

Mason's mark. Simple mark, shallowly cut, used by a mason to identify his work. Sometimes found on tombs and ledger stones.

Merlon. Raised part of the parapet in a battlement.

Double hammerbeam roof, late sixteenth century, St Andrew's, Shifnal, Salop

Lantern tower, c.1400, All Saints Pavement, York

Lavatorium, c.1220, Much Wenlock Priory, Salop

Lesenes, c.1050, St Peter's, Stanton Lacy, Salop

Mason's mark, ? fourteenth century, Selby Abbey, N Yorks

Nave of Canterbury Cathedral, Kent, 1405, by Henry Yevele

Parvis, 1488, St Michael's, Aylsham, Norfolk

Pedilavium, the only one in the United Kingdom, thirteenth century, Lichfield Cathedral, Staffs

Piscina and sedilia, c.1240, St Lawrence's, South Cove, Suffolk

Porch, fourteenth century, protecting an early twelfth century doorway, St Michael's, Upton Cressett, Salop

Minster. Church which was originally part of a monastery.
Mullion. Vertical bar which divides a window into two or more lights.
Narthex. Vestibule or porch at the west end of a church.
Nave. The western part of a church where the public stood, or these days, sits, the quire, the eastern part, being reserved for the clergy. The nave was commonly used, like the churchyard, for a variety of secular purposes as well.
Octagonal tower. See Tower.
Oculus. Circular window.
Ogee. See Arches, doors and windows.
Oratory. A chapel.
Ossuary. See Charnel house.
Painted roof. The only painted roof from the thirteenth century is the nave roof in Peterborough Cathedral, Cambs, dating from about 1250. Remnants of mediaeval painting survive on the vaults of St Mary's, Ottery St Mary, Devon, but they were overpainted in 1847–50 and in 1977. This story could be repeated many times elsewhere. See, for example, the fifteenth century roof of St Cuthbert's, Wells, Som, which was restored in 1963. There is an impressive painted chancel ceiling, dated 1672, at St Mary's, Bromfield, Salop. St Michael's, Llanyblodwel, Salop (c.1847), is worth seeing. A good example of an original nineteenth century roof, painted in 1859–66, is in St Mary's, Huntingfield, Suffolk, painted by the vicar's wife, Mildred Holland.
Pargetting. Decorative plasterwork on the outside wall of a timber-framed building, usually formed with carved wooden stamps.
Parvis. An open space outside the entrance to a church. More commonly, the room above the porch of a church.
Pedilavium. Foot-washing on Maundy Thursday, in commemoration of St John's Gospel, 13, 1–17. Also, a part of a building specially designed for this. Only one survives in the United Kingdom (or, perhaps, was ever built): the pedilavium in Lichfield Cathedral, Staffs (thirteenth century).
Perpendicular. See Arches, doors and windows.
Pilaster. A semi-column, a column attached to a wall.
Pinnacle. A small spire on top of a buttress, at the corners of towers, on gables, on roof-lines etc. A pinnacle could be decorative or could be built to add downward weight.
Piscina. Bowl, usually with a drain, built into the south wall near the altar. Piscinas often come in pairs or even sets of three. They were for washing hands and holy vessels. The drain leads to the outside of the church, so that the water falls on consecrated ground.
Plate tracery. See Tracery.
Porches. In cathedrals, most porches protect the west door and in churches, the south door; but there are many exceptions. They came into use from the late twelfth century (and sometimes protected earlier work, such as tympanums, columns, sundials and scratchdials), to shelter churchgoers from the weather, but they rapidly acquired other uses. Banns of marriage were called there, the churching of women took place in the porch, contracts were signed, executors distributed legacies there, and public notices were displayed. Larger porches served as meeting places, lock-ups and temporary lodgings; and the largest, of two or three storeys, accommodated living quarters for the priest, meeting rooms, libraries, school rooms and strong rooms. The many two-storey porches include St Mary's, Nantwich, Ches and St Mary's, Pulham St Mary, Norfolk, and three-storey porches include St John's, Cirencester, Glos and St John's, Burford, Oxon.

Presbytery. Area at the east end of a church, reserved for the clergy, in which the main altar stands. Also, a Roman Catholic priest's house (see entry in Other religious buildings).

Priest's door. In mediaeval churches, a door used by the priest in the south wall of the chancel, to which the public were rarely admitted. Now, often bricked up or kept locked.

Pulpitum. Stone screen separating the chancel from the nave. Where there is both a pulpitum and a rood screen (see the Church Furnishings section), the rood screen is one bay west of the pulpitum.

Respond. Half-column built against a wall at the end of an arcade.

Retrochoir. Part of a cathedral or larger church to the east of the main altar, behind the presbytery.

Rhenish helm. Four-sided tower roof with gables on all four sides. The only mediaeval Rhenish helm roof is at St Mary's, Sompting, Sussex (c.1000). Rhenish helm roofs went through something of a revival in the nineteenth century: St Mary's, Mulberry Street, Manchester (1848); St Peter and St Paul's, Hawkley, Hants (1865); St Andrew's, Churcham, Glos (1878).

Rib tracery. See Tracery.

Ribs. See Vault.

Roof. See Angel roof, Hammerbeam roof, Painted roof, Rhenish helm, Saddleback roof, Single framed roof, Tie beam roof.

Roof coverings. Most roof coverings used on houses are also used on churches: slates, clay tiles, stone tiles, concrete tiles, lead sheeting, copper sheeting and stainless steel sheeting. Wooden shingles and thatch are more uncommon. Shingles are found in southern England, though more often on spires than roofs as the steeper roofs of spires allow swifter run-off of water and so prevent damp and rot.

For shingled roofs see: St Peter's, North Tawton, Devon, St Dubricius's, Porlock, Som, All Saints', Herstmonceux, Sussex, St Mary's, Bexley, London, and All Saints', Woodchurch, Kent. Thatched churches are rare except in Norfolk and Suffolk, though there are a few modern ones elsewhere: see All Saints', Brockhampton, Herefs, built by William Lethaby in 1902. For thatched churches in Norfolk, see St Edmund's, Acle; St Edmund's, Thurne; St Peter and St Paul's, Mautby; St Margaret's, Hales; St Nicholas's, Potter Heigham. For Suffolk, see St Peter's, Theberton; St Andrew's, Covehithe; St Lawrence's, South Cove; All Saints', Icklingham; St Margaret's, Herringfleet.

Rose window, wheel window. A large circular window. More exactly, a wheel window has tracery radiating from the centre, while a rose window has tracery which does not radiate from the centre.

See Canterbury Cathedral, Kent (c.1170); The Dean's Eye (c.1210) and The Bishop's Eye (1325–50), Lincoln Cathedral; York Minster (thirteenth century); Beverley Minster, E Yorks (mid thirteenth century); Durham Cathedral (fifteenth century, rebuilt in the nineteenth century).

Round churches. See Church plans.

Round tower. See Tower.

Roundel. A circular window; an oculus; or a circular moulding containing a decorative motif.

Sacristy. Room in a church in which the church valuables were kept: a vestry.

Saddleback roof. Tower roof with a ridge between two gables, such as that at St James's, Kinnersley, Herefs (fourteenth century); St Cenydd's, Llangennith, Glam; and, both in Glos, St Peter's, Duntisbourne Abbotts and St Andrew's, Eastleach Turville.

Sanctuary. Area immediately surrounding the main altar. See also Sanctuary ring in the Church furnishings section.

Scissors arch. See Strainer arch.

Priest's door with carved corbels, c.1330, St Mary's, Dennington, Suffolk

Rhenish helm tower roof, shingled, eleventh century, St Mary's, Sompting, Sussex

Thatched roof (roof undated, but probably thirteenth century, thatch many times renewed) with octagonal tower (early sixteenth century), St Mary's, Ashby, Suffolk

Late fifteenth century brick sacristy built against a stone fourteenth century chancel, St Mary's, Dennington, Suffolk

Saddleback tower roof, fourteenth century, St James's, Kinnersley, Herefs

Broach spire with lucarnes, St Andrew's, Barnwell, Northants

Candle-snuffer spire, shingled, fourteenth century, St Mary's, Bexley, London

Squint, c.1300, St Michael's, Aylsham, Norfolk

Stair turret, fifteenth century, St Nicholas and St Cyriac's, South Pool, Devon

Strainer arch, 1348, Wells Cathedral, Som

Sedilia. A set of two, three or four seats set in niches at the south side of the chancel. They were used by the priests during services.

Single cell churches. See Church plans.

Single-framed roof, trussed rafter roof. Timber roof in which the rafters are joined high up with a collar-beam, often supported by struts. It was often boarded.

Slype. A covered passage leading from the cloisters to the chapter house, infirmary or cemetery. See the slypes at Winchester, Gloucester, Exeter and St Albans Cathedrals.

Sound hole. Opening made in a belfry wall for ventilation.

Spandrel. The triangular space on either side of the head of an arch, or the triangular spaces between two arches in an arcade.

Spire. Spires made their appearance in the twelfth century. They may be made of timber (mostly clad with copper, lead, shingles or tiles), stone, or occasionally brick.

Broach spire: octagonal spire rising from the tower walls: the spaces immediately above the corners of the tower are filled with a half-pyramid of masonry (the broach).

All Saints', Patcham, Sussex, St Andrew's, Broughton, Northants, St Mary's, New Mills, Derbys.

Splay-foot spire: broach spire with its base opening out and forming eaves over the tower.

St Mary's, Molesey, Manchester; Wishaw Church, East Lanarkshire, St Mary's, Gladestry, Powys (thirteenth century), St Mary's, Fordwich, Kent (thirteenth century), St John's, Kingsley, Ches (1849–50).

Crown spire: open-work spire formed by connected arches.

St Giles's Cathedral, Edinburgh (1495), Newcastle Cathedral, Tyne & W (1448), St Dunstan-in-the-East, London (1695–1701).

Needle spire: a narrow spire, set in from the tower parapets.

St Andrew's, Worcester (Glover's Needle), St Mary's, Ashwell, Herts (fourteenth century), All Saints', Sudbourne, Suffolk (1878), St Anne's Cathedral, Belfast.

Parapet spire: a wider spire which is also built wholly within the parapet of the tower. The dividing line between needle spires and parapet spires perhaps is rather grey.

Lichfield Cathedral, Staffs, St Wulfram's, Grantham, Lincs, St Edwin's, Coniscliffe, Durham.

Candle-snuffer spire: wooden spire in two or three parts, each resting on the other, like petticoats.

See (both now shingled) St Mary's, Bexley, London (fourteenth century; the top part is octagonal and the lower part four-sided); and St Augustine's, Brookland, Kent (c.1260, a detached bell tower).

Spire light. See Lucarne.

Squinch. Masonry filling in the upper corners of a square room so as to form the base of a dome.

Squint, hagioscope, leper's window. Low window on the south side of the chancel through which (so it is said) lepers who could not enter the church, and nuns, who lived secluded, could view mass. More likely, the hagioscope would enable the chantry priest to synchronise his mass with the priest officiating at the high altar. The longest squint in England is reputed to be at Holy Trinity, Bradford-on-Avon, Wilts.

See also Holy Trinity, Goodramgate, York; St Mary's, Lytchett Maltravers, Dorset; St Helen's, Bishopsgate, London; St Mary's, West Chiltington, Sussex; St Oswald's, Sowerby, N Yorks.

Stair turret, vice. Turret attached to the outside of a tower, containing a spiral staircase giving access to different levels of the tower and usually leading to the tower roof.

All Saints', Brixworth, Northants; St Andrew's, Brigstock, Northants; St Cuthburga's, Wimborne Minster, Dorset; All Saints', Hough on the Hill, Lincs; St Mary's, Broughton, Lincs.

Steeple. Church tower and spire together.

Strainer arch, scissors arch. Arch inserted between two walls or columns to prevent them from leaning towards each other. The best known strainer arches are the arches stabilising the tower piers at Wells Cathedral, Som (1338–48).

Stripwork. See Lesene.

Three-cell churches. See Church plans.

Tie beam roof. A roof consisting of rafters linked with beams joining their feet (tie beams), or simply pinned to the wall plates. This is the earliest form of timber roof, dating from the eleventh century.

Tierceron vaulting. See Vault.

Tower. Towers first appeared in Britain in the tenth century. Most were built of wood and so, over the years, were replaced. Some Saxon stone towers still survive.

St John's, Barnack, Cambs; St Andrew's, Bywell, Northumb (now redundant); St Mary's, Sompting, Sussex.

Most early towers were built as defensive structures, with just ladders for entrances, and also carried bells. The vast majority are square and at the west end of the church. Larger churches may have axial towers, which are central towers, above the crossing. St Edith's, Eaton-under-Heywood, Salop, unusually has the tower in the middle of the south wall. There are 182 churches with round towers, mostly Saxon and mostly in East Anglia: 126 in Norfolk, forty-two in Suffolk, two in Cambs, seven in Essex, and only five in the rest of England – three in Sussex and two in Berkshire.

St Margaret's, Burnham Norton; St Andrew's, Bedingham, St Mary's, Haddiscoe; St Mary's, Roughton; all in Norfolk; and All Saints', Ramsholt, Suffolk.

Some churches have hexagonal towers.

St Nicholas's, Ozleworth (twelfth century) and St Lawrence's, Swindon Village, both in Glos.

Some have octagonal towers.

St Nicholas's, Buckenham, Norfolk; St Mary's, Ashby, Suffolk; All Saints', Kettesworth, Norfolk; St Peter and St Paul's, South Petherton (crossing tower), and St Mary Major's, Ilchester, both in Som; St Luke's, Hodnet, Salop; St Michael's, Coxwold, N Yorks.

Only one church in the United Kingdom has a triangular tower: All Saints', Maldon, Essex.

Some churches have detached towers.

St Mary's, Marston Moretaine, Beds; St Mary's, Berkeley, and St Peter and St Paul's, Westbury on Severn, both in Glos; Holy Trinity, Bosbury, Herefs; St Augustine's, Brookland, Kent; St Mary's, West Walton, Norfolk; St Andrew's, Bramfield, Suffolk and St Andrew's, Little Snoring, Norfolk (which are also round towers).

See also Saddleback roof and Rhenish helm roof.

Tracery. Ornamental stonework in a window, screen etc.

Plate tracery appeared c.1200 and has its openings cut through, or apparently cut through, solid masonry: the stone rather than the glass dominates the window.

Bar or rib tracery, introduced c.1250, has its openings defined by thin stone members: the glass rather than the stone dominates the window.

Transept. In a cruciform church, the structure which runs (usually) north-south across the eastern end of the nave to form the crossing.

Transom. Horizontal bar in windows, screens, the tops of doors etc.

Triforium. Gallery above the aisle and below the clerestorey, with open or glazed arches looking down into the nave.

Trussed rafter roof. See Single framed roof.

Two-cell churches. See Church plans.

Collar-beam and tie beam roof, fifteenth century, St Edith's, Eaton-under-Heywood, Salop

Thirteenth century tower in the middle of the south wall, St Edith's, Eaton-under-Heywood, Salop

Detached round tower, c.eleventh century, St Andrew's, Little Snoring, Norfolk

Nave arcade, triforium and clerestorey, twelfth century, Selby Abbey, N Yorks

Norman tympanum, c.1100, St Giles's, Pipe Aston, Herefs

Fan vaulting in the south aisle, c.1530, Bath Abbey, Som

Lierne vaulting, 1340, choir, Wells Cathedral, Som

Wind braces, ? fourteenth century, St Michael's, Stanton Long, Salop

Tympanum. The space between the lintel at the top of a doorway and the semi-circular arch above it. Normally applied to Norman architecture.

Undercroft. See Crypt.

Vault. An arched stone roof. The earliest form of vaulting was based on the semicircular arch: the barrel vault, or cylindrical, cradle, wagon or tunnel vaulting. See, for example, St Hubert's, Corfe Mullen, Dorset (thirteenth century). Where two barrel vaults intersect, this is called *cross vaulting* or *groined vaulting*. Cross vaulting can only be used when both the intersecting barrel vaults are the same height.

Diagonal ribbed vaulting is a vault with ribs which stretch from corner to corner of a bay, as well as all four sides, dividing the vault into four triangles. See Durham Cathedral (c.1120).

Tierceron vaulting has tierceron ribs, which stretch from the wall column to the roof rib or transverse rib, but do not meet the central boss. Tierceron vaulting is more decorative and structural, and where the tierceron ribs meet others, subordinate bosses were created. See Exeter Cathedral, Devon (1353–69).

Lierne vaulting took things a stage further: a lierne rib does not spring from the wall or join the ridge rib, but joins two ribs that do, giving even further opportunities for decoration and subordinate bosses. See Gloucester Cathedral (c.1350).

Fan vaulting is considered by some the ultimate achievement of rib vaulting and the only purely English invention. It is shaped like a series of fans, formed of half conoids (cones with concave sides), each touching the extreme edge of the next. The earliest examples are both from Glos, where the style seems to have originated: they are claimed to be the east cloister of Gloucester Cathedral (1351–77) and the canopy over the tomb of Edward, Lord Despenser (died 1375) in Tewkesbury Abbey, Glos. The largest is in King's College Chapel, Cambridge (1446–1515).

Vault, burial. See Burial vault.

Vestry. Place where the church vestments, plate and the parish chest used to be kept, and where the clergy robe.

Vice. See Stair turret.

Wagon roof, cradle roof, barrel roof. A timber roof with rafters closely spaced and collar beams strengthened by curved braces underneath, so that it presents a semicircular appearance. It is often boarded underneath, sometimes painted, and seen most often in the West Country.

St Mary's, Croscombe, Som; St Andrew's, Winterborne Tomson, Dorset; St Ia's, St Ives, Cornwall; St Mary Magdalene's, Helmsley, N Yorks.

Webbing. The infill between the ribs of a vault.

Wheel window. See Rose window.

Windows. See Arches, doors and windows.

Wind brace. In roof construction, a strut joining a principal rafter to a purlin, to give the roof more rigidity.

OTHER RELIGIOUS BUILDINGS

Some of these terms may be well-known, but they are sometimes misunderstood. What is the difference, for example, between an abbey, a priory, a friary and a monastery – if any?

Abbey. A monastery or convent, led by an abbot or an abbess.

Bishop's Palace. Nowadays, simply the residence of a bishop, but in the past, an extensive fortified house. Most of them are ruinous today, many having been destroyed in the Civil War (1642–6). The earliest is probably Sherborne Castle (1122–37), built by Roger de Caen, Bishop of Salisbury. The rise in lawlessness in the early fourteenth century, following the Great Famine (1315–17) and the Black Death (1348–50), gave rise to much stronger fortifications. The Bishop's Palace at Wells, Som (1340) and the Bishop's Palace St Davids, Pembs (1347), date from this time. See also Lincoln (twelfth to thirteenth century, home of the bishops of Lincoln); Wolvesley Castle (1130–40) and Bishops Waltham (1160–80), both in Hants, homes of the bishops of Winchester; Rose Castle, Dalston, Cumbria (from 1340, home of the bishops of Carlisle); and Auckland Castle, Bishop Auckland, Durham (c.1180, home of the bishops of Durham).

Campanile. Bell tower standing apart from the church. See the introductory notes to the section on Bells.

Chapel of ease. A chapel for those living some distance from the parish church. Most services could be performed, except burial. Many chapels of ease were abolished by the Dissolution of Collegiate Churches and Chantries Act in 1547.

Collegiate church. Church which is governed by a college of canons, often presided over by a dean or provost, though it is not the seat of a bishop and has no diocesan responsibilities. Most collegiate churches were abolished in 1547 by the Dissolution of Collegiate Churches and Chantries Act and the rest in 1840 by the Cathedrals Act. Only three remain in England: Westminster Abbey, London; the Royal Chapel of St George's at Windsor Castle, Berks; and St Endelienta's, Endellion, Cornwall (which was overlooked both in 1547 and 1840). Nonetheless, nearly seventy churches in England, half a dozen in Wales, some forty in Scotland, and a handful in Northern Ireland still hold on to the title.

Convent. House occupied by a community of nuns.

Daughter church. A church in a parish which is not the parish church.

Double monastery. See Monastery.

Friary. Usually situated in towns, since friars worked in the community, not in

Ruins of the Bishop's Palace, c.1340, St Davids Cathedral, Pembs

A Royal Peculiar: St Edward's, Cambridge (c.1400)

The Bishop's Barn, fifteenth century, Wells, Som

monasteries. A friar is a member of a mendicant ('begging' – they were forbidden to own property) order. The four 'great orders' are the Carmelites (White Friars, founded c.1155); the Franciscans (Grey Friars, founded 1209); the Dominicans (Black Friars, founded c.1216); and the Augustinians (Austin Friars, founded 1244). There are many minor orders, some of them for women (eg the Capuchines (Poor Clares), founded 1538).

Glebe. Church property and land. Nowadays this is administered centrally by each diocese for the financial benefit of all its clergy.

Monastery. A self-supporting community of monks or nuns. The first to be established in the UK were Benedictine monasteries, in the sixth century. Later came Cluniac (eleventh century), Carthusians and Cistercian (both twelfth century). The Dissolution of the Monasteries (1536–40) destroyed or secularised all of them, and their churches sometimes became parish churches or, with five of them, cathedrals (see the section on The rise and fall of church buildings). A double monastery was a monastery for men and women, who lived separately under the governance of a common superior.

Nunnery. See Convent.

Parsonage, rectory, vicarage, presbytery (Roman Catholic), manse (normally in Scotland), chapel house (in Scotland). The residence of the parish priest or minister, maintained by the church.

Priory. A monastery whose head is a prior or prioress. Some orders, such as the Dominicans and the Carthusians, call all their monasteries priories. The Benedictines distinguish between two kinds of priories: conventual, which have less than the canonically required twelve monks living in them and so have no abbot; and obedientary priories, which are subordinate to abbeys. The Cluniac order has only one abbey (at Cluny) and all their other houses are obedientary priories.

Royal Peculiar or Peculier. A church which is under the direct jurisdiction of the crown and is not part of any diocese. There are thirteen Royal Peculiars at present.

In London: Westminster Abbey; The Chapel Royal, St James's Palace; The Queen's Chapel, St James's Palace; The Chapel Royal, Hampton Court; The Chapel of St John the Evangelist, Tower of London; The Chapel Royal, St Peter ad Vincula, Tower of London; The Queen's Chapel of the Savoy; The Chapel of St Mary Undercroft, Palace of Westminster; The Royal Foundation of St Katharine, Tower of London. At Windsor, Berks: St George's Chapel, Windsor Castle, Berks; The Royal Chapel of All Saints, Windsor. In Cambridge, St Edward's, Cambridge. In Edinburgh, the Chapel Royal, Holyrood Palace.

Tithe barn. Mediaeval barn for storing tithes – one-tenth of farming produce, given to the church. Tithes were abolished in 1936. Most surviving tithe barns have been converted to residences, function rooms, community centres, and heritage centres, though some of of them still exist in something like their original form.

Harmondsworth Great Barn, London (the largest in Britain); Swalcliffe tithe barn, Oxon; Dunster Priory tithe barn, Dunster, Som; East Riddlesden Hall, Keighley, W Yorks; Great Coxwell Barn, Oxon; Nether Poppleton tithe barn, York; the Bishop's Barn, Wells, Som; The Tithe Barn, Bishop's Cleeve, Glos.

ARCHITECTS AND MASTER CRAFTSMEN

Until the early seventeenth century buildings in the United Kingdom, including churches, were built by master craftsmen, usually masons but sometimes carpenters. The names of many of them are known, though not many personal details, usually following the indefatigable research of John Harvey (1911–97, for whom the Renaissance was a 'catastrophe') and Arthur Oswald (1904–79). After the Commonwealth (1649–60), architects' careers and a growing number of biographical facts become known. But a glance through this list confirms that relatively few churches were built between the Great Fire of London (1666) and the end of the eighteenth century. With the Commissioners' churches (from 1818), the floodgates opened. Thousands of churches were built in the next hundred years, mostly to indifferent neo-Gothic designs, though with many glorious exceptions.

Alan of Walsingham (fl. 1314, died 1364). Goldsmith, architect, sacrist (from 1321) and prior (from 1341) at Ely Cathedral, Cambs. Designed St Mary's Chapel, Ely Cathedral (now Holy Trinity Church), the Lady Chapel there (1321–49) and, after the crossing tower had collapsed in 1322, supervised building of the Octagon (1322–8), Lantern (1328–42, under the direction of William Hurley), Prior Crauden's Chapel (1330) and the choir (1338–50).

Alexander the Mason (fl. 1235–57). Master of the Work at Lincoln Cathedral from 1240, responsible for the nave, chapter house, the galilee chapel, the upper part of the west front, and the lower stage of the central tower after its collapse in 1237. He is said to be the first to introduce lierne vaulting (to the nave roof). Perhaps also worked on the towers of St Mary Magdalene's, Newark, Notts and St Wulfram's, Grantham, Lincs.

Archer, Thomas (c.1668–1743). Amateur baroque architect. In addition to country houses for friends, he designed St Philip's, Birmingham, W Mid (1710–15, now a cathedral); St Paul's, Deptford, London (1713–30); St John's, Smith Square, London (1713–28; gutted 1742 and 1941, restored 1965–8); and St Mary's, Hale, Hants (1717).

Atkinson, Peter (c.1776–1843). Son of architect of the same name and did most of his work in York. Built twelve churches, all Gothic, from 1821 to 1831, for the Commissioners for Building New Churches, five of them in partnership with his pupil R H Sharp (1793–1853). Among them were St Paul's, Alverthorpe, W Yorks (1823–5) and St John's, Cleckheaton, W Yorks (1830–1). Retired in 1833, lived abroad and died in Calcutta.

Austin and Paley (1868–1944). Neo-Gothic architectural partnership, going by various combinations of the names Paley and Austin, based in Lancaster. The original Austin and Paley were Hubert Austin (1841–1915) and E(dward) G(raham) Paley (1823–95). Paley's son Henry joined the partnership in 1886, and Austin's son Geoffrey in 1914. E G Paley designed many churches, including Lancaster Cathedral (1859) before Austin joined him, and together they were involved in the design of over a hundred churches and some eighty other buildings. Their new (as opposed to restored) churches include:

Christ Church, Ashford, Kent (1867); St Michael's, Grimsargh, Lancs (1871); St John the Evangelist's, Cheetham Hill, Manchester (1871); St Mary's, Betws-y-Coed, Conwy (1873); Holy Trinity, Seathwaite, Cumbria (1874); St Michael and All Angels, Atherton, Manchester (1877); St Maxentius's, Bradshaw, Manchester (1878); St John's, Hutton Roof, Cumbria (1881); St John the Evangelist's, Warrington, Ches (1884); Good Shepherd's, Tatham, Lancs (1888).

Barry, Sir Charles (1795–1860). Neo-classical architect, most famous for, oddly, designing the Houses of Parliament in the neo-Gothic style (1840–60). But his earlier work was designing churches in the neo-Gothic style.

St Matthew's, Campfield, Manchester (1821–2); All Saints', Whitefield, Manchester (1822–5); St Peter's, Brighton, Sussex (1824–8); St Saviour's, Ringley, Manchester (1826, demolished except for the tower, rebuilt 1851–4 by Sharpe and Paley); St Andrew's, Hove, Sussex (1827–8); Unitarian Chapel, Manchester (1837–9, in poor condition, roof removed 2005).

In later life he said he wished he could destroy all of them, which has at least partly come to pass. Nevertheless, some twenty years later, he built Holy Trinity, Hurstpierpoint, Sussex (1843–5), again in the neo-Gothic style.

Beke, Richard (fl. 1409, died 1458). Master mason, master of the works at Canterbury Cathedral from 1434/5 until his death. He was responsible for building the lowest stage of Bell Harry tower, the completion of the northwest transept and the Lady Chapel (1448–55) and the pulpitum (c.1455).

Bentley, John Francis (1839–1902). Catholic convert (1862) and neo-Gothic architect whose claim to fame is designing the neo-Byzantine Westminster Cathedral (although he never went to Byzantium). Also designed the Sacred Heart seminary, Hammersmith, London (1876–84, now a Catholic high school); Church of the Holy Rood, Watford, Herts (1887–92); also St John's Beaumont, Old Windsor, Berks (1888), a Catholic preparatory school).

Blomfield, Sir Arthur (1829–99). One of the last, and most prolific, neo-Gothic architects. He was the son of the Bishop of London. His assistant architect was, briefly, Thomas Hardy.

All Saints', Windsor, Berks (1862–4); St Mark's, Binfield, Berks (1866); St Barnabas's, Jericho, Oxford (1869); St Andrew's, Surbiton, London (1872); St Michael's, Hughenden, Bucks (1874–90); St Nicholas's, Heythrop, Oxon (1880); St Andrew's, Worthing, Sussex (1882); St Mary's, Walmer, Kent (1887); St Mary's, Liss, Hants (1892); St Mary's, Swansea, Glam (1896).

He restored Southwark Cathedral and also designed the Royal College of Music, London (1882).

Blore, Edward (1787–1879). Illustrator, and from the 1820s, prolific architect, mostly in the neo-Gothic style. As well as a good number of country houses, he worked on or in nearly fifty churches (including nine Commissioners' churches), a dozen of which were later destroyed or demolished. Among those which survive are:

Richard Beke's pulpitum, Canterbury Cathedral, Kent (c.1455)

Portrait almost certainly of Adam Lock, died 1229, architect of the nave of Wells Cathedral, Som

Portrait almost certainly of Henry Yevele (c.1320-1400), architect of the nave of Canterbury Cathedral, Kent

The cloisters, Canterbury Cathedral, Kent, completed in 1414 by Stephen Lote (died 1417/18)

The quire, Canterbury Cathedral, Kent, by William of Sens (c.1178)

Holy Trinity, Waltham Cross, Herts (1831–2); St John's, Leytonstone, London (1832–3); Christ Church, Croft, Lancs (1832–3); St Peter's, Stepney, London (1837–8); Holy Trinity, Barkingside, Essex (1839–40); St John's, Cinderford, Glos (1843–4).

Howard Colvin remarks: 'A dull competence pervades all his work'.

Bodley, George Frederick (1827–1907). Neo-Gothic architect. Articled to Sir Gilbert Scott and for nearly thirty years (1868–97) partner of Thomas Garner (1839–1906, also articled to Sir Gilbert Scott). Bodley's and Garner's work is mostly indistinguishable one from the other. Their many churches include:

St Michael and All Angels, Brighton, Sussex (1858–62); All Saints', Selsey, Glos (1858–62); St Martin's, Scarborough, N Yorks (1860–3); All Saints', Jesus Lane, Cambridge (1861–6); St John the Baptist's, Liverpool, Mersey (1868–70); St Augustine's, Pendlebury, Lancs (1870–4); Holy Angels, Hoar Cross, Staffs, (1871–6); St German's, Roath, Cardiff, Glam (1880–6); St Mary's, Clumber, Notts (1886–8); St Aidan's, Skelmanthorpe, W Yorks (1892–5); Holy Trinity, South Kensington, London (1901–6).

Bonomi, Ignatius (1787–1870). Greek revival and neo-Gothic architect. Son of Joseph Bonomi, Italian architect domiciled in England. Surveyor of Bridges for Co Durham, where he practised. Set up in 1821; took John Augustus Cory (1819–87) into partnership in 1842; retired in 1850.

St Augustine's, Darlington, Durham (1826–7); St Andrew's new church, Upleatham, N Yorks (1834–5); St Mary's, Sunderland, Durham (1835); St Cuthbert's, Wigton, Cumbria (1837); St Peter's, Scremerston, Northumb (1840–3); St John's, Upper Hopton, W Yorks (1845–6); St Mary's, Oxenhope, W Yorks (1848–9).

Bray, Sir Reginald (c.1440–1503). Architect of the Henry VII Chapel, Westminster Abbey, London (1503–9), and was Henry VII's Chancellor of the Duchy of Lancaster. Also designed St George's Chapel, Windsor Castle, Berks (before 1503) and Great Malvern Priory (before 1502). The nave and aisles of St Mary's, Oxford (1490s) and the tower of St Mary Magdalene's, Taunton, Som (c.1503) have been attributed to him.

Bucknall, Benjamin (1833–95). Neo-Gothic architect. Converted to Catholicism 1852. Pupil of Charles Francis Hansom whom he superseded as designer of the unfinished Woodchester Mansion, Nympsfield, Glos (1858–70). In 1878 he settled in Algiers, some say because of ill-health, leaving his wife and four children behind, and changed his style to neo-Moorish. He designed churches, most of them Catholic, before leaving England.

Our Lady and St Michael's, Abergavenny, Mon (1858); St George's, Taunton, Som (1860); St Mary's (RC), Monmouth (1861–71); St Wulfstan's, Malvern, Worcs (1862); Holy Trinity, Llanegwad, Carms (1865–78).

Burges, William (1827–81). Neo-Gothic architect and furniture, stained glass and jewellery designer. Rich ('Good art is far too rare and far too precious ever to be cheap'), articled to Edward Blore (1843), and then (1848) to Matthew Wyatt. In 1856 he established his own practice in London and in 1863 fulfilled his first major commission, St Finbarre's Cathedral, Cork, which considerably exceeded its budget. Later famous for rebuilding Cardiff Castle and Castell Coch, he designed several churches.

All Saints', Fleet, Hants (1862); St Michael and All Angels, Lowfield Heath, Sussex (1868); Christ the Consoler, Skelton-on-Ure, N Yorks (1876); St Mary's, Fountains Abbey, Ripon, N Yorks (1878); and All Saints', Murston, Kent (1873).

Burn, William (1789–1870). Scottish architect, born in Edinburgh, went to London where he was apprenticed to Sir Robert Smirke, returned to Edinburgh and established a practice there. By 1830 he had the biggest practice in Scotland.

In 1844 he again moved to London to take advantage of increasing English commissions. He designed or worked on some forty churches, almost all neo-Gothic; but see North Leith Parish Church, Edinburgh which is neo-classical (1816). 'Most of his country churches', Howard Colvin comments, 'are of slight architectural merit'.

Keir Church, Dumfries and Galloway (1814); St John's, Edinburgh (1818); New Abbey Church, Dunfermline, Fife (1821); St Peter's, Peebles, Borders (1831); Portpatrick Church, Dumfries and Galloway (1842).

Butterfield, William (1814–1900). Very High Church, very neo-Gothic architect with very nonconformist parents. Set up his own practice in London in 1840, his first commission being Cotham Church, Bristol (1842–3). Designed, restored or extended some hundred churches.

St Ninian's Cathedral, Perth and Kinross (1850); Cathedral of the Isles, Great Cumbrae, Argyll and Bute (1851); Balliol College chapel, Oxford (1856–7); All Saints', Margaret Street, London (1859); St Cross, Clayton, Manchester (1863–6); St Barnabas's, Horton-cum-Studley, Oxon (1867); Rugby School chapel, Warwicks (1875); St Mary Brookfield, Camden, London (1875); Keble College chapel, Oxford (1876).

Also designed St Paul's Cathedral, Melbourne, Victoria, Australia.

Canterbury, Michael of. See Michael of Canterbury.

Caröe, W(illiam) D(ouglas) (1857–1938). Conservation architect, specialising in conserving and restoring cathedrals and churches. Son of the Danish consul at Liverpool (hence the surname) and pupil of J L Pearson. He became architect to the cathedrals of Brecon, Canterbury, Durham, St Davids and Southwell. He founded the firm of Caroe and Partners in 1884; it is now amalgamated with Stainburn Taylor Architects.

His new churches include the Swedish Church, Liverpool, Mersey (1883–4); St Barnabas's, Walthamstow, London (1902–23); St Ninian's, Douglas, IoM (1913); and chapels at St Mary's, Gillingham, Dorset (1921) and Holy Trinity, Eccleshall, Staffs (1929–31).

A(lban) D(ouglas) R(endell) Caroe (1901–91) was W D Caröe's third son (he dropped the diacritical mark on his surname) and ran Caroe and Partners after his father's death. His best-known work was the conservation of the west front of Wells Cathedral, Som (1973–86), on which he worked with his son, Martin (1933–99), and the eastern extension of Newport Cathedral, Glam (1961–2); but see also his St Catherine's, Norwich, Norfolk (1936). Martin Caroe was also a noted conservation architect. See St Helen's, Abingdon, Oxon (the fourteenth-century painted ceiling) and St Peter's, Hascombe, Surrey, where he conserved the wallpaintings.

Carver, Richard (c.1792–1862). Pupil of Sir Jeffrey Wyatville, who established himself in Taunton, Som and held the post of country surveyor. He worked almost entirely in Somerset. He was, said *The Ecclesiologist* (1844), 'entirely ignorant of the principles of Ecclesiastical Architecture'. It is hard to say that *The Ecclesiologist* was wrong.

Holy Trinity, Blackford, near Wedmore (1823); Christ Church, Theale (1828); St Michael's, Burrowbridge (1838); Holy Trinity, Taunton (1842); all in Somerset; St James's, Chedington, Dorset (1841, now a private house).

Chalmers, James (1858–1927). Glagow architect about whose personal life little is known. He mainly designed churches in the neo-Norman or Romanesque style, including Grantshouse Free Church, Borders (1888, his first); Kirriemuir Baptist Church, Angus (1893); St Gabriel's, Govan, Glasgow (1902); Scotstoun Parish

Church, Whiteinch, Glasgow (1906); Oban Cathedral, Argyll and Bute (1908); All Saints', Jordanhill, Glasgow (1910).

Chantrell, Robert Dennis (1793–1872). Neo-Gothic church architect, working in Yorkshire, mostly in the West Riding. Pupil of Sir Robert Soane (1807–14). Set up practice in Leeds, W Yorks (1819) and moved back to London in 1846.

Emmanuel Church, Lockwood, W Yorks (1829); St George's, New Mills, Derbys (1830); Christ Church, Skipton, W Yorks (1839); St Lucius's, Farnley Tyas, W Yorks (1840); St Peter's, Leeds, W Yorks (1841); Holy Trinity, Leven, E Yorks (1845);;St Mary's, Middleton, W Yorks (1846).

Christian, Ewan (1814–95). Vastly prolific neo-Gothic architect. A Manxman, pupil of Matthew Habershon, teacher of W D Caröe and President of the RIBA. There are still mixed views about him: some call him 'the callous Mr Christian'; others 'a revolutionary with a touch of genius'. His best-known work is the National Portrait Gallery, London (1896), but he also designed some ninety new churches and carried out around 1,300 church restorations.

His restorations include Southwell Minster, Notts (1848–88); Carlisle Cathedral, Cumbria (1853–70); St Mary's, Scarborough, N Yorks (1848–52); St Peter's, Wolverhampton, W Mid (1852–65); St Giles's, Skelton, N Yorks (1882); St Bartholomew's, Tong, Salop (1892). New churches include St John's, Hildenborough, Kent (1844); St Stephen's, Tonbridge, Kent (1852); Christ Church, Lewisham, London (1862); St Mark's, Leicester (1872); Holy Trinity, Sunk Island, E Yorks (1877); St Dionis's, Fulham, London (1885); St John's, Locks Heath, Hants (1895).

Clerk, Simon (fl. 1434, died 1489). Master mason who is known to have worked on Bury St Edmunds Abbey, Suffolk from 1445 (it was dissolved in 1539) and King's College Chapel, Cambridge from 1477 to 1485, where he worked with John Wastell on the fan vaulting. Probably involved in the tower of St Peter and St Paul's, Lavenham, Suffolk (c.1486–1525, again with John Wastell), and Great St Mary's, Cambridge (1478–1519).

Clyve, John (fl. 1362–92). Architect working in the Perpendicular style and master mason at Worcester Cathedral (1366–7), where he probably designed the south arcade and the vault of the nave, tower, the north porch and the east cloister.

Cole, John (fl. 1501–5). Master mason responsible for the planning and the early stages of the construction (1501–5) of the spire of St James's, Louth, Lincs, the United Kingdom's second highest parish church spire.

Comper, Sir (John) Ninian (1864–1960). Scottish architect, church interior designer and stained glass artist: some say, the last of the great neo-Gothic figures. Worked in partnership with William Bucknall (1888–1905).

Most notable works are St Cyprian's, Clarence Gate, London (1903); St Mary's, Wellingborough, Northants (1904–31); St Michael and All Angels, Inverness, Highland (1904–28); St Philip's, Cosham, Portsmouth, Hants (1937).

Cottingham, Lewis Nockalls (1787–1847). Conscientious restorer of cathedrals and churches and architectural author. Started in practice 1814.

Cathedrals he restored were Rochester, Kent (1825–30); St Albans, Herts (1832–3); Armagh (1834–7); and Hereford (1841–7, completed by his son). Among the churches he restored were St Mary's, Bury St Edmunds, Suffolk (1843); All Saints', Great Chesterford, Essex (1842) St James's, Louth, Lincs (1844); All Saints', Roos, E Yorks (1847).

Cowper, John (fl. 1453–84). Master mason who was largely responsible for introducing the use of decorative brickwork to England. First mentioned (1453) as working on Eton College. From 1475 he worked on Holy Trinity, Tattershall, Lincs (about 1475 to 1500), and possibly Wayneflete's chantry chapel at Winchester Cathedral, Hants (?1480s) and St George's Chapel, Windsor Castle, Berks (1475–1528).

Crowther, J(oseph) S(tretch) (1820–93). Manchester neo-Gothic architect and church restorer.

Among his new churches were St Philip's, Alderley Edge, Manchester (1853); St Mary's, Hulme, Manchester (1853–8, now converted into flats); St James's, Staveley, Cumbria (1865); and among his restorations were Manchester Cathedral (1850–70); Holy Trinity, Kendal, Cumbria (1869); St Wilfrid's, Northenden, Manchester (1873–6); St Benedict's, Manchester (1880, made redundant 2002, now a climbing centre); St Chad's, Poulton-le-Fylde, Lancs (1881); St George's, Hulme, Manchester (1884).

Dobson, John (1787–1865). Neo-classical, and later neo-Gothic, architect and Newcastle city planner; best known for designing Newcastle Central Station. His daughter said he 'never exceeded an estimate', and he was also a teetotaller and an insomniac. Designed or adapted over sixty churches, as well as over a hundred houses and many public and commercial buildings.

Churches include: Scottish Presbyterian Church, North Shields, Tyne & W (1811, later a Salvation Army hall); St Thomas the Martyr's, Barras Bridge, Newcastle, Tyne & W (1825); Independent Chapel, Sunderland, Durham (1825); St Cuthbert's, Cowpen, Northumb (1840); St Paul's, Hendon, Durham (1852); St Columba's Presbyterian Church, North Shields, Tyne & W (1857); Jesmond Parish Church, Newcastle, Tyne & W (1861).

Douglas, John (1830–1911). Architect working largely in Cheshire, Lancashire and North Wales. Began working in the neo-Gothic style, but soon included vernacular elements such as timber framing, pargetting and tile hanging. Established a practice in Chester in either 1855 or 1860, and designed some 500 buildings of all kinds.

His new churches include (grade I and II* only): St Anne's, Warrington, Ches (1869); St Mary the Virgin's, Halkyn, Flint (1877–88); St Michael's, Altcar, Lancs (1879); St Mary's, Pulford, Ches (1884); St Paul's, Colwyn Bay, Conwy (nave 1888, chancel 1895, tower 1911); St John's, Barmouth, Gwynnedd (1889–95); Christ Church, Bryn-y-Maen, Conwy (1899); All Saints', Deganwy, Conwy (1899); St John's, Weston, Ches (1900); St John the Baptist's, Old Colwyn, Conwy (1899–1903).

Drew, Sir Thomas (1838–1910). Immensely energetic Irish neo-Gothic eccesiastical architect. Architect for the diocese of Down, Connor and Dromore from 1865 and consultant architect to Christ Church and St Patrick's Cathedrals, Dublin, Armagh Protestant Cathedral and St Columb's Cathedral, Derry; responsible for the restoration of Holy Trinity Cathedral, Waterford. Designed St Anne's Cathedral, Belfast (1899).

His many churches include Kilmore Church, Crossgar, (1866–8); Drumbeg Parish Church (1868–70); St Donard's, Dundrum (1886), all in Co Down; and St Jude's, Ormeau Road, Belfast (1869–75).

Dunn, Archibald M(atthias) (1832–1917). Catholic neo-Gothic architect working in north-east England. Apprenticed to C F Hansom and later went into partnership with his son, E J Hansom.

His churches (all Catholic) include: St Mary's, Blackhill, Durham (1854); St Joseph's, Gateshead, Tyne & W (1858); Our Lady and St Wilfrid's, Blyth, Northumb (1858); St Anthony of Padua's, Walker, Newcastle, Tyne & W (1860); St George's, Bells Close, Lemington, Tyne & W (1869); St Dominic's, Newcastle, Tyne & W (1873).

Dykes Bower, Stephen (1903–94). Architect and church restorer. Neo-Gothic by taste, through thick and thin. Surveyor to the Fabric, Westminster Abbey, London, 1951–73.

New churches include All Saints', Hockerill, Herts (1937); St John the Evangelist's, Newbury, Berks (1957); Holy Spirit, Southsea, Hants (1958); and St Nicholas's, Great Yarmouth, Norfolk (1961). His restorations were mostly due to Second World War damage and include St Alban's Copnor, Portsmouth, Hants (1950?); St Edmundsbury Cathedral, Bury St Edmunds, Suffolk (from 1960, chancel, transepts and side chapels).

Ely, Reginald or Reynold (fl. 1438–71). Master mason responsible for the design of King's College Chapel, Cambridge from 1446 to 1461, when work ceased. (It recommenced in 1483 and was finished in 1515). He may also have designed St Mary's, Burwell, Cambs and the lower stage of the tower at St Botolph's, Boston, Lincs (both mid-fifteenth century.

Englishman, William the. See William the Englishman.

Everard, Robert (fl. 1440–85). Worked at Norwich Cathedral, Norfolk, from c.1452 and is credited with building the spire and the nave vaulting. He may also have worked on St Mary's, Martham, Norfolk (1456–69: the chancel was demolished 1855–61); St John's, Norwich, Norfolk (1470, now St Andrew's Hall); and St Margaret's, Hardley, Norfolk (1458–62).

Ferrey, Benjamin (1810–80). Neo-Gothic architect. Studied with A W N Pugin under Pugin's father, A C Pugin. Started his own practice in 1834 in London, which grew to a prodigious size. Diocesan architect for Bath and Wells from 1841 to his death. Designed or restored over fifty churches.

His new churches include: All Saints', Dogmersfield, Hants (1843); St Barnabas's, Swanmore, Hants (1846); Holy Trinity, Wood Green, Witney, Oxon (1849); Holy Trinity, Deanshanger, Northants (1853); St Mary's, Fairfield, Worcs (1854); Christ Church, Colbury, Hants (1870).

Flockton, William (1804–64) and **Flockton, Thomas James** (1823–99). Father and son. Neo-Gothic architects in the Sheffield area. William Flockton set up as an architect in 1833, in partnership with his son from 1849–64. Thomas James Flockton was joined by George Lewslie Abbott, who retired in 1877, then by Edward Mitchel Gibbs (1847–1935).

They designed (all in Sheffield, S Yorks): Holy Trinity (1848, now the New Testament Church of God); Christ Church, Pitsmoor Road (1850); St Thomas's, Brightside (1854); St Matthew's (1855); St Stephen's (1857), St Barnabas's, Highfield Place (1876); St Thomas's, Newman Road (1876); St John's, Ranmoor (1887). Flockton and Gibbs also carried out a sizeable restoration of Sheffield Cathedral (1880).

Foster, James (c.1748–1823). Bristol architect with an odd mix of neo-classical and neo-Gothic. His sons James II (died 1836), another son, Thomas (1793–1846), his grandson John (died 1880), and William Ignatius Okeley (dates unknown: he left the firm after 1840) joined the practice after James Foster's death.

His, and later their, churches include St Andrew's, Clifton, Bristol (1822, destroyed 1940, demolished 1956); and, all in Glos, St John's, Beachley (1833); Holy Trinity, Brimscombe (1839); Christ Church, Hanham (1842).

Fowler, C(harles) Hodgson (1840–1910). Neo-Gothic church restorer and architect working mostly in Co Durham, Yorkshire, Lincolnshire and Nottinghamshire. Articled to Sir Gilbert Scott, and at different times architect to Rochester, Lincoln and Durham Cathedrals.

New churches include St Mary's, South Hylton, Sunderland, Tyne & W (1880); St

Helen's, Grove, Notts (1882); St Andrew's, Bishopthorpe, York (1898–1902).

Gabriel, S(amuel) B(urleigh) (?–1866). Neo-Gothic church architect about whom little is known. He worked mostly in Bristol and mostly in partnership with another architect called S J Hicks.

New churches (all in Bristol) include: St Mark's, Easton (1848, now supported housing); St Simon the Apostle's, Baptist Mills (1848, since 1960 St Peter and St Paul Greek Orthodox church); St Jude the Apostle with St Matthias-on-the-Weir, Old Market, (1849); St Michael the Archangel's, Two-Mile-Hill (1849); St John the Evangelist's, Clifton (1858–69).

Garner, Thomas (1839–1906). See under G F Bodley.

Gibbons, Grinling (1648–1721). Wood carver and sculptor. Born in Rotterdam and came to England in 1667. Evelyn the diarist first discovered him in 1671 and recommended him to Sir Christopher Wren. By the late1680s he was working for Charles II and went on to work for James II, William III (who gave him the title Master Carver) and George I. In addition to much work in palaces and country houses, he was employed by Wren on (all in London) St Paul's Cathedral (choir stalls and organ case); Westminster Abbey (monument to Sir Cloudesley Shovell); St James's, Piccadilly (font and reredos); St Mary Abchurch (reredos); St Alfege's, Greenwich (pulpit, column capitals); St Paul's, Covent Garden (where he is buried: pulpit). He also carved the archbishop's throne in Canterbury Cathedral, Kent, and the statue of Archbishop Lamplugh in York Minster.

Gibbs, James (1682–1754). Baroque architect. He was sent to the Scots College in Rome in 1703 to train for the priesthood but abandoned his studies within a year and devoted himself to architecture. Returned to England in 1709 with a thorough knowledge of Italian Baroque and a deep admiration for Sir Christopher Wren. Published *A Book of Architecture* (1728), possibly the most widely read book on the subject in the eighteenth century.

His churches were: St Mary-le-Strand, London (1717); Shipbourne Church, Kent (1722, rebuilt 1879); St Peter's, Vere Street, London (1724, now deconsecrated); St Martin-in-the-Fields, London (1726); All Saints', Derby (1725, now Derby Cathedral); St Mary's, Patshull, Staffs (1743, now redundant). The Hospital Chapel, Kirkleatham, N Yorks (1741–8) is attributed to him. After his death, St Nicholas's West, Aberdeen (now Kirk of St Nicholas Uniting) was rebuilt in 1751–5 from Gibbs's own drawings.

Goldie, George (1828–87). Neo-Gothic architect specialising in Roman Catholic churches. (He was a Catholic himself).

St Mungo's Cathedral, Glasgow (1850); St Vincent's, Sheffield, S Yorks (1856); St Pancras's, Ipswich, Suffolk (1861); St Wilfrid's, York (1864); St Mary and St Augustine's, Stamford, Lincs (1865); and Our Lady of Victories, Kensington, London (1869).

Goodwin, Francis (1784–1835). Importunate Midlands architect, going in for every competition he could. It is unsurprising that he died (insolvent) of insomnia followed by apoplexy, working on the competition for the new Houses of Parliament in 1835. (He did not win it).

Holy Trinity, Bordesley, Birmingham, W Mid (1823, deconsecrated in 1970, now empty); St John's, Derby (1828); St Mary's, Bilston, W Mid (1830, a Commissioners' church).

Graham, James Gillespie (1776–1855). Scottish neo-Gothic architect, born James Gillespie. His early career is unknown, but in 1815 he married an heiress, Margaret Graham, and added her surname to his own. Howard Colvin describes him as 'ambitious, pushing and none too scrupulous'; he once used virtually the same floor plans for country houses in Lanarkshire and Argyll and Bute. He was a prolific church architect.

Clackmannan Church, Clackmannanshire (1815); Kilmadock Church, Perth and Kinross (1822); Dunino Church, Fife (1826); Errol Church, Perth and Kinross (1833); Tolbooth St John's Church, Edinburgh (1844, built as Victoria Hall, now The Hub).

Green, John (1787–1852) and **Benjamin Green** (1813–58). Father and son, neo-Gothic architects in Northumberland and Co Durham. The father's and the son's buildings are indistinguishable from each other (except that John Green specialised in bridges) and usually indifferent. Worked occasionally with John Dobson.

All in Northumberland: United Secession Meeting House, Clavering Place, Newcastle (1822); St Mary's Chapel, Alnwick (1836, now the Bailiffgate Museum); Holy Trinity, Dalton (1837); Holy Saviour, Sugley (1837); Holy Trinity, Cambo (1842); Holy Trinity, Horsley (1844); Holy Trinity, Seghill (1849).

Grimthorpe, Lord (1816–1905). Edmund Beckett (Denison), first Baron Grimthorpe. Architect who said (with some reason) 'I am the only architect with whom I have never quarrelled'. Pevsner calls him a 'pompous, righteous, bully'. Famous for designing the clock mechanism for the Houses of Parliament (1851); infamous (in the view of contemporaries) for his restoration of St Albans Cathedral, Herts, and also St Peter's (1893) and St Michael's (1896), both in St Albans and both restored at his own expense. Less controversially, he worked with W H Crossland on designing St Chad's, Far Headingly, Leeds, W Yorks (1868). See also the section on Clocks.

Gwilt, George (1775–1856) the Younger. Son of George Gwilt the Elder, a respected surveyor. Best known for the restoration of the steeple and foundations of St Mary-le-Bow, Cheapside, London (1818–20) and the restoration of the choir and tower of St Saviour's, Southwark (1822–5, now Southwark Cathedral) and its Lady Chapel (1832–3).

Habershon, W(illiam) G(illbee) (1818–92) and **Matthew Edward** (1828–1900). Neo-Gothic architects, sons of Matthew Habershon (1789–1852), a respected architect to whom Ewan Christian was articled, opponent of A W N Pugin and pioneering expert on timber-framed buildings. W G and E Habershon were partners from 1852 to 1863, when they separated and took other partners.

W G and E Habershon's churches include St John's, Hove, Sussex (1856); St Augustine's, Scaynes Hill, Sussex (1858); St Michael's, Boulge, Suffolk (1858) and St Michael's, Newhaven, Sussex (1854, restoration).

W G Habershon's churches include St Peter's, Sandy, Beds (1859); All Saints', Challoch, Dumfries and Galloway (1872); St Dunstan's, Ashhurst Wood, Sussex (1886); St Peter's, Shelley, Essex (1888); St Michael's, Partridge Green, Sussex (1890); Roath Park Presbyterian Chapel, Cardiff, Glam (1897); St James's, Warter, E Yorks (1863); Holy Trinity, Lower Beeding, Sussex (1862 and 1884, both extensions).

E Habershon's churches include St Giles's, Dallington, Sussex (1864, restoration); Holy Trinity, Ebernoe, Sussex (1867); St John's, Copthorne, Sussex (1877).

Hadfield, Matthew Ellison (1812–85). Catholic, mostly neo-Gothic, architect specialising in Roman Catholic churches, and from 1850 to 1860 partner of his former pupil George Goldie. He designed three Catholic cathedrals: St John's, Salford, Manchester (1848); St Marie's, Sheffield, S Yorks (1850); and the Cathedral of the Annunciation and St Nathy, Ballaghaderreen, Co Roscommon (1860).

His churches include St Vincent's, Sheffield, S Yorks (1853, expanded by George Goldie 1856, disused since 1998); St Catherine's, Littlehampton, Sussex (1863); St Hilda's, Whitby, N Yorks (1867); St Bede's, Rotherham, S Yorks (date not known). But his All Saints', Glossop, Derbys (1834–7) is neo-classical.

Hamilton, David (1768–1843). Glasgow architect, mostly neo-Gothic, but also indulging in Greek Revival, neo-Jacobean, Italianate and neo-Norman. He designed public, commercial and domestic buildings and country houses as well as churches. Many of his churches have been demolished, but those surviving include: Ayr New Church (1812); Larbert Old Church, Stirling (1820); Campsie High Church, Lennoxtown, Stirling (1828, ruinous, damaged by fire); Bothwell Church, Lanarkshire (1833).

Hamilton, Thomas (1784–1858). Edinburgh architect, son of an architect, also Thomas. He was the leading Greek Revivalist architect in Scotland, though his churches are mostly neo-Gothic. His churches are indifferent.

St John's (now St Columba's) Free Church, Johnston Terrace, Edinburgh (1845); New North Free Church, Forrest Row, Edinburgh (1846, now the student-run Bedlam Theatre, owned by Edinburgh University); St Mary's, South Leith, Edinburgh (1848, rebuilt); Free Church, Dunbar, East Lothian (1850, later Abbey Church; disused and now (2013) for sale); St Kenneth's, Kennoway, Fife (1850).

Hansom, Charles Francis (1817–88) Neo-Gothic architect. Roman Catholic, brother of J A Hansom with whom he was in partnership 1854–9, when he established his own practice in Bath with his son, E J Hansom. Known as 'Francis the Handsome'. Designed solely Roman Catholic churches and one Roman Catholic cathedral (with his brother), Plymouth (1856–8).

Churches include Our Lady and St Alphonsus's, Hanley Swan, Worcs (1846); St Gregory's, Cheltenham, Glos (1854–77); St John's, Bath, Som (1863); Holy Family, Broxwood, Herefs, (1863); Annunciation to the Blessed Virgin Mary, Souldern, Oxon (1867). Also designed Clifton College, Bristol (1860s and 1873–5) and Malvern College, Worcs (1863–71).

Hansom, Joseph (Aloysius) (1803–82). Prolific (he designed over 200 buildings), neo-Gothic, and on occasion neo-classical, Roman Catholic architect. He also invented the hansom cab (1834) and founded *The Builder* (1843), renamed *Building* in 1966 and still going strong. From neither the hansom cab nor *The Builder* did he make any money. In partnership with Edward Welch, 1828–34, with whom he designed Birmingham Town Hall, W Mid, in 1831, which led to their bankruptcy. Churches by Hansom and Welch appear under Welch.

His many churches include St Edward King and Confessor, Clifford, W Yorks (1848); St Beuno's Theologate, St Asaph, Den (1848); St George's, Peel Street, York (1850); Mount St Mary's, the 'Famine Church', Leeds, W Yorks (1852, now empty and stripped); St Walburge's, Preston, Lancs (1854: it has the tallest church spire in England); Plymouth Cathedral (built 1858, with his brother C F Hansom); Our Lady and St Neot's, Liskeard, Cornwall (1863).St Mary Immaculate, Falmouth, Cornwall (1868); Church of the Holy Name of Jesus, Manchester (1871); The Oxford Oratory, Oxford (1875); St Mary's Priory, Fulham Road, London (1876).

Hardwick, Thomas (1752–1829). Neo-classical (though sometimes neo-Gothic) architect, specialising in churches. A pupil of Sir William Chambers, visited Italy 1776–9; J M W Turner was in his office for a time.

St Mary's, Wanstead, Essex (1790); St Mary's, Marylebone Road, London (1817); St John's, Workington, Cumbria (1823); Holy Trinity, Bolton, Lancs (1825); St John's, Farnworth, Lancs (1826, a Commissioners' church); St Barnabas's, King Square, Finsbury, London (1826, now St Clement's).

Harrison, James (1814–66). Chester architect about whom little is known. In his secular buildings he favoured the neo-Tudor, black-and-white, style; but his churches, several of which are no longer used for worship, are neo-Gothic.

St Michael's, Chester, Ches (1850, made redundant 1972, now a heritage centre); Holy Ascension, Upton, Ches (1854); All Saints', Handley, Ches (1855); Holy Trinity, Capenhurst, Ches (1859); St Luke's, Dunham on the Hill, Ches (1861); Holy Trinity, Chester, Ches (1869, made redundant 1960s, now the Guildhall).

Hawksmoor, Nicholas (1661–1736). Baroque architect. Worked with Sir Christopher Wren, c.1679 until about 1700, working on Chelsea Hospital, St Paul's Cathedral, Hampton Court Palace and Greenwich Hospital, all in London. Clerk of the Works at Kensington Palace (1689) and Deputy Surveyor of Works at Greenwich (1705), also in London. Later worked with Sir John Vanbrugh, whose assistant (some say mentor) he became, working with him on Blenheim Palace, Oxon (1705–16) and then in sole charge (1722–5); and Castle Howard, N Yorks (1728–36). Made his name with his six London churches: St Alfege's, Greenwich (1712–4, completed by John James 1730. Gutted 1941, reopened after restoration 1963); St Anne's, Limehouse (1714–30, damaged by fire 1850); St George-in-the-East, Wapping (1714–29, gutted 1941 but exterior restored 1960–4); Christ Church, Spitalfields (1714–29, much altered 1822–3, 1851 and 1866); St Mary Woolnoth (1716–24, altered by Butterfield 1875–6); St George's, Bloomsbury (1716–31). Also worked with John James on St Luke Old Street (1727–33) and St John Horsleydown (1727–33) and on the west towers of Westminster Abbey, London (1734–c.1745, completed by John James), all in London.

Haycock, Edward (1790–1870). Born in Shrewsbury, pupil of Sir Jeffrey Wyatville in London, and in about 1814 returned to Shrewsbury to join his father's building business. After about 1845 he devoted himself entirely to architecture. He became a town stalwart: County Surveyor, 1834–66, Conservative Councillor for thirty-four years and mayor in 1842. Howard Colvin says, 'His numerous Gothic churches…do nothing to enhance his reputation.'

St Peter's, Machynlleth, Powys (1827); St George's, Frankwell, Shrewbury, Salop (1832); St David's, Carmarthen, Carms (1836); Christ Church, Cressage, Salop (1841); St Edward's, Dorrington, Salop (1845).

Hayward, John (1807–91). West of England neo-Gothic architect, specialising, though not exclusively, in designing and restoring churches. Trained under Sir Charles Barry and in 1834 set up his practice in Exeter. His most noticeable building is the Royal Albert Memorial Museum, Exeter.

Churches in Devon include St John the Evangelist's, Tipton St John (1839); St Andrew's, Exwick (1841); St Mary's, Bickleigh (1843, restoration); All Saints', Okehampton (1844); St Mary's, Bicton (1850); St Michael's, Sowton (1845); St Mary's, Uffculme (?1850, restoration); St Philip and St James's, Ilfracombe (1856); St Michael and All Angels, Alphington, Exeter (date not known, restoration). He also designed several churches in Jersey.

Herland, Hugh (c.1330–1411). Richard II's master carpenter. He designed and built the hammerbeam roof of Westminster Hall, London, 1393–1400. Though not part of a church building, its influence was immense.

Honeyman, John (1831–1914). Mostly neo-Gothic architect, born in Glasgow and did most of his work there. Set up in practice in 1861 and made his name with designs for Free West Church, Greenock, Renfrewshire (1861) and Lansdowne United Presbyterian Church, Glasgow (1862). The practice expanded rapidly.

Park Free Church, Helensborough, Argyll and Bute (1862); Cathcart Free Church, Glasgow (1865); Free West Church, Perth,

Perth and Kinross (1869–72, alterations and additions by Honeyman, 1895); Kirkcudbright Free Church, Dumfries and Galloway (1874, alterations and additions by Honeyman, 1886, 1894, converted into flats 1987); St Anthony's, Glasgow (1879, Roman Catholic).

In 1888 he took into partnership the wealthy architect John Keppie, who hired in turn Charles Rennie Mackintosh (1889). By this time Honeyman's sight was failing. He went blind in about 1902. Towards the end of his life he was involved in the restoration of two cathedrals, Brechin Cathedral, Angus (1898–1902) and Iona Abbey, Argyll and Bute (1902–4).

Hopkins, William (J) (1820–91). Worcs architect who became Worcester Diocesan Architect. He designed, renovated and rebuilt many Worcestershire churches.

Cow Honeybourne parish church, Honeybourne (1863, rebuilt; now private houses); St Peter ad Vincula, Tibberton (1868); All Saints', Wilden (1880); St Mathias and St George's, Astwood Bank (1884).

Hugall, John West. Indifferent neo-Gothic architect about whom nothing is known, not even his dates. He seems to have been active from about 1848–78.

His new churches include: All Saints', Durrington, Wilts (1851, largely rebuilt); St James's, Bourton, Oxon (1860); St Michael and All Angels, Little Marcle, Herefs (1870); St James's, Welland, Worcs (1875).

Hurley, William (fl. 1319, died 1394). Edward III's master carpenter, in charge of all royal timber works. Consultant who designed, and maybe worked on, the Lantern and the misericords at Ely Cathedral, Cambs.

Hurst, William (1787–1844). Born, worked and died in Doncaster, S Yorks, first in partnership with John Woodhead (died c.1838) and, after his death, with William Lambie Moffat, or Moffatt (1808–82). Built many neo-Gothic churches, particularly churches financed by The Incorporated Church Building Society.

He designed, as Woodhead and Hurst, St George's, Portobello, Sheffield, S Yorks (1825, a Commissioners' church, now part of the University of Sheffield); St Thomas's, New Brampton, Derbys (1831); St John's, Ridgeway, Derbys (1840). As Hurst and Moffat, he designed St George's, Woodsetts, W Yorks (1841); St John's, Goole, W Yorks (1848); St Peter's, Rock Ferry, Ches (1842).

Hussey, R(ichard) C(harles) (1806–87). Architect and partner (from 1835) of Thomas Rickman. He inherited Rickman's practice on Rickman's terminal illness (1838).

Churches include: St John the Evangelist's, Stoke Row, Oxon (1846); St Mary's, Frittenden, Kent (1848); St Laurence's, South Weston, Oxon (1860); St John the Evangelist's, Knypersley, Staffs (date not known)

Inwood, William (c.1771–1843) and Inwood, Henry William (1794–1843). Neo-classical and sometimes neo-Gothic architects, father and son, who seem to have always worked together. Their St Pancras's New Church, London (1822, neo-classical) was much admired, as was their Camden Chapel, London (1824, neo-classical, later St Stephen's, after 1920 All Saints'). St Mary's, Somers Town, London (1827, neo-Gothic); St Stephen's, Islington, London (1839, neo-Gothic) were less admired. H W Inwood was drowned at sea.

Jackson, Sir Thomas Graham (1835–1924). Primarily a school and college architect but also a church restorer. Pupil of Sir Gilbert Scott's (1858–61). Set up his own practice in 1862 and carried out a substantial body of work in what he himself called a 'refined English Renaissance' style in Oxford, Cambridge and various public schools, including chapels at Radley College, Berks (1891–1910) and Giggleswick School, N Yorks (1897).

James, John (c.1673–1746). Carpenter (Master of the Carpenters' Company, 1734) and baroque architect. He was one of the two Commissioners for Building Fifty New Churches (1716; the other one was Nicholas Hawksmoor). Joint Clerk of the Works at Greenwich Hospital (with Nicholas Hawksmoor) from 1718 until his, James's, death. Surveyor to the Fabric, St Paul's Cathedral on Wren's death (1723). Surveyor to the Fabric, Westminster Abbey from 1736.

Churches include St Mary's, Twickenham, London (1715); St Mary's, Rotherhithe, London (1715); St Lawrence's, Little Stanmore, London (1716); St George's, Hanover Square, London (1725).

Janyns, Robert (fl. 1438–64) and his sons Henry (fl. 1453–83) and Robert II (fl. 1499–1506). Family of masons and master masons working in the Perpendicular tradition. The father worked on All Souls College, the chapel of Merton College and the Divinity School, Oxford. Henry became Chief Master of the Works at St George's Chapel, Windsor Castle, Berks in about 1475. His brother Robert was chief mason during the building of Henry VII's tower at Windsor Castle, Berks (1499–1505) and probably worked on the Lady Chapel at Burford Church, Oxon (1490s).

Jenkins, William (c.1763–1844). Methodist minister, c.1790–1810. When he retired due to ill-health, he began a second career as an architect in London. He designed solely Methodist chapels.

Carver St, Sheffield, S Yorks (1804, now a pub); St Peter's, St Peters St, Canterbury, Kent (1811); Bondgate, Darlington, Co Durham (1812); Bishop St, Leicester (1815); Walcot, Bath, Som (1816); Gold St, Northampton (1816, now closed).

Joy, William (fl. 1329–47). Master mason at Wells Cathedral, Som, from 1329. He created the strainer arches at the crossing (1338–48), the pulpitum, the presbytery, the vaulting over the presbytery and choir, and the retrochoir. He also worked at Exeter Cathedral from 1342 until his death, which was before 1352; and probably at St Mary's, Ottery St Mary, Devon (1337–45). He may have worked at St Augustine's Abbey, Bristol (now Bristol Cathedral).

Kirby, Edmund (1838–1920). Neo-Gothic Catholic architect. Worked for John Douglas and by 1863 set up his own practice. Most of his work was in Liverpool, the northwest of England and North Wales. His practice still exists.

St Werburgh's, Chester, Ches (1875); St Michael and All Angels, Little Leigh, Ches (1879); Our Lady and All Saints', Parbold, Lancs (1884); St Cross, Appleton Thorn, Ches (1887); St John's, High Legh, Macclesfield, Ches (1893); St Joseph's, Tranmere, Birkenhead, Mersey (1900); St Peter and St Francis's, Prestatyn, Den (1903); St John the Baptist's, Meols, Mersey (1913).

Lindsay, Ian G(ordon) (1906–66). Scottish conservation architect. Worked for Orphoot and Whiting from 1933–52, when he set up his own practice, restoring many houses for the National Trust for Scotland, and Pluscarden Abbey, Elgin, Moray.

He restored St Mahew's Church, Cardross, Argyll and Bute (1953); St Mary's-by-the-sea, Wemyss, Fife (1954); Craigmillar Park Church, Edinburgh (1956); Newcastle Cathedral, Tyne & W (1961); Canongate Church, Edinburgh (1963); Iona Abbey, Argyll and Bute (1965); Oban Cathedral, Argyll and Bute (1968).

Lock, Adam (fl. 1215–c.1229). Master mason; architect of much of Wells Cathedral (1207–29) except the West Front, and thought to have been the architect of the Elder Lady Chapel, St Augustine's Abbey, Bristol (now Bristol Cathedral).

Lote, Stephen (fl. 1381–1417/8). Assistant and successor to Henry Yevele at Canterbury Cathedral, Kent, Westminster Abbey and the Tower of London. At

Canterbury Cathedral he was responsible for the cloisters, continuing the work on the transepts, the pulpitum and the tomb of Henry IV. He probably continued Yevele's work at All Saints', Maidstone, Kent, and probably designed St Mary and All Saints', Fotheringhay, Northants (c.1415).

Manners, George Phillips (c.1789–1866). Indifferent neo-Gothic architect who worked in Bath and held the post of city architect from 1823 till his retirement in 1862.

St Michael's, Bath, Som (1836); St John's, Weston, Bath, Som (1838); All Saints', East Huntspill, Som (1839); Holy Trinity, Cleeve, Som (1840); Christ Church, Bradford-on-Avon, Wilts (1840).

Mapilton, Thomas (fl. 1408, died 1438). Master mason at Durham Cathedral where he designed the cloisters (1408–16). Appointed King's Master Mason in 1421. Consultant to Canterbury Cathedral, Kent, where he designed the south western tower. In 1429 he was responsible for old St Stephen's, Walbrook, London (completed 1439), and in 1429–30 he was consultant to Bury St Edmunds Abbey. He may have visited Florence Cathedral in 1420 as a consultant on the vaulting.

Maufe, Sir Edward (Brantwood) (1883–1974, originally surnamed Muff). Restrained and correct architect, most famous for designing Guildford Cathedral (1936–61). Went to St John's College, Oxford, where he later designed the Dolphin Quad (1947).

St Bede's, Clapham Road, London (1924); St Saviour's Church for the Deaf, Acton, London (1926); St Thomas the Apostle's, Hanwell, London (1934); St John the Evangelist's, Hook, Hants (1938); St Columba's, Knightbridge, London (1955); St Nicholas's, Saltdean, Sussex (1964).

Michael of Canterbury (fl. 1275–1321). Master mason, who is said to have invented the ogee arch. Worked at Canterbury Cathedral, Kent, designed St Stephen's Chapel, Westminster, London (from 1292, destroyed by fire, 1834) and probably also the Chapel of St Etheldreda, Ely Place, London (1290–8). He also designed memorials: the Eleanor Cross, Cheapside, London (1290–4, destroyed 1642); the tombs of Edmund Crouchback and Aveline of Lancaster in Westminster Abbey, London (both c.1296); Bishop William of Louth, Ely Cathedral, Cambs (c.1298); and probably Archbishop Peckham in Canterbury Cathedral, Kent (died 1292).

Moffat, William Lambie (1808–82). See Hurst, William.

Moore, Temple (Lushington) (1856–1920). Neo-Gothic architect, assistant to George Gilbert Scott Jnr from 1879 to 1890, when he set up his own practice.

St Aidan's, Carlton, N Yorks (1886); St Mark's, Mansfield, Notts (1894); St John the Evangelist's, West Hendon, London (1896); St Wilfrid's, Harrogate, N Yorks (1908); St Margaret of Antioch, Leeds, W Yorks (1908); St Augustine's, Gillingham, Kent (1916).

Newall, Walter (1780–1863). Greek Revival and neo-Gothic architect. Born, worked and died in Dumfries, and during the middle of the nineteenth century was the area's leading architect, building small-scale public buildings, farmsteads and churches.

His churches include Buittle (1819); Kirkmahoe (1823); New Abbey (1824); Anwoth (1827); Parton (1834); Kirkpatrick Durham (1850); all in Dumfries and Galloway.

Nicholson, Sir Charles Archibald (1867–1949). Neo-Gothic and Arts and Crafts architect. Consultant cathedral architect to Belfast (west front, 1925–7), Lincoln (towers, 1922), Lichfield, Llandaff, Portsmouth (1935, westwards extension), Sheffield and Wells (Crucifixion, 1920), and diocesan architect for Chelmsford (extension of the choir, 1923–6), Wakefield and Winchester, He also worked on Brecon (the Havard chapel, 1922), Leicester (bishop's throne and choir stalls1927), and Carlisle (high altar and baldacchino, 1936).

New churches include St Matthew's, Chelston, Torquay, Devon (1904); St Alban's, Westcliffe-on-Sea, Essex (1908); St Paul's, Yelverton, Devon (1912); St Luke's, Downham, Lewisham, London (1928); St Andrew's, Bromley, London (1929); St Elisabeth's, Dagenham, London (1932); All Saints', Hillingdon, London (1932); St Lawrence's, Eastcote, London (1932); St Mary's, Bournemouth, Hants (1934, now redundant).

Norreys, Thomas (fl. 1229–49). Master mason, deputy to Adam Lock at Wells Cathedral, Som, and succeeded him after his death. Responsible for the western end of the nave and the west front of Wells Cathedral.

Oates, John (1793–1831). Neo-Gothic church architect who was born, worked and died in Halifax, W Yorks. He designed ten churches for the Commissioners for Church Building, eight of which survive. The earliest was St Matthew's, Buckley, Flint (1822) and the last that he personally supervised was Holy Trinity, Idle, W Yorks. His last two Commissioners' churches, St Mark's, Shelton, Staffs (1833) and St James's, Hebden Bridge, W Yorks (1833), were erected after his death by his brother Matthew and Thomas Pickersgill, Matthew's partner.

Orchard, William (fl. 1468, died 1504). Master mason, responsible for Magdalen College, Oxford (from 1467), the pendant vaults (and possibly the chancel vaults, 1478–1503) of the Divinity School, Oxford (1480–3), the cloisters of Christ Church Cathedral, Oxford (c.1489–99) and parts of the Cistercian College of St Bernard, Oxford (from 1502; now incorporated in the Front Quad of St John's College, Oxford). He also designed St Leonard's, Waterstock, Oxon (1500–2, nave and chancel rebuilt 1790, restored by G E Street 1858) and possibly designed the Harcourt Chapel at St Michael's, Stanton Harcourt, Oxon (c.1470).

Owen, T(homas) E(llis) (1804–62). Town developer, successful speculative builder and architect. Trained in London, went to Italy and when he returned saw Southsea, Hants, then marshland, as a prime development site, which he worked on from 1834 to 1850. Nonetheless, he began and ended by building churches.

St Mary's, East Stoke, Dorset (1829, now converted to three houses); Holy Trinity, Fareham, Hants (1836, a Commissioners' church); St Jude's, Southsea, Hants (1851); Holy Trinity, Hadley, Salop (1856).

Pace, George (Gaze) (1915–75). Architect, restorer, church furnisher and cathedral architect to York Minster. He restored Llandaff Cathedral, Cardiff, Glam, after war damage, including the pulpitum (1955–60).

Chapel at Scargill House, Kettlewell, N Yorks (1960); St Mark's, Chadderton, Manchester (1963); William Temple Memorial Church, Wythenshawe, Manchester (1965); Keele University Chapel, Newcastle-under-Lyme, Staffs (1965); extension to St Andrew's, Rushmere St Andrew, Ipswich, Suffolk (1968); Bell Tower at Chester Cathedral, Ches (1969–75).

Paley, E(dward) G(raham) (1823–95). Neo-Gothic architect, partner of Edmund Sharpe and later (1868) of Hubert Austin. Lived and worked in Lancashire, though he was a Yorkshireman. He himself designed or restored over fifty churches.

All in Lancashire: St Mary's, Yealand Conyers (1852); St James's, Wrightington Bar (1857); St Mary and St Michael's, Bonds (1858); St Peter's (now Lancaster Cathedral), Lancaster (1859); St Peter's, Quernmore (1860); St Anne's, Singleton (1861); All Saints', Higher Walton (1862); St Saviour's, Aughton 1864); St Andrew's, Livesey, Blackburn (1867).

Palmer, John (1785–1846). Neo-Gothic, Roman Catholic, solely ecclesiastical architect.

Pleasington Priory (or St Mary and St John's), Pleasington, Lancs (1818); St Mary's, Blackburn, Lancs (1826, now Blackburn Cathedral); Holy Trinity, Ashton-in-Makerfield, Lancs (1838).

Pearson, Frank Loughborough (1864–1947). Only son of J L Pearson. Joined his father's office in 1881; made a partner 1890; completed several buildings after his father's death (see below).

Pearson, John Loughborough (1817–97). Conservative, not to say cautious, neo-Gothic architect. Born in Durham, where he trained under Bonomi, and moved to London, where he trained under Philip Hardwick (1792–1870). Restored or worked on Bristol, Chichester (Sussex), Exeter (Devon), Lincoln and Peterborough (Cambs) cathedrals, St George's Chapel, Windsor Castle, Berks, and Westminster Abbey, London.

His many churches include St Anne's, Ellerker, E Yorkshire (1843); St Matthew's, Landscove, Devon (1850); St Peter's, Daylesford, Glos (1863); St Peter's, Vauxhall, London (1864); St Augustine's, Kilburn, London (designed 1870, but not completed until 1897); St Michael and All Angels, Croydon, London (1881); Truro Cathedral, Cornwall (1880–1910, completed by his son, Frank Pearson); St Agnes, Toxteth Park, Liverpool, Mersey (1885); All Saints', Hove, Sussex (1887, completed by Frank Pearson); St John's, Friern Barnet, London (designed 1889, completed by Frank Pearson); St Mary's, Laverstoke, Hants (1895); St Stephen's, Bournemouth, Dorset (1898).

Pinch, John, the younger (1786–1849). Architect based in Bath. Son of John Pinch the elder (1769–1827) who was a builder-architect (St Mary's, Bathwick, 1817–20). Worked with his father from about 1820 and succeeded to his father's practice.

Churches (all except the last in the neo-Gothic style) include St Saviour's, Walcot, Bath, Som (1831); St John the Baptist's, Midsomer Norton, Som (1831); All Saints', Weston, Som (1832); Christ Church, Downside, Som (1838, made redundant 1983); Holy Trinity, Paulton, Som (1839); and St John the Baptist's, Farrington Gurney, Som (1844, neo-Norman).

Ponting, Charles (1850–1932). West Country neo-Gothic architect, mainly engaged in restorations.

His new churches include St Michael's, West Overton, Wilts (1878); St Birinus's, Redlynch, Wilts (1896); St John the Evangelist's, Ford, Wilts (1897); St Thomas's, Southwick, Wilts (1904); Christ Church, Shaw, Wilts (1905); St Aldhelm's, Sandleheath, Hants (1907); St Stephen's, Kingston Lacy, Dorset (1907); St Mary's, West Fordington, Dorchester, Dorset (1912).

Prichard, John (1817–86). Welsh neo-Gothic architect, based in Llandaff, Cardiff, specialising in restoration work, notably at Llandaff Cathedral (1843–69) where he preceded George Pace.

His new churches include St Swithin's, Ganarew, Herefs (1850) and St Margaret's, Roath, Cardiff (1870). Restorations include St John's, Llandenny, Mon (1860–5); St Thomas's, Monmouth (1876); and St Catherine's, Baglan, Glam (1875–82).

Prior, Edward (Shroeder) (1857–1932). Arts and Crafts theorist, writer (*A History of Gothic Art in England*, 1900), academic and architect. Pupil of Norman Shaw, 1874–80.

He worked at St Michael's, Framlingham, Suffolk (1889); St Mary's, Burton Bradstock, Dorset (1897); and St Mary and All Saints', Whalley, Lancs (1909). He designed Holy Trinity, Bothenhampton, Dorset; St Andrew's, Roker, Tyne & W, where he used reinforced concrete (1907); St Osmund's, Parkstone, Poole, Dorset (1916, now occupied by the Society of St Stephen the Great).

Pritchett, James Piggot (1789–1868). Undistinguished neo-Gothic architect.

Born in Pembs, trained in London and worked in York. He was in partnership with Charles Watson, 1813–31, but thereafter worked on his own. His first ecclesiastical building was Lendal Independent Chapel, York (1816, closed 1929, now a restaurant).

Other churches include St Peter's, Nether Hoyland, W Yorks (1830); St John's, Brearton, N Yorks (1836); Ebenezer Chapel, Little Stonegate, York (1851, now a shop); Christ Church, Brampton Bierlow, W Yorks (1855).

Pugin, Augustus Welby Northmore (1812–52). Immensely prolific ('Clerk, my dear sir, clerk, I never employ one. I should kill him in a week'), draughtsman, writer, teacher, architect and wrecker (off the Godwin Sands). Thrice married (first married and a father at the age of twenty); converted to Catholicism in 1835. Most famous for assisting Sir Charles Barry with the Houses of Parliament, London (1840–52). Designed a phenomenal number of houses, presbyteries, convents, colleges, cathedrals and churches, in Ireland, Guernsey and Australia as well as England. He made his name with *Contrasts* (1836) formulating the neo-Gothic ideal. He influenced John Ruskin and William Morris and his theories held sway well into the twentieth century. He died at the age of forty following a stroke, caused by the effects of syphilis.

Among his many churches are: St Peter and St Paul's, Newport, Salop (1832); St Mary's, Derby (1839); St Alban's, Macclesfield, Ches (1838); St Wilfred's, Hulme, Manchester (1839); St Chad's Cathedral, Birmingham, W Mid (1839); Holy Trinity, Radford, Oxon (1839); St Giles's, Cheadle, Staffs (1840); Our Lady and St Wilfrid's, Warwick Bridge, Cumbria (1840); St Marie's, Brewood, Staffs (1840); St Augustine's, Kenilworth, Warwicks (1841); Nottingham Cathedral (1841); St Mary's, Stockton-on-Tees, Durham (1841); St James the Less, Rawtenstall, Lancs (1844); St Peter's, Marlow, Bucks (1845); St John the Evangelist's ('The Willows'), Kirkham, Lancs (1845); St Augustine's, Ramsgate, Kent (1845); St Lawrence's, Tubney, Oxon (1845); St Thomas of Canterbury's, Fulham, London (1847).

Pugin, E(dward) W(elby) (1834–75). A W N Pugin's eldest son by his second marriage. Catholic neo-Gothic architect who designed well over a hundred churches in England, Scotland, Ireland, Scandinavia and the United States.

His many churches include: Shrewsbury Cathedral, Salop (1856); St Edward's, Rusholme, Manchester (1861); St Catherine's, Kingsdown, Kent (1865: his only surviving Anglican church, now redundant); St Mary of Furness, Barrow-in-Furness, Lancs (1867); Our Lady and St Paulinus's, Dewsbury, W Yorks (1871); St Mary's, Cleator, Cumbria (1872); Our Lady and St Michael's, Workington, Cumbria (1876, completed after his death).

Pugin, (Edmund) Peter Paul (1851–1904). Neo-Gothic architect, largely working in Scotland. He was baptised Edmund Peter but took the name Paul when he grew up. A W N Pugin's only son by his third marriage; his father died when he was a year old. Became a partner with his half-brother, E W Pugin. When E W Pugin died, Peter Paul Pugin assumed responsibility.

His many churches (all Catholic) included St Mary and St Finnan's, Glenfinnan, Highland (1873); St Mary's, Cleland, North Lanarkshire (1873); St Francis Xavier's, Carfin, North Lanarkshire (1881); Holy Family, Mossend, North Lanarkshire (1884); St David's Cathedral, Cardiff, Glam (1887); St Joseph's Cathedral, Swansea, Glam (1889); St Andrew's Cathedral, Glasgow (1889); Holy Family and St Ninian's, Kirkintilloch, East Dunbartonshire (1891); St Agnes's, Lambhill, Glasgow (1893); St Augustine's, Langloan, Coatbridge, North Lanarkshire (1896–1907); Our Lady of Good Aid, Motherwell, North Lanarkshire (1900, now Motherwell Cathedral); Holy Redeemer,

Clydebank, East Dunbartonshire (1901–3); St Peter's, Dowanhill, Glasgow (1903).

Raghton, Ivo de (fl. 1317–c.1339). Master mason. He almost certainly designed the west front of York Minster, including the great west window (1338–9). He probably had a hand in the design of the east front of Carlisle Cathedral, Cumbria (1318–22), the reredos at Beverley Minster, E Yorks (1324–34), the east window of Selby Abbey, N Yorks (begun c.1330), the pulpitum at Southwell Minster, Notts (c.1320–35), and the south transept rose window at Lincoln Cathedral (c.1320–35).

Railton, William (c.1801–77). His one claim to fame is to have designed Nelson's Column (1843). Otherwise, writes Howard Colvin, 'His Gothic churches…do not reward the architecturally minded visitor'.

St Peter's, Duddon, Ches (1835); St Philip and St James's, Groby, Leics (1840); All Saints', Thorpe Acre, Loughborough, Leics (1845).

Ramsey, William (de) (fl. 1323, died 1349). Master mason and probable creator, or one of the creators, of the Perpendicular style. Worked at the cloisters at Norwich Cathedral (1320s); on St Stephen's Chapel, Westminster, London (from 1323, destroyed in the fire of 1834); Visiting Master Mason (ie consultant) at Norwich Cathedral (1326–31); Master Mason at St Paul's Cathedral, London where he worked on the chapter house and cloister (1332 onwards, both destroyed by fire in 1666); Chief Surveyor of all castles south of the Trent (1336, for life); consulted about the presbytery of Lichfield Cathedral, Staffs (1337); in charge of St Stephen's Chapel, Westminster (1337).

Rawstorne, Walker (c.1807–67). Architect practising in Bradford from c.1835–54, designing mostly neo-Gothic churches, including a handful of Commissioners' churches.

St Paul's, Buttershaw, W Yorks (1838); St Mary's, Burley in Wharfedale, W Yorks (1843); St Luke's, Eccleshill, W Yorks (1848, a Commissioners' church).

Redman, Henry (c.1495–1528). Master Mason of the King's Works and son of the master mason at Westminster Abbey, London. By 1495 he was working there on the nave. In 1501–4 he built the Friary of the Observant Franciscans at Richmond (now destroyed). Other works included the cloister and gatehouse at Eton College (1516), and control of the works at York Place (1511, later part of Whitehall Palace, destroyed by fire 1698), and Hampton Court for Cardinal Wolsey.

Reyns, Henry de (fl. 1243–c.1253). Master of the King's Masons. Almost certainly an Englishman, who almost certainly visited Rheims (Reyns) in France. He advised on the defences at Windsor Castle in 1243 and York Castle in 1244–5. In 1245 the rebuilding of Westminster Abbey began, with the demolition of the east end, and Henry was put in charge, beginning with the crypt of the new chapter house (1246), and proceeding with the cloister, the chancel and the transepts. By 1253, when Henry de Reyns probably died, the first stage was virtually completed. (Henry III died in 1272, and work on the Abbey came to a halt).

Richard of Farleigh (1332–65). Master-Mason of Salisbury Cathedral, Wilts, from 1334. He almost certainly built the tower and spire at Salisbury, and may have designed St Anne's Gate and Chapel in the Close (1350–4). Before this, he was in charge of work at the abbeys of Reading, Berks (made ruinous in 1538), and Bath, Som (rebuilt c.1500–35), and he may also have been responsible for the tower of Pershore Abbey, Worcs (c.1330). In 1352–3 he was Master of the Works at Exeter Cathedral, Devon.

Rickman, Thomas (1776–1841). Self-taught neo-Gothic architect with an enormous appetite for work. Invented the terms Norman, Early English, Decorated and Perpendicular to describe English mediaeval architecture, in *An Attempt to discriminate the Styles of English Architecture from the Conquest to the Reformation*, 1817, and became a specialist in English mediaeval church buildings. Having built three churches with John Cragg, a Liverpool ironmaster (St George's, Everton, (1813), St Michael's, Aigburth, (1813) and St Philip's (1815–6, demolished 1882)), he opened an architect's office in Liverpool, Mersey, in 1817, followed by another in Birmingham, W Mid, in 1820. Built New Court, St John's College, Cambridge (1827–31) and many public and private buildings.

His many churches include St George's, Birmingham, W Mid (1822, where he is buried, demolished 1960); St Paul's, Preston, Lancs (1823, now home to 97.4 Rock FM); St Peter's, Preston, Lancs (1825); St David's, Glasgow (1826); St Peter ad Vincula, Hampton Lucy, Warwicks (1826); St Andrew's, Ombersley, Worcs (1829); Holy Trinity, Lawrence Hill, Bristol (1832, deconsecrated about 1960, now the Trinity Centre); St Matthew's, Bristol (1835); All Saints', Stretton-on-Dunsmore, Warwicks (1837); St Stephen's, Sneinton, Notts (1837).

Robert the Mason (fl. 1077–1119). Designed and built St Albans Abbey church, later St Albans Cathedral. His tower, which still stands, is the only eleventh century crossing tower to survive in England.

Roberts, Henry (1803–76). Trained under **Sir Robert Smirke**, travelled abroad, and went into practice designing buildings for Evangelicals. This abruptly ceased when, in 1852 or 1853, he was discovered to have had an affair 'with a member of the lower orders'. He spent the last twenty years of his life in Italy.

St Philip and St James's, Escot, Devon (1840); St Paul's Church for Seamen, Whitechapel, London (1847, closed 1990, now a nursery); Wigtown Parish Church, Dumfries and Galloway (1853).

Robertson, William (1786–1841). Neo-classical and neo-Gothic Scottish architect. Little is known about his life until he established himself in Elgin in about 1823. Worked on public and domestic buildings, mausolea and manses, and churches.

Churches include: Holy Trinity, Elgin, Moray (?1829); St John's, Gamrie, Moray (1830); St Thomas's, Keith, Moray (1831), all neo-classical; St Mary's, Inverness, Highland (1836, Roman Catholic, neo-Gothic); Urquhart Parish Church, Drumnadrochit, Highland (1838); Seafield Church, Portnockie, Moray (1838, converted to Kirk House 1971–2, neo-Tudor).

Ross, Alexander (1834–1925). Prolific (he is said to have built 450 schools alone), mostly neo-Gothic architect, known (to some) as 'the Christopher Wren of the North'. Lived much of his life in Inverness and he carried out much of his work there. Son of James Ross (c.1781–1853), also an architect, and at the age of 19 took over his father's practice on his father's death. Commissioned to design St Andrew's Cathedral, Inverness in 1866.

The many churches he designed include St Ninian's, Kilmartin, Glenurquhart, Highland (1853); Kilmuir Free Church, Skye, Highland (1860); Avoch Parish Church, Highland (1870); St Michael's, Dufftown, Moray (1880); Episcopal Mission Church, Inverness, Highland (1890); Courthill Chapel, Lochcarron, Highland (1901); St Finnbarr's, Dornoch, Highland (1912).

Russell, Richard (fl. 1490, died 1517). Master carpenter. From 1490 to 1516 he was chief carpenter at Westminster Abbey, and probably built the timber roof of Henry VII's Chapel. He also worked at St Margaret's, Westminster, London, probably from c.1490 to his death. From 1509 to 1515 he was master carpenter at King's College Chapel, Cambridge.

St Aubyn, J(ames) P(iers) (1815–95). Well-connected neo-Gothic, mainly ecclesiastical, and, some say, deeply indifferent, architect. Worked mostly but not exclusively in the south-west, where his family was a major landowner and built and restored over sixty churches.

New churches include: St Illogan's, Illogan, Cornwall (1846); St Mary's, Devonport, Devon (1850); St John the Baptist's, Godolphin Cross, Cornwall (1851); St James the Less, Plymouth, Devon (1856); St Andrew's, Thringstone, Leics (1862); Holy Innocents', Tuck Hill, Salop (1865); St Clement's, Kensington, London (1869); St Mary's, Tyndalls Park, Bristol (1870–81); St Michael and All Angels, Galleywood Common, Essex (1873); St Peter's, Noss Mayo, Devon (1882); St Michael's, Silverstone, Northants (1884).

Salvin, Anthony (1799–1881). Neo-Gothic architect who developed a large practice, building and restoring castles, country houses and some sixty churches. Born in Co Durham, he moved to London in his twenties and, some say, worked initially in the office of John Nash. Made his name designing country houses and restoring castles, including the Tower of London (1851–76) and Windsor Castle, Berks (1856–67). Worked on Norwich, Norfolk (1830), Durham (1842) and Wells, Som (1847) cathedrals.

Among his thirty-five new churches were (listed I and II* only) were St John's, Keswick, Cumbria (1838); Christ Church, Kilndown, Kent (1839–41); St John the Evangelist's, Grantham, Lincs (1840–1); St Mary Magdalene's, Torquay, Devon (1843–9); St Paul's, Alnwick, Northumb (1846); All Saints', Runcorn, Ches (1849); Holy Trinity, Darlington, Durham (1856); St Matthew's, Torquay, Devon (1858); St John's, Perlethorpe, Notts (1876).

Savage, James (1779–1852). Bridge-builder (eg Richmond Bridge, Dublin, 1816) and neo-Gothic architect. He was appointed to restore Temple Church, London (1840), but was dismissed (and ruined) in 1842 for wildly exceeding his estimates.

His churches include St Luke's, Chelsea, London (1824); Holy Trinity, Tottenham Green, London (1829), St Mary's, Ilford, Essex (1831); St Paul's, Addlestone, Surrey (1838). His only classical church is St James's, Bermondsey, London (1829, a Commissioners' church).

Scoles, Joseph John (1798–1863). Neo-Gothic Roman Catholic architect, almost entirely designing Roman Catholic churches. From 1822–6 he travelled in Sicily, Greece, Egypt and Syria with Joseph Bonomi the Younger, devoting himself to architectural and archaeological research.

His churches include St Peter's, Yarmouth, Norfolk (1833); St James's, Colchester, Essex (1837); St Mary's, Newport, Mon (1840); St Alban's, Pontypool, Mon (1846); Our Lady of the Snows, Prior Park College, Bath, Som (1844–67); St Mary's, Yarmouth, Norfolk (1850); Our Lady's, Lydiate, Lancs (1855); Holy Cross, St Helens, Lancs (1862).

Scott, Sir (George) Gilbert (1811–78). Also known as 'Great' Scott. Astoundingly prolific, neo-Gothic architect (his only famous neo-classical building is the Foreign Office, Whitehall, London, 1861–8), credited with somewhere between eight hundred and a thousand buildings and restorations. Besides his enormous volume of public and domestic building work, such as the Albert Memorial, Kensington, London (1864–72) and the Midland Grand Hotel, St Pancras, London (1865), he was involved in over three hundred churches, and most English and Welsh cathedrals, as well as abbeys, priories, collegiate churches and Oxford and Cambridge college chapels. The only county of England and Wales in which he did not work was Cered. He also worked in Australia (St Alban's Anglican Church, Muswellbrook,

NSW), Germany (St Nikolaus's, Hamburg, 1844), India (University of Bombay, 1875), Scotland (St Mary's Cathedral, Edinburgh, 1879; St Paul's Cathedral, Dundee, 1855), Newfoundland (St John's Cathedral, (1846–80), New Zealand (Christ Church Cathedral, Christchurch, 1864–94) and South Africa (new tower and spire, Cathedral of St Michael and St George, Grahamstown, 1879). Set up his own practice in 1835, specialising in workhouses, of which he designed over forty; and designed his first church in 1838 (St Mary Magdalene's, Flaunden, Herts). His first success was winning the competition (1840) to design the Martyrs' Memorial in Oxford (1840–2). From then on, there was no stopping him.

Designed St Giles's, Camberwell, London (1844); St George's, Doncaster, S Yorks (1858);St Mary Abbots, Kensington, London (1872) and hundreds more. His last church was All Souls, Blackman Lane, Leeds, W Yorks (1876–80: his son Oldrid Scott supervised the completion). Restored cathedrals at Ely, Cambs (1848); Gloucester (1854–76); Peterborough, Cambs (1855–60); Lichfield, Staffs (1855–61, Hereford (1855–63); Wakefield, W Yorks (1858–60, 1865–9, 1872–4); Durham (1859, 1874–6); Brecon, Powys (1860–2, 1872–5); Canterbury, Kent (1860, 1877–80); Chichester, Sussex (1861–7, 1872); Ripon, N Yorks (1862–74); Worcester (1863–4, 1868, 1874); St Edmundsbury, Bury St Edmunds, Suffolk (1863–4, 1867–9); St Davids, Pembs (1864–76); Salisbury, Wilts (1865–71); St Asaph, Den (1866–9, 1871); Newcastle, Tyne & W (1866–71, 1872–6); Chester (1868–75); Exeter, Devon (1869–77); 1877–81); Christ Church, Oxford (1870–2, 1874–6); Rochester, Kent (1871–4); St Albans, Herts (1871–80); Manchester (1872); and Winchester, Hants (1875).

Scott, George Gilbert (1839–97). Architect, called 'Middle' Scott to distinguish him from his far more successful father (Sir Gilbert Scott) and son (Sir Giles Scott). Converted to Catholicism in 1880, turned to drink a year or two later, was certified insane in 1884, moved to Rouen and was declared sane, and died of cirrhosis of the liver in his father's Midland Grand Hotel, London.

St John the Baptist's, Norwich, Norfolk (since 1976 Norwich RC Cathedral); St Agnes's, Kennington, London (1877, blitzed and demolished); All Hallows, Southwark, London (1880, blitzed and demolished); St Mary Magdalene's, East Moors, N Yorks (1882, sometimes attributed to Temple Moore).

Scott, Sir Giles Gilbert (1880–1960). Slightly conservative Roman Catholic architect, disparaging both the traditionalist and the modernist, hewing to the middle line. Third son of 'Middle' Scott. Most famous for designing, at the age of 21, Liverpool Anglican Cathedral (1903–78); also Battersea Power Station (1930–3), the K2 (1924) and K6 (1935) red telephone kiosks; and Cambridge University Library (1931–4). Designed his first church in 1905–6, the Church of the Annunciation in Bournemouth, Dorset, and he was working on his last, the Church of Christ the King, Plymouth, Devon (1961–2) on his deathbed.

Our Lady Star of the Sea and St Maughold Church, Ramsey, IoM, (1912); St Paul's, Stoneycroft, Liverpool, Mersey (1916); Our Lady and St Alphege's, Bath, Som (1929); St Columba's Cathedral, Oban, Argyll and Bute (1930–53); St Andrew's, Luton, Beds (1932); St Alban and St Michael's, Golders Green, London (1933);St Leonard's, St Leonards-on-Sea, Sussex (1953–61, with his brother Adrian); the Carmelite Church, Kensington, London and St Anthony's, Preston, Lancs (both 1959).

Scott, (John) Oldrid (1841–1913). Mostly ecclesiastical architect, second son of Sir Gilbert Scott. He rebuilt the west front of

Hereford Cathedral (1902–8) and carried out considerable restoration of St Albans Cathedral (c.1890–1907).

His new churches include St Stephen's Greek Orthodox Chapel, West Norwood Cemetery, London (begun c.1873); St Sophia Greek Orthodox Cathedral, Bayswater, London (1879); St Philip's, Hove, Sussex (1895); St Giles's, Wendlebury, Oxon (1901); St John the Evangelist's, Palmers Green, London (1908).

Scune, Christopher (fl. 1505–21). Master mason. He designed the nave of Ripon Cathedral, N Yorks (1503–21) He succeeded John Cole on the spire at St James's, Louth, Lincs (1505–13), but there was evidently a falling out because he left before the spire was complete. Master of masons at Durham Cathedral from about 1515 to 1519. He was almost certainly responsible for the tower and the tower arch of Fountains Abbey (1494–1526).

Sens, William of. See William of Sens.

Sharpe, Edmund (1809–77). Early neo-Gothic architect. Started in practice in Lancaster in 1836 and was joined in 1838 by E G Paley who became his partner in 1845. In 1851 he abandoned architecture to become a railway engineer, designing thereafter only St Paul's, Scotforth, Lancaster (1874–6). However, between 1836 and 1851 he designed churches almost exclusively. He pioneered the use of terra cotta as a building medium: St Stephen and All Martyrs, Bolton (1846) and Holy Trinity, Rusholme (1846), both in Manchester. Early churches (and his last, St Paul's) were in the neo-Romanesque style, such as St Mark's, Blackburn, Lancs (1838). He designed five Commissioners' churches, including St Paul's, Farington, Lancs (1840) and Holy Trinity, Blackburn, Lancs (1849; made redundant 1981).

Shaw, (Richard) Norman (1831–1912). Eclectic vernacular architect, assistant to G E Street (from 1858), whom he acknowledged as his mentor. Set up in practice in 1862. He worked mostly on country houses and public buildings, but he designed Holy Trinity, Bingley, W Yorks (1868, demolished 1974); St Margaret's, Ilkley, W Yorks (1879); All Saints', Leek, Staffs (1885); St Michael and All Angels, Bedford Park, London (1880); All Saints', Richard's Castle, Salop (1893).

Simon the Mason (fl. 1291, died 1322). Master mason. Almost certainly in charge of the building of the nave of York Minster from 1291.

Simpson, Archibald (1790–1847). Scottish architect: born, worked and died in Aberdeen, where he had an extensive practice, designing public buildings, houses and country houses as well as churches. Worked in several styles, including neo-Gothic, neo-Tudor and neo-classical.

Kintore Parish Church, Aberdeenshire (1819); St Giles's, Elgin, Moray (1828); Gordon Chapel, Fochabers, Moray (1833); Rothesay Free Church, Argyll and Bute (1844); Woodside Church, Aberdeen (1846).

Sims, Ronald (1926–2007). Church restorer and interior designer. Joined George Pace's practice and inherited it after his death.

Worked on St Mary's, Clifton, Bristol (1969–79); St Mary's, South Hylton, Sunderland, Tyne & W (1970); St Mary's, Putney, London (1983); chapter house, Southwark Cathedral, London (1989).

Smirke, Sir Robert (1780–1867). Neo-classical architect (though occasionally neo-Gothic), and also a pioneer of concrete and cast iron beams. Most famous for designing the British Museum, London, but he designed or re-modelled over fifty public buildings and sixty private houses, as well as more than twenty churches. He had powerful friends. He trained under George Dance the Younger (1797–1801); went to Italy and Greece (1801–5); made official architect to the Office of Works

(1813–32), with John Nash and Sir John Soane; architect to the Duchy of Lancaster and treasurer to the Royal Academy 1820); knighted in 1832; retired from practice 1845. From 1818 he was adviser to the Commissioners for the Church Building Act (1818), for whom he designed seven Commissioners' churches.

His churches include Luton Hoo Park Chapel, Beds (1816); St Anne's, Wandsworth, London (1822); St George's, Brandon Hill, Bristol (1823, now a concert venue); St George's, Tyldesley, Lancs (1824); St Mary's, Bryanston Square, London (1824); St Philip's, Salford, Manchester (1824, a copy of St Mary's, Bryanston Square); Grosvenor Chapel, Chapel St, London (c.1825); Milton Mausoleum, Markham Clinton, Notts (1832); Askham Church, Cumbria (1832).

Smith, George (1782–1869). A careful architect, who moved in style from restrained neo-classical to restrained neo-Gothic, Italianate and Jacobethan in the course of his career, which included being District Surveyor to the Southern District of the City of London (1810) and surveyor to the Mercers' Company (1814), posts which he held until his death.

Many of his churches have been destroyed, but those that survive are St Peter and St Paul's, Mitcham, Surrey (1822); St Peter's, London Colney, Herts (1826); St Michael and All Angels Chapel, Blackheath, London (1830); St George's Wesleyan Chapel, Stepney, London (1840); St Thomas's, Noak Hill, Essex (1841); St Patrick's, Kilrea, Co Londonderry (1842).

Smith, John (1781–1852). Aberdeen architect, an earlier competitor of Archibald Simpson, and, like him, was born, worked and died in Aberdeen. Trained in London and returned to Aberdeen in 1804. Appointed City Architect in 1824. His earlier work was Greek Revival, but later (from about 1820) he was known as 'Tudor Johnny' for his essays into sixteenth and seventeenth century revivalist styles.

The following are all in Aberdeenshire: Fintray Church (1821); St Clement's Church, Footdee (1827); North Church (1829, now Aberdeen Arts Centre); Longside Parish Church (1835); Aboyne Church (1841); Kincardine O'Neil Church (1846).

Smith, S(amuel) Pountney, 1812–83. Neo-Gothic architect who was born, worked and died in Salop. Became a Shrewsbury stalwart: JP, conservative borough councillor, mayor, and later alderman. Worked mainly in the Early English style, and mainly designing, rebuilding and restoring churches.

All these are in Salop: designed Christ Church, Little Drayton (1847), Holy Trinity, Uffington (1856), Holy Trinity, Leaton (1859); rebuilt St Mary's, Harley (1846) and St Andrew's, Hope Bowdler (1863); restored St Peter and St Paul's, Sheinton (1854), St Giles's, Shrewsbury (1863), St John's, Ruyton XI Towns (1862, 1868), St Mary's, Battlefield (1862), St Michael's, Munslow (1870), St Mary's, Highley (1881).

Smith, William (1661–1724, who lived in Staffs) and Francis Smith (1672–1738, 'Smith of Warwick'). Brothers who frequently worked together. Master masons and architects who altered, designed or built country houses, public buildings and churches. William rebuilt Warwick after the great fire of 1694 (including, with his brother, St Mary's Church).

Churches they added to or designed include St Peter and St Paul's, Coleshill, Warwicks (1714, tower); St Modwen's, Burton-on-Trent, Staffs (1719–26); All Saints', Derby (1723–5, designed by James Gibbs, now Derby Cathedral); All Saints', Gainsborough, Lincs (1736–44); St Mary's, Monmouth (1737, remodelled by G E Street 1881–2).

Smyth, William (fl. 1465, died 1490). Master mason in the Perpendicular style at Wells Cathedral, Som (before 1480) and was probably responsible there for the fan vaulting in the crossing and the Sugar Chantry Chapel. Probably responsible for the vaulting at Sherborne Abbey (1486–93) and Milton Abbey (after 1481, now a school), both in Dorset. He may also have been the architect of St Bartholomew's, Crewkerne, Som (1475–90).

Spence, Sir Basil (Urwin) (1907–76). Scottish architect, most famous for designing Coventry Cathedral, W Mid (1956–62), for which he was knighted; but otherwise not really a church architect. Apart from Coventry Cathedral, he designed St Oswald's, St Chad's and St John the Divine's, all in Coventry and all in 1957, and St Paul's, Sheffield, S Yorks (1959).

Sponlee, John de (fl. 1350, died c.1386). Mason working in the Perpendicular style, mostly at St George's Chapel, Windsor Castle, Berks, where he began the vestry and the chapter house in 1350 and built the Canons' Lodgings (1353), the treasury (1353–4), the cloisters (1356), the Spicery Gate (1357–8), New Gate and Belfry Tower (1359–60). Also, following William de Ramsey, continued St George's Chapel (1348–9).

Stirling, William (1772–1838). Perthshire builder and architect of stables, farms, offices, manses and country churches. He usually designed churches in a simplified neo-Gothic style.

See Logie Parish Church, Stirling (1805); Airth Parish Church, Stirling (1818); Rattray Parish Church, Perth and Kinross (1820); Dron Parish Church, Perth and Kinross (c.1825); Tillicoultry Parish Church, Clackmannanshire(1827); Dunipace (Old) Parish Church, Stirling (1832).

Stow, Richard de (fl. 1270–1307). Master mason at Lincoln Cathedral at the turn of the thirteenth and fourteenth centuries and responsible for designing and building the upper stage of the cathedral's central tower (1306–11).

Street, G(eorge) E(dmund) (1824–81). Neo-Gothic architect. Studied under Sir Gilbert Scott (1840s), set up in practice in 1849 in Oxford, had Philip Webb as senior clerk (1852–9) and William Morris as apprentice (1855–6) and moved to London in 1856. In addition to the Royal Courts of Justice, Strand, London (1868–82), he designed some 180 ecclesiastical buildings.

St Simon and St Jude's, Milton under Wychwood, Oxon (1854); All Saints, Maidenhead, Berks (1857); St James the Less, Pimlico, London (1861); St Philip and St James's, Oxford (1860–2 and 1864–6, since 1983 the Oxford Centre for Mission Studies); St Mary Magdalene's, Paddington, London (1867–73). Also carefully restored Bristol Cathedral (1867–88) and relentlessly restored Christ Church Cathedral, Dublin (1871–8).

Tarring, John (1805–75). Neo-Gothic architect who designed nonconformist chapels, sometimes called 'the Gilbert Scott of the Dissenters'. He worked mainly in southeast England.

St Michael and All Angels, Thornton, Bucks (1850: Tarring largely rebuilt it); Weybridge United Reformed Church, Surrey (1864); Methodist Chapel, Lady Margaret Road, Kentish Town, London (1867, now Our Lady Help of Christians); Methodist Church, Ealing Broadway, London (1869, with Charles Jones, now a Polish Catholic church); Christ Church United Reformed Church, Enfield, London (1875); United Reformed Church, Dawlish, Devon (1871, now The Strand Church); Congregational Memorial Hall, Farringdon Street, London (1875).

Taylor, Thomas (c.1778–1826). Yorkshire neo-Gothic architect operating from Leeds, mostly as a church architect. His first church, Christ Church, Liversedge, W Yorks, was designed in 1816. Many of his churches have been demolished or altered.

Only two of his seven Commissioners' churches survive: St Lawrence's, Pudsey, W Yorks (1824); and St John's, Dewsbury Moor, W Yorks (1827).

Other surviving churches include Holy Trinity, Huddersfield, W Yorks (1819); and Holy Trinity, Ripon, N Yorks (1827).

Telford, Thomas (1757–1834). Surveyor, bridge builder (he became Surveyor of Bridges, Salop in 1788 and built over a thousand bridges, including the Menai and Conwy Suspension Bridges, both 1826), canal maker (surveyor, engineer and architect to the Ellesmere Canal (1793 onwards. See his aqueducts at Pontcysyllte, near Llangollen, Den (1795–1805) and Chirk, Den (1796–1801), road engineer (the A5, 1815–26), dock builder (St Katherine's Dock 1827–8, now mostly demolished; Whitstable Harbour, 1832) and, in his early years, a neo-classical architect. Born in Scotland but moved to London in 1782, then Portsmouth (Commissioner's House, 1784–6, to designs by Samuel Wyatt), then to Shrewsbury and died in London.

St Mary Magdalene's, Bridgnorth, Salop (1792–4); St Michael's, Madeley, Salop (1794-6); perhaps St Leonard's, Malinslee, Salop (1805); and thirty-two churches (1823 onwards, mostly mass-produced), in the Scottish Highlands as a result of the Commission for Parliamentary Churches.

Tempas, John (fl. 1514–5). Master mason from Boston, Lincs, where he probably designed and built the octagonal lantern at St Botolph's. He was called in to finish the spire at St James's, Louth, Lincs, when Christopher Scune walked out and stayed with it until its completion in 1515.

Teulon, S(amuel) S(anders) (1812–73). Inventive neo-Gothic architect. In practice from 1838 and designed country houses, estate cottages and a hundred and fourteen churches. He died insane, probably from syphilis.

Holy Trinity, Hastings, Sussex (1858); St James's, Leckhampstead, Berks (1860); St John the Baptist's, Huntley, Glos (1863); St Mary's, Ealing, London (1866–74); St Stephen's, Rosslyn Hill, Hampstead, London (1871).

Thomas de Cambridge (fl. 1364–70). The 'Cambridge' is in Gloucestershire, not Cambridgeshire. Master builder of Hereford, contracted to build the fan vaulted chapter house of Hereford Cathedral (destroyed in the Civil War) and, some suspect, built the east cloister of Gloucester Cathedral, which is probably the earliest fan vaulted structure in England.

Thomas of Witney (fl. 1292–1342). He began working at Exeter Cathedral, Devon, in 1313, having previously worked at St Stephen's Chapel, Westminster, London (1292, 1294, later rebuilt), and Winchester Cathedral, Hants, carrying out alterations to the presbytery (around 1311). By 1316 or earlier he was in charge of Exeter Cathedral, building the pulpitum, the crossing, the nave, the high altar and the reredos (both mostly destroyed), the sedilia (1316–26), and designing the bishop's throne (1313–19). He may have designed the Lady Chapel and the retrochoir at Wells Cathedral, Som (completed by 1326), and the crossing at Merton College chapel, Oxford (1330–2).

Thomson, David (1831–1910). Scottish neo-Gothic architect, largely ecclesiastical. Chief assistant, later partner and successor, to Charles Wilson. Executed Wilson's designs for Eastwood Parish Church, Pollokshaws, Glasgow (1863) and Oban Cathedral, Argyll and Bute(1864).

Balfron Chapel, Stirling (1866); St Mary's, Glasgow (1867); Dennistoun Church, Glasgow (1870); St Margaret's, Dalry, N Ayrshire (1873); Sorbie Parish Church, Dumfries and Galloway (1876); West Calder

Parish Church, Midlothian (1877); Chryston Parish Church, North Lanarkshire (1878); Milton of Campsie Church, Stirling (1888); Addiewell Parish Church, Motherwell, North Lanarkshire (1889); Thornliebank Church, Renfrewshire (1891).

Tresk, Simon de (fl. 1255–c.1291). Stonemason. Responsible for designing and building the Angel Choir in Lincoln Cathedral (1256–80).

Trubshaw, James (1777–1853). Staffordshire builder, civil engineer and neo-Gothic architect, most famous for designing the Grosvenor Bridge, Chester (1833) and inventing under-excavation to straighten the tower of St Chad's, Wybunbury, Ches (1832). (It was used on the Leaning Tower of Pisa, 1999–2001).

He designed several Commissioners' churches, including St Lawrence's, Chapel Chorlton, Staffs (1827); St James's, Longton, Stoke-on-Trent, Staffs (1834); St Michael's, Great Wolford, Warwicks (1835); St James's, Congleton, Ches (1848); Holy Trinity, Hanley, Staffs (1849).

Trubshaw, Thomas (1802–42). Neo-Gothic architect and landscape gardener, eldest son of James Trubshaw; he died young. All his buildings, including churches, are in Staffordshire.

Christ Church, Hilderstone (1829); St Lawrence's, Biddulph (1833); St Michael's, Brereton (1837); St Mary's, Moreton (1838); Christ Church, Knightley (1841); St James's, Salt (1842).

Underwood, Henry Jones (1804–52). Neo-Gothic architect working mainly in Oxford. He committed suicide at the White Hart Hotel in Bath, possibly while insane.

St Mary and St Nicholas's, Littlemore, Oxon, (1835); St Paul's, Walton Street, Oxford (1836, neo-classical, now Freud's bar); St Peter's, Bushey Heath, Herts (1837); Church of the Ascension, Littleworth, Oxon (1839); Holy Trinity, Burdrop, Oxon (1840); Holy Trinity, Sibford Gower, Oxon (1840).

Vertue, Robert (fl. 1475, died 1506). Master mason who worked on the nave of Westminster Abbey, London (1475–90). With his brother William he designed Bath Abbey, Som (1501). Designed the Henry VII chapel at Westminster Abbey (begun 1503) and was involved in the king's tomb. Also involved in St George's Chapel, Windsor Castle, Berks (c.1500).

Vertue, Robert II (fl. 1506–55). Son of Robert Vertue and Master of the Works, Evesham Abbey, Worcs. There he designed the belltower (1529–39), the Mortuary Chapel at All Saints' (before 1513) and the chantry chapel of St Clement at St Lawrence's (c.1520, rebuilt 1836–7, made redundant 1979).

Vertue, William (fl. 1501, died 1527). Master mason, brother of Robert Vertue, with whom he was involved with Bath Abbey, Som from 1501. Worked on the choir fan vaulting of St George's Chapel, Windsor Castle, Berks (from 1503) and also the flying buttresses and the carvings. He advised John Wastell on the design for the fan vaulted ceiling at King's College Chapel, Cambridge (1507, 1509, 1512). In charge of Henry VII's Chapel, Westminster Abbey, after the death of his brother (1506). Probably designed the church of St Peter ad Vincula, Tower of London (1512–20) and Lupton's Chantry Chapel, Eton College chapel, Berks (1515). Designed the cloister and the Chapel of St Stephen, Westminster, London (1526, destroyed by fire 1834).

Vulliamy, Lewis (1791–1871). Son of Benjamin Vulliamy and brother of Benjamin Lewis Vulliamy, the clockmakers (see section on Clocks). Trained under Sir Robert Smirke and spent four years (1818–21) abroad, mostly in Italy. Soon acquired an extensive practice, designing with equal facility in the neo-classical, Romanesque, Italianate, neo-Tudor and neo-Gothic styles. He was said to be 'peculiar in his notions' and quarrelled with all four of his sons. He mostly designed houses, but also many public buildings and churches.

St Bartholomew's, Sydenham, London (1831); St Clement's, Spotland, Lancs (1834); St Nicholas's, Winterborne Clenston, Dorset 1840); St Peter and St Paul's, Chingford, Essex (1844); All Saints', Ennismore Gardens, London (1849); St Mary's, Lasborough, Glos (1862).

Walsingham, Alan of. See **Alan of Walsingham**.

Wastell, John (c.1460–c.1515). Master mason, of Bury St Edmunds, Suffolk. He worked with **Simon Clerk** at St Edmund's Abbey, Bury St Edmunds, Suffolk (from c.1450; the Abbey was destroyed in the Dissolution of the Monasteries, 1539), St Mary's, Saffron Walden, Essex (1485), and King's College Chapel, Cambridge (from 1486). He was summoned to Kent in 1494, where he designed the crossing tower (Bell Harry Tower) of Canterbury Cathedral, Kent (1494–1505).

He also worked on Great St Mary's, Cambridge (1491–1514); St Mary's, Dedham, Essex (1494); the lower stages of the tower at St Andrew's, Soham, Cambs (c.1496). He probably worked on St Peter and St Paul's, Lavenham, Suffolk (1495–1515); the retrochoir (the New Building) at Peterborough Cathedral, Cambs (1496–c.1528); St James's, Nayland, Suffolk (?1500); St James's, Bury St Edmunds, Suffolk (1503–21, now St Edmundsbury Cathedral). He returned to King's College Chapel, Cambridge, in 1508 and stayed until the chapel was finished in 1515.

Watson, Charles (c.1770–1836). Yorkshire architect. Lived in Wakefield until 1807 and then moved to York. He worked first in partnership with William Lindley (St John's, Wakefield, W Yorks, 1795) and then in partnership with **J P Pritchett**. He retired in 1831.

With Pritchett, all neo-Gothic: Lendal Independent Chapel, York (1816); Friends' Meeting House, Friargate, York (1819); St Mary's, Greasbrough, W Yorks (1828); St Peter's, Nether Hoyland, W Yorks (1830).

Webster, George (1797–1864). Neo-Gothic church architect (but neo-classical architect of public buildings), of Kendal, Cumbria, almost all of whose work is in Cumbria.

All in Cumbria: St Mary's, Rydal (1824); St Paul's, Lindale (1829, where he is buried); St Stephen's, New Hutton (1829); Holy Trinity, Kendal (1837); St Thomas's, Kendal (1837); St George's, Kendal (1841); St Leonard's, Cleator (1842); Holy Trinity, Bardsea (1843–53).

Welch, Edward (1806–68). Partner and fellow-bankrupt (1834) with **J A Hansom**, 1828–34, with whom he designed several churches, all neo-Gothic.

Acomb Church, W Yorks (1831); St John's, Toxteth Park, Liverpool, Mersey (1832); St Peter's, Onchan, IoM (1833). When the partnership was dissolved, he designed, among others, Rhos-y-Medre Church, Den (1837); Ysgeiviog Church, Flint (1837); Christ Church, Adlington, Lancs (1838); St George's, Quarry Hill, Sowerbury, W Yorks (1840); St James's, West Derby, Lancs (1846).

Welch, John (1810–55). Neo-Gothic architect, younger brother of **Edward Welch**, working mostly in the Isle of Man (1830–88), and St Asaph, Den (1839–?).

Holy Trinity, Lezayre, IoM (1833); St Michael's, Kirk Michael, IoM (1835); St Michael's, Bettws yn Rhos, Conwy (1838); St Mary's, Bagillt, Flint (1839); St George's, Llandudno, Conwy (1840, since 2002 a business centre); St Ffinan's, Llanffinan, Anglesey (1841); St Nidan's, Llanidan, Anglesey (1843).

White, William (1825–1900). Neo-Gothic church architect (and inventor of the framed rucksack) who studied under **Sir Gilbert Scott**, along with **Street** and **Butterfield**. He set up in practice in Truro, Cornwall (1846) and moved to London in 1851.

St Michael's, Baldhu (1848) and St Peter's, Mithian (1861), both Cornwall; Holy Trinity, Barnstaple, Devon (1867); St Michael and All Angels, Lyndhurst (1858–70), and Christ Church, Freemantle (1866), both in Hampshire; All Saints', Notting Hill, London (started c.1850, eventually completed 1861); St John's, Felbridge, East Grinstead, Sussex (mid 1860s).

Wightwick, George (1802–72). Eclectic architect, dramatist, amateur thespian and possibly the first architectural journalist. Born in Flintshire and later moved to Plymouth, Devon (1829) where he set up his own successful practice. Eventually he fell out with the ecclesiologists of Exeter and retired in 1851.

St Michael and All Angels, Bude, Cornwall (1835); Christ Church, Lanner, Cornwall (1840); St Mary's, Portreath, Cornwall (1841); St John's, Treslothan, Cornwall (1842); St John's, Brownston, Devon (1844, now a residence).

William the Englishman (fl. 1174, died c.1214). Master mason who worked on Canterbury Cathedral, Kent (1177–84) after the original architect, **William of Sens**, was crippled falling from a scaffold. He built the Corona at the east end and the Trinity Chapel. Said to have worked also at Chichester Cathedral, Sussex (1187–99).

William of Sens (fl. 1174, died 1180). French master mason who was summoned from France in 1174 to work on Canterbury Cathedral, Kent. He rebuilt the choir in three years, but in 1177 was crippled in a fall from the scaffolding and returned to France, where he died.

Willson, Edward James (1787–1854). Antiquary and self-trained neo-Gothic architect who was born, worked and died in Lincoln. Howard Colvin says he 'was, for his time, a relatively careful and scholarly restorer of churches'.

Holy Trinity, Messingham, Lincs (1818); St Saviour's, East Retford, Notts (1829);

St Mary's, Grantham, Lincs (1832); St Mary's, Louth, Lincs (1833); St John's, Thorpe End, Melton Mowbray, Leics (1840).

Wilson, Charles (1810–63). Glasgow neo-classical and Italianate architect. Most of his churches have been demolished or massively altered, but those which survive are:

West Church of Scotland, Rothesay, Argyll and Bute (1845); Helensburgh Parish Church, Argyll and Bute (1846, nave demolished, now an information centre); Maryhill Free Church, Glasgow (1847); Rutherglen Free Church, South Lanarkshire (1850); Melrose Free Church, Borders (1851); St Paul's, Meadowside, Dundee (1852); Eastwood Parish Church, Pollokshaws, Glasgow (1863, completed by **David Thomson**).

He prepared designs for Oban Cathedral, Argyll and Bute (1863) just before his death; the cathedral was also built by David Thomson (1864).

Witney, Thomas of. See **Thomas of Witney**.

Wodehirst, Robert (de) (fl. 1351, died 1401). Norwich master mason. After working at St Stephen's Chapel, Westminster, London and Westminster Abbey, London (1357–8), he built the presbytery clerestory windows (1361–9) at Norwich Cathedral, Norfolk. He is credited with the aisle windows at All Saints', Swanton Morley, Norfolk (about 1370). He was working in Norwich again, as master mason for the cloisters, in 1385–6. From 1387–93, he was working on the reredos of the high altar and (probably) completing the west tower at Ely Cathedral, Cambs. In 1394 he was again in Norwich, rebuilding St Gregory's.

Woodhead, John (died c.1838). See **William Hurst**.

Woodyer, Henry (1816–96). High church neo-Gothic gentleman architect and church restorer, pupil of **William Butterfield** and follower of **A W N Pugin**.

Holy Innocents', Highnam, Glos (1851); St Paul's, Sketty, Glam (1853); Holy Jesus's, Lydbrook, Glos (1851); St Martin's, Dorking, Surrey (1868–77); St John the Baptist's, Hafod, Swansea, Glam (1880).

Wren, Sir Christopher (1632–1723). Anatomist, mathematician, astronomer, physicist, meteorologist and, later, baroque architect, some say England's greatest. Studied at Wadham College, Oxford (c.1649, BA 1650, MA 1653) and All Souls (1653–57). Professor of Astronomy at Gresham's College, London (1657–61); Savilian Professor of Astronomy at Oxford (1661–73). Turned to architecture in 1663, when he designed the chapel of Pembroke College, Cambridge (1663–5) and the Sheldonian Theatre, Oxford (1664–9). In 1666, following the Great Fire of London, Wren was appointed, with Sir Roger Pratt and Hugh May, as Royal Commissioners to oversee the rebuilding of the city. Wren was responsible for the fifty-one churches, of which a great number have been altered, demolished or destroyed by bombing in the Second World War.

The only ones substantially intact are St Benet's, Paul's Wharf (1677–83); St Clement's, Eastcheap (1683–7); St James Garlickhythe (1676–83); St Margaret's Lothbury (1686–90); St Margaret Pattens, Eastcheap (1684–7); St Martin's, Ludgate (1677–84); St Peter's, Cornhill (1675–81); St Stephen Walbrook (1672–9); and St Paul's Cathedral (1675–1710). He also designed St James's, Piccadilly (1676–84) and St Clement Danes, Strand (1680–2).

Wyatt, James (1746–1813). Prolific neo-classical and neo-Gothic architect, who designed and altered some forty public buildings, over a hundred country houses, about twenty town houses, a dozen monuments and some twenty-five churches and cathedrals (including Lichfield, Staffs, Salisbury, Wilts and Hereford). He was killed when his carriage overturned near Marlborough, Wilts, whilst travelling from Bath to London. Only six churches that he designed himself survive (the rest are all alterations and adaptations).

St James's, Milton Abbas, Dorset (1786); St Swithun's, East Grinstead, Sussex (1789); St Mary's, Weeford, Staffs (1804); St Michael and All Angels, Hafod, Cered (1803, damaged by fire 1932); St Mary's, Dodington, Glos (1796–1816); St George's, Hanworth, London (1816, but designed 1808).

Wynford, William (fl. 1360–1405). Architect using the then new Perpendicular style. First mentioned in 1360 when he was warden of the masons at Windsor Castle. His two major ecclesiastical works were Wells Cathedral, Som, to which he was master mason (1364) and consultant architect from 1365 until his death, and to which he contributed the south-west tower (1385–95); and Winchester Cathedral, Hants (1390s), where he probably spent most of the rest of his life. He also worked at Abingdon Abbey, Oxon (1375–6), New College, Oxford (1379) and Winchester College, Hants (1382). Worked on occasion with **Henry Yevele**.

Yevele or **Yeveley, Henry** (c.1320–1400). Prolific master-mason, King's Principal Mason from 1378, a leading proponent of the new Perpendicular style, and, some say (though they would have to argue with Wren's supporters) England's greatest architect. Born perhaps at Yeaveley in Derbys, may have learned his trade on Lichfield Cathedral, Staffs, and moved to London after the Black Death around 1353. By about 1360 he was in the king's service. Worked for the Black Prince, for whom he designed a tomb in Canterbury Cathedral, Kent, then Edward III, for whom he probably designed the tomb in Westminster Abbey, London, and lastly Richard II, for whom he certainly designed the tomb in Westminster Abbey.

He designed the nave and west cloister of Westminster Abbey (1360s) and the nave and south cloister of Canterbury Cathedral, Kent (1377–1400), and in the 1370s he designed the Neville screen in Durham Cathedral. Said to have worked on St Albans Cathedral, Herts (the south and east cloister, late 1350s), and Selby Abbey, N Yorks (1379? – the sedilia). In Kent he may have designed St John the Baptist's, Meopham (1381–96) and All Saints' church and college, Maidstone (founded 1395). As well as churches and cathedrals, he worked on Westminster Palace (1360s), the Tower of London (The Bloody Tower, 1361), Windsor Castle, palaces, manor houses, castles and fortifications.

Bell Harry tower, Canterbury Cathedral, Kent: fan vaulting by John Wastell (c.1460–c.1515), above arches by Henry Yevele

CHURCH FURNISHINGS

Mediaeval churches were a mass of colour: almost every surface, and every statue, was painted, and most windows were filled with stained glass. This was mostly destroyed by the Puritans. in the hundred and thirty years between about 1530 and 1660. The altars and altar rails, rood lofts, stoups, crucifixes, crosses, pictures, stained glass, brasses, and statues were smashed, removed or decapitated. Only patches of paintings remain today, mostly rediscovered in the course of nineteenth century restoration. William Dowsing (1596–1668), a Puritan iconoclast, has chronicled his trail of destruction through Cambridgeshire and Suffolk in 1643–4 in his *Journal*, but the sheer apocalyptic fury of the Puritan revolution, the Taleban of the sixteenth and seventeenth centuries, is still difficult to imagine.

Alms box. See Poor box.

Altar. Stone or wooden table, normally at the east end of the church, at which mass or holy communion is celebrated. In larger churches and cathedrals there are, or were, several altars in chapels and transepts, as well as the high altar. Early altars were wooden; stone altars are found dating from the early sixth century (see St Laurence's, Bradford-on-Avon, Wilts), usually built over the relics of a saint. (The wooden altar made something of a return after the Reformation). The position of the main altar has changed from time to time: some say that Anglo-Saxon altars, like modern altars, were situated at the east end of the nave. These days most main altars, whether made use of or not, stand at the east end of the chancel. See also Communion table.

Altar rails or communion rails. Made of wood or metal, they divide the sanctuary (the immediate altar area) from the rest of the chancel. Archbishop Laud (Archbishop of Canterbury 1633–45) instituted altar rails, some say to protect the altar from dogs.

Altar stone, portable altar. Small stone altar which could be inserted into the top of a wooden altar table. It is usually marked with five crosses, one at each corner and one in the middle. Altar stones were abolished by Edward VI (reigned 1547–53), but were often concealed. See Holy Trinity, Goodramgate, York; St Mary's, Great Milton, Oxon; St Mary's, Cleobury Mortimer, Salop.

Altar frontal. Richly-decorated cloth which covers the altar. The colour is changed with the liturgical season (see section on Calendar and colours).

Super-frontal: a kind of fringed pelmet at the top of a frontal.

Baldacchino. A canopy over an altar, usually made of fabric but often of metal or stone. The baldacchino in St Paul's

Altar stone, perhaps sixth century, St Davids Cathedral, Pembs

Bequest board, 1687, St Nicholas and St Cyriac's, South Pool, Devon

Brass, fifteenth century, St Mary's, Wiveton, Norfolk

Brass, sixteenth century, St Mary's, Wiveton, Norfolk

Cathedral, London, is modern (1958) and built of stone.

Bench-ends. See Pew.

Bequest board, donations board. A wooden board containing details of donors to charities, usually fastened to a wall beneath the tower.

Bible box. Lockable, richly carved box in which the church bible used to be kept, popular in the seventeenth century.

Brass. A metal plate (about 80% copper and 20% zinc), usually fastened to a monument on the church floor, church wall or tomb chest. Brasses date from the second half of the thirteenth century to about 1650, though there are some modern ones. See, for example, the brass to Robert Stephenson, died 1859, designed by Sir Gilbert Scott, and to Sir Gilbert Scott himself, died 1878, designed by G E Street, both in Westminster Abbey, London. About eight thousand mediaeval brasses survive, around thirty of them monastic brasses. About half are engraved with a stylised representation of the person (or persons) buried, or (from c.1440) a skeleton or a corpse in a shroud. Skeletons and corpses may be seen in the brasses of Bernard Brocas (died 1488), St Andrew's, Sherborne St John, Hants; Richard Howard (died 1499) and his wife, St Michael's, Aylsham, Norfolk; John Symonds and his wife (1512), St Margaret's, Cley, Norfolk. Others carry heraldic devices, Christian symbols or biblical scenes. The oldest is probably the head of a priest, part of a brass of 1282, at St Mary's, Ashford, Kent. The earliest brass to a woman is to Joan de Cobham in St Mary's, Cobham, Kent (died before 1298, brass engraved c.1305). Monumental brasses originated in Flanders in the thirteenth century, and Flemish brasses may be seen at St Albans Cathedral, Herts (Abbot Thomas de la Mare, died 1396); King's Lynn Minster, Norfolk (Adam de Walsoken, died 1349, and Robert Braunche, died 1364) and two brasses in Holy Trinity, Wensley, N Yorks (1395, church now redundant). As with so many church furnishings, the Reformation, the rise of Puritanism and the Commonwealth (ie from c.1530 to 1660) meant the wholesale destruction of thousands of brasses, though Elizabeth I attempted to have brasses returned to their churches. Many brasses were also destroyed in the refurbishments of the eighteenth and nineteenth centuries.

Bread shelf. See Dole cupboard.

Cartouche, cartouche tablet. Memorial tablet, popular in the seventeenth and eighteenth centuries, usually made of marble, in the form of a sheet of paper with the sides curled up.

Chest tomb. See Tomb.

Choir stalls. Stalls built in the chancel facing each other (ie facing north and south). They are usually far grander than the seating in the nave. See also Misericord.

Collar: SS or ss collar, Yorkist collar. A collar around the necks of some effigies on tombs and brasses, often having a pendant. The SS collar, composed of esses, denotes adherence to the house of Lancaster and its origin is unknown. Henry IV (reigned 1399–1413) gave such collars to his eminent retainers, and it may have been used earlier by John of Gaunt. The Yorkist equivalent was a collar composed of suns and roses. See an SS collar on the tomb of Lord Bardolph, c.1440s, St Mary's, Dennington, Suffolk; and a Yorkist collar on the tomb of Sir Nicholas Fitzherbert, died 1473, St Mary and St Barlock's, Norbury, Derbys. Collars died out under Henry VII.

Communion rails. See Altar rails.

Communion table. A wooden table used by Puritans in the sixteenth and seventeenth centuries in place of an altar.

Cope chest. A cope is a clerical vestment shaped like a cloak made out of a semicircular piece of fabric. A cope chest is a piece of furniture, semi-circular or quadrant-shaped in plan, in which the copes could be stored flat or folded once. See the mediaeval cope chests at Wells Cathedral, Som (the oldest, c.1120); Salisbury Cathedral, Wilts (thirteenth century); Gloucester Cathedral (fourteenth century). There is a modern cope chest at Tewkesbury Abbey, Glos (1990s).

Credence table, credence shelf. Table or shelf for keeping holy vessels on. Sometimes built into the walls near the piscina: an aumbry.

Cresset stone. Stone slab which has hollows for holding candles. Some were small enough to be portable; others were fixed. See examples at Brecon Cathedral, Powys (the biggest, with holes for thirty candles); St Oswald's, Collingham, W Yorks; St Martin's, Lewannick, Cornwall; St Pancras's, Alton Pancras, Dorset; St Bees Priory Church, Cumbria.

Dole cupboard, dole shelf, bread shelf, dole table. To hold loaves of bread for the poor, usually near the entrance to a church and usually provided by a local benefactor. They became widespread after the Dissolution of the Monasteries (1536–40) because there were no longer any religious houses to look after the poor. See All Saints', Hereford; St Mary's, Warwick; All Saints', Milton Ernest, Beds; St Martin's, Ruislip, London. Dole tables (as opposed to shelves) are rare. See the thirteenth century example in St Mary's churchyard, Powerstock, Devon.

Donations board. See Bequest board.

Doom painting. Somewhat frightening painting of the Day of Judgement, with souls being conveyed to heaven or hell, often painted by a local artist on wet plaster, usually on the west wall or the chancel arch. Most of them were painted over or destroyed during the Reformation and the Commonwealth (c.1530–1660) and only about sixty survive. See St John's, Clayton, Sussex (twelfth century); St Andrew's, Pickworth, Lincs (fourteenth century); St Thomas of Canterbury's, Salisbury, Wilts and St Andrew's, Chesterton, Cambs (both fifteenth century); St Mary's, Warwick (1449, restored 1678); St Peter's, Wenhaston, Suffolk (early sixteenth century). See also Wallpainting.

Family pew ('parlour pew'). A type of elaborate box pew dating from the end of the sixteenth century. and owned or rented (though renting pews was abolished in the middle of the nineteenth century) by the local dignitaries. Their fittings may include stairs and a roof; they sometimes had a carpet, curtains, a table, comfortable armchairs and a fireplace. See Holy Trinity, Wensley, N Yorks; St Mary's, Langley Marish, Berks; St Peter's, Croft-on-Tees, N Yorks; St Andrew's, Gatton, Surrey; St Mary's, Whitby, N Yorks.

Feretory. A shrine.

Font. Often the oldest piece of furniture in a church, sometimes ante-dating the church itself. The font is usually placed inside the south door (or west, where there is one). Fonts are normally made of stone, though lead fonts do exist (one is in Gloucester Cathedral and another, twelfth century, in St Augustine's, Brookland, Kent) and a very few wooden ones (see St Andrew's, Marks Tey, Essex, fifteenth century).

Seven sacraments fonts exist only in East Anglia. They are fonts on which are carved illustrations of baptism, confirmation, holy eucharist, penance, extreme unction, matrimony and holy orders. See St Margaret's, Cley, Norfolk; St Peter Mancroft, Norwich, Norfolk; St Edmund's, Southwold and Holy Trinity, Blythburgh, both in Suffolk.

Font cover, font canopy. Usually wooden, font covers were introduced in 1236, by a decree of the Archbishiop of Canterbury,

An SS collar on the tomb of Lord Bardolph, c.1440s, St Mary's, Dennington, Suffolk. His wife Joan also wears one.

Oak cope chest, c.1120, Wells Cathedral, Som

Cresset stone, twelfth century, Brecon Cathedral, Powys

Bread shelf, eighteenth century, All Saints', Hereford

Part of the doom painting, c.1480, St Peter's, Wenhaston, Suffolk

Seven sacraments font, late fifteenth century, Norwich Cathedral, Norfolk

Family pew with canopy, ? 1664, St John's, Stokesay, Salop

Norman font with eighteenth century font cover, Beverley Minster, E Yorks

West gallery, 1766, St Andrew's, Quatt, Salop

View from the west gallery, 1588, St Peter's, Melverley, Salop

padlocked to stop holy water being stolen. (The water appears to have been rarely changed). They were often tall and elaborately carved. See St Nicholas's, North Walsham (fifteenth century); St Peter Mancroft, Norwich; St Botolph's, Trunch; St Mary's, Elsing, (all in Norfolk); Church of the Assumption, Ufford, (fifteenth century) and St Mary's, Bramford (sixteenth century), both in Suffolk; Holy Trinity, Balsham, Cambs; St Mary's, Garthorpe, Leics; St James's, Swimbridge, Devon.

Foramina. A shrine with holes in the long sides into which people would put their heads or hands, in order to get as close as possible to the relics (see St Osmond's tomb, Salisbury Cathedral, Wilts).

Gallery. *Side galleries* were built or added to provide extra seating. A few are mediaeval (see St Agnes's, Cawston, Norfolk); most are much later (see St Chad's, Shrewsbury, Salop, 1792).

A *west gallery* is a gallery at the west end of the church, usually in the space beneath the tower. The earliest dated west gallery is from 1588 (St Peter's, Melverley, Salop) and many date from the seventeenth century. See St Giles and St Peter's, Sidbury, Devon (1620), St Mary and St David's, Kilpeck, Herefs (seventeenth century?); All Saints', Wilby, Norfolk (1637), St Helen's, Berrick Salome, Oxon (1676). A number were built in the eighteenth century, usually for the choir and the musicians (see the section on Music and singing). See St Mary's, Abbotts Ann, Hants (1716), Dore Abbey, Abbeydore, Herefs (about 1720), St John's, Crosscanonby, Cumbria (1730), All Saints', North Cerney, Glos (1754), St Mary's, Avington, Hants (1771). With the spread of the organ, which was less trouble than a band, most of them were taken out in the course of Victorian restoration, though a number still exist.

Glastonbury chair. A wooden armchair common since the sixteenth century. It has two X-shaped legs, like a director's chair, but it does not fold. Sixteenth century examples – perhaps the original examples – are in the Bishop's Palace, Wells, Som, and St John's, Glastonbury, Som.

Gradine. A shelf behind the altar, often part of the reredos, for standing the cross and candlesticks on on.

Hatchment, funeral hatchment. Diamond-shaped board fixed on a church wall on which the coat of arms of the deceased were painted. See also Royal arms.

Hearse, herse. 1 A wooden or metal framework fixed over a tomb to carry candles and a pall, which were only removed on special occasions. See the tomb of Robert Curthose of Normandy, Gloucester Cathedral (died 1134, about 1230) and Richard Beauchamp, St Mary's, Warwick (died 1439, about 1450). 2 A carriage for carrying a coffin at a funeral. See also Hearse in the section on Churchyards.

Heart burial. Usually marked by a small niche in the church wall and maybe two hands holding a heart. Popular in the thirteenth and fourteenth century and was reputedly to commemorate crusaders who died abroad. The memorials in St Peter and St Paul's, Mappowder, Dorset, St Peter and St Paul's, Leybourne, Kent, St Michael's, Castle Frome, Herefs, St Giles's, Horstead Keynes, Sussex and St Giles's, Bredon, Worcs, are almost certainly memorials to crusaders, unlike those in St Peter's, Yaxley, Cambs, Dore Abbey, Abbeydore, Herefs; St Alkmund's, Whitchurch, Salop, and St Mary's, Brabourne, Kent. Some famous people had their hearts buried separately for quite other reasons: for example, King John (1167–1216): buried in Worcester Cathedral, heart in Croxton Abbey, Lincs (now destroyed); Eleanor of Castile (1241–

90): body in Westminster Abbey, London, heart in Blackfriars Priory, London (now destroyed), entrails in Lincoln Cathedral; Robert Bruce (1274–1329): buried in Dunfermline Abbey, Fife, heart in Melrose Abbey, Borders (ruinous); Prince Arthur (1486–1502): buried in Worcester Cathedral, heart (or possibly intestines) in St Laurence's, Ludlow, Salop; Percy Bysshe Shelley (1792–1822): ashes buried in Rome Protestant Cemetery, heart in St Peter's, Bournemouth, Hants; Thomas Hardy (1840–1928): ashes in Westminster Abbey, heart at St Michael's, Stinsford, Dorset (although it is in the churchyard, not the church).

Hour glass. See Sermon timer.

Jesse window. See Tree of Jesse.

Kneeler. Wooden shelf or, more commonly, a hassock, for kneeling on when praying.

Lectern. Reading stand on which the church bible is placed, usually to the south of the chancel arch, and usually in the shape of an eagle. Passages from the Bible are read from it (as opposed to the pulpit, which is mainly for sermons). The oldest lecterns date from about 1200 and are made of stone. See St John's, Crowle and St James's, Norton, both in Worcestershire (both lecterns are in the churchyards), and St Mary's, Crich and St Helen's, Etwall, both in Derbyshire (lecterns are in the chancels). Slightly later examples may be seen in St Margaret's, King's Lynn, Norfolk and St Mary's, Ottery St Mary, Devon.

Ledger, ledger slab, grave slab, ledger stone. Rectangular slab of stone covering a grave or graves, set in the church floor. Earlier ones are simply marked with a cross, but from the seventeenth century they are normally inscribed with details of the deceased. About 250,000 survive.

Lent veil. Veil covering the crucifix and other images during Lent. Usually a Roman Catholic custom.

Memorials, monuments. See Wall monuments.

Misericord. A tip-up seat, normally in the choir, with a shallow ledge beneath on which the monks could rest while standing during the long services. The ledge is usually carved, with animals, grotesques and scenes of everyday life: the carvers seem to have given free expression to their imaginations. Misericords date from about 1250 to about 1500, though many are by later imitators. They were carved from a solid piece of oak (or sometimes chestnut), usually by travelling bands of craftsmen: for example, the same group carved the misericords at Lincoln Cathedral, followed by (probably) the Carmelite monastery at Coventry, followed by Chester Cathedral, followed by Roche Abbey, S Yorks. The most common arrangement is a centre piece with a carving on each side of it (the supporters or ears), all three parts connected in theme. Many survive: at the Dissolution of the Monasteries, a number of misericords from abbeys found their way into parish churches, and during the Puritan period, they seem to have been relatively unnoticed. The oldest misericords in the United Kingdom are in Exeter Cathedral, Devon (c.1230). The largest sets can be seen at Salisbury Cathedral, Wilts (thirteenth century, 106 misericords, unusual in that they are all similar designs of foliage), St George's Chapel, Windsor Castle, Berks (c.1480, ninety-six), Lincoln Cathedral (fourteenth century, ninety-two), and Beverley Minster, E Yorks and King's College Chapel, Cambridge (both early sixteenth century, both sixty-eight). Most misericords, about 3,500, are in England. Wales, Scotland and Northern Ireland have only 179 between them. There are about 8,000 in France and a very small number in Belgium, Germany and Switzerland.

Hearse above the tomb of Richard Beauchamp, died 1439, St Mary's, Warwick

Grave slab, eleventh century, Chester Cathedral, Ches

Misericord, crawling man, fourteenth century, All Saints', Hereford

Parclose screen enclosing the Birde chantry chapel, 1515, Bath Abbey, Som

Parish chest, sixteenth century, St James's, Louth, Lincs

Bench-end by Richard Bird and John Haynes, 1449, St Mary's, Warwick

Poor box, ? sixteenth century, St Agnes's, Cawston, Norfolk

Riddel and riddel posts, twentieth century, Wells Cathedral, Som

Pulpit, 1625, converted into a three-decker 1628, St Mary's, Dennington, Suffolk

Fine sets can be seen at All Saints', Hereford; St Laurence's, Ludlow, Salop (c.1430); St Botolph's, Boston, Lincs (late fourteenth century); St Mary and All Saints', Whalley, Lancs (early fifteenth century); Ripon Cathedral (1489–94); and Manchester Cathedral (c.1510).

Pall. A large piece of cloth covering a coffin at funerals. One, made in 1774 from a cope, may be seen at St John's, Glastonbury, Som.

Parclose screen. Screen of stone, wood or metal separating a chapel or a shrine from the body of the church. (A parclose is an enclosure).

Parish chest. Chest for keeping parish records and valuables in. In 1538 it was made compulsory for all churches to have a parish chest with a slot in the top (for alms) and at least three locks. The key holders were the vicar, a churchwarden and a respectable lay person.

Many still survive: St Peter and St Paul's, Little Gaddesden, Herts, St Mary's, Bradford Abbas, Dorset, and St James's, Louth, Lincs (all mediaeval); St Mary's, Kempley, Glos and St Mary's, Prescot, Lancs (both early sixteenth century); St Mary's, Houghton-on-the-Hill, Norfolk (1724).

Parlour pew. See Family pew.

Pew. In early churches, the only form of seating might have been a stone shelf around the wall of the nave: this was for the elderly and infirm ('the weakest go to the wall'). Seating in the body of the nave (bench pews) was introduced in the fourteenth century and gradually became common in the sixteenth century. Elaborately carved bench-ends are found in most parts of Britain, but particularly in East Anglia and the West Country. The West Country bench-end tends to be square-topped, and the East Anglian with a poppy head (resembling a fleur-de-lys) at the top, and animals, figures, saints or grotesques were carved below.

For West Country bench-ends, see St Meubred's, Cardinham and St Morwenna and St John's, Morwenstow, both in Cornwall; St Brannock's, Braunton and All Saints', East Budleigh, both in Devon; St Mary's, Bishop's Lydeard and St Margaret's, Spaxton, both in Som. For East Anglian bench-ends, see St Mary's, Feltwell and St Mary's, Wiggenhall in Norfolk, St Mary's, Woolpit, St Mary's, Dennington and Church of the Assumption, Ufford in Suffolk, and St Mary's, Fen Ditton in Cambs.

Box pews date from the end of the seventeenth century. These had high sides and a door to keep the draught out, and ranged from the simple (see Holy Trinity, Goodramgate, York and St Mary's, Molland, Devon) to the spectacularly elaborate (see Family pew).

Poor box, alms box. A locked box with a slot in the top, used to collect money for the poor or for charity.

Portable altar. See Altar stone.

Predella. A panel behind the altar which forms the base of the reredos.

Pulpit. Pulpits became common in the seventeenth century. In previous centuries, preaching (if any) had mostly been done by friars at the village or churchyard cross. With the rise of Puritanism, preaching became the most important part of the liturgy, and so pulpits appeared in most churches: raised platforms made of stone or wood and reached by steps on which the priest stood to address the congregation. Pulpits were usually placed to the north of the chancel arch. Wealthier churches had double-decker pulpits (the lower usually for the use of the parish clerk) or three-deckers, in which the bottom deck was used by the parish clerk for community announcements, the middle deck from which the priest conducted the service, and the top deck for sermons. See, for example, Greatham Parish Church, Sussex, St Peter's, Cretingham, Suffolk, St John's,

Stokesay, Salop, and St James's, Idlicote, Warwicks, for a double-decker; and Holy Trinity, Teigh, Rut, St Saviour's, Foremark, Derbys, St Winifred's, Branscombe, Devon, St Edith's, Eaton-under-Heywood, Salop, and St Andrew's, Bayvil, Pembs (now redundant) for a three-decker.

Reredos. Decorative screen behind the altar, sometimes stone (in which case they are most likely to have been defaced at the Reformation or by the Puritans), sometimes painted or carved wood, sometimes fabric (see Riddel). A rare example of a mediaeval stone reredos which survived is at Christchurch Priory, Dorset (c.1360).

Retable. A reredos (Westminster Abbey, London, has the remains of a retable dating from c.1270); or, a carved shelf behind the altar, used for placing candlesticks and other ornaments on.

Riddel, riddel posts. Riddels (from French *rideaux*, curtains) are curtains at the back and sides of an altar. Riddel posts are the four posts at the corners of an altar from which rails supporting them are held. They were a mediaeval feature extensively revived by Sir Ninian Comper (1864–1960).

Rood. Large crucifix flanked by statues of The Virgin Mary and St John the Evangelist, standing on a rood beam which stretched from one side of the chancel to the other. All mediaeval roods were destroyed at the Reformation or the Commonwealth, but a few rood beams still exist. See the Church of the Assumption, Ufford, St Nicholas's, Denston and St Mary Magdalene's, Westerfield, all in Suffolk, and All Saints', Theddlethorpe, Lincs (now redundant). All roods and most rood beams that can be seen today are nineteenth or twentieth century recreations.

Rood loft. A gallery on top of the rood screen, used for cleaning and painting the rood, and sometimes for singing. Most mediaeval rood lofts were destroyed by law in 1548 and 1561, and almost all the rest during the Commonwealth period (1645–60), and their presence is usually only attested by stairs leading to a high-level doorway (see, for example, St Peter's, Hereford) or by Victorian reconstructions. There are very few mediaeval survivals, including St Edith's, Coates-by-Stow, Lincs, St Oswald's, Flamborough, E Yorks, St Mary's, Atherington, Devon, and St Margaret's, St Margarets, Herefs.

Rood screen. Elaborately carved screen separating the nave from the chancel, in the past usually topped by a rood loft and usually made of wood but sometimes stone. Many mediaeval wooden screens survive.

See St Andrew's, Pickworth, Lincs; St Michael's, Kirk Langley, Derbys; St Agnes's, Cawston, Norfolk; St Peter, St Paul and St Thomas of Canterbury's, Bovey Tracey, Devon; St Mary's, Staindrop, Durham; St Mary's, Baldock, Herts; St Stephen's, Old Radnor, Powys.

Mediaeval stone screens are much rarer. See Holy Trinity, Bottisham, Cambs; St Mary's, Totnes, Devon; St Mary's, Berkeley, Glos; Holy Trinity, Tattershall, Lincs; St Nicholas's, Baulking, Oxon; St Mary's, Bramford, Suffolk.

Royal arms. From 1660 it was compulsory by law for churches to display the royal arms on the chancel arch or over the rood beam, though the practice may have started in Henry VIII's reign or even earlier. Today this law is 'probably not still in force', says Bluemantle Pursuivant. The royal arms were usually painted on wooden boards, though sometimes on plaster panels. Most royal arms date from after 1660, but see the arms of Henry VIII at St Nicholas's, Rushbrooke, Suffolk (though this may be a nineteenth century forgery), of Edward VI at St Mary's, Westerham, Kent, and of Elizabeth I at St Mary Magdalene's, Himbleton, Worcs. Changes of sovereign

Reredos, nineteenth century, St Laurence's, Ludlow, Salop

Rood loft, c.1520, St Margaret's, St Margarets, Herefs

Rood screen, late fifteenth or early sixteenth century, St Andrew's, Bramfield, Suffolk

Sanctuary knocker, fourteenth century, St Peter's, Cound, Salop

Stations of the Cross, fifteenth century, Lincoln Cathedral

Sermon timer, ? seventeenth century, St Lawrence's, Ingworth, Norfolk

Tomb of Bishop Richard Fleming, died 1431, with cadaver in a shroud below, Lincoln Cathedral

Stoup, ? twelfth century, St Mary's, Abbeydore, Herefs

Gurney stove, c.1870

Tomb of Sir Edward Stanley (below, d.1632) and his parents (above), Sir Edward Stanley (d. 1576) Margaret Vernon (d. 1596), c.1602, St Bartholomew's, Tong, Salop

often meant changes in the royal arms, so the original version may be difficult to date accurately.

Sanctuary chair. Chair within the sanctuary, to be used by a visiting bishop.

Sanctuary ring, sanctuary knocker. A ring or knocker on the outside of a church door, laying hands on which gave sanctuary to the fugitive who could reach it. In 1540, most forms of sanctuary were abolished, and James I abolished all forms of ecclesiastical sanctuary in 1623.

Sermon timer. A hour-glass attached to, or near, the pulpit so that the preacher could keep an eye on the length of his sermon. See St Lawrence's, Ingworth, and St Edmund's, South Burlingham, both eighteenth century and both in Norfolk.

Seven sacraments font. See Font.

Shrine. A tomb or other building within a church where the relics, or supposed relics, of a saint, and sometimes others, were kept. (The Second Council of Nicaea (787), somewhat oddly, forbade the consecration of the church unless it contained a relic). Shrines became objects of pilgrimage from about the fifth century until the sixteenth, and some still continue today. In the United Kingdom, shrines were mostly looted during the Reformation (it is said that twenty-six cartloads of treasure were removed from the shrine of St Thomas a Becket at Canterbury Cathedral, Kent) and the relics destroyed.

Some shrines, nonetheless, survived: Westminster Abbey, London (Edward the Confessor's body); St Albans Cathedral, Herts (St Alban's scapula and maybe other bones); St Denys's, Stanford-in-the-Vale, Berks (St Denys, on the piscina); St Magnus's Cathedral, Kirkwall, Orkney (some of St Magnus's bones and part of a skull); St Melangell's, Pennant Melangell, Powys (her bones); St Candida and Holy Cross, Whitchurch Canonicorum, Dorset (St Wite's bones).

Of non-saints, the tomb of Edward II in Gloucester Cathedral attracted pilgrims throughout the fourteenth and fifteenth centuries.

Shroud. You are unlikely to see a real example of a shroud, though shrouds are often depicted in pictures, statues or brasses. A shroud was a cloth in which a corpse was wrapped for burial, knotted above the head and beneath the feet, until the seventeenth century, when coffins became common. It had to be made of natural fibre, preferably wool, if not, cotton or linen.

Side galleries. See Galleries.

Sounding board, tester. A horizontal canopy above a pulpit, designed to deflect the speaker's voice towards the congregation, dating from the late sixteenth to eighteenth centuries, and commonly found above two- and three-storey pulpits.

Stations of the Cross. A series of pictures or sculptures depicting scenes from Christ's crucifixion, very common in Roman Catholic churches. The traditional fourteen stations are: Jesus is condemned to death; Jesus carries His cross; Jesus falls the first time; Jesus meets His mother; Simon of Cyrene helps Jesus to carry the cross; Veronica wipes the face of Jesus; Jesus falls the second time; Jesus meets the women of Jerusalem; Jesus falls the third time; Jesus is stripped of his garments; Jesus is nailed to the cross; Jesus dies on the cross; Jesus is taken down from the cross; Jesus is laid in the tomb. Lincoln Cathedral possesses two Stations of the Cross: part of a fine fourteenth century series, and a twentieth century series.

Stoup. A vessel containing holy water, placed near the entrance to a church, for dipping your finger in before crossing yourself. Most stoups were destroyed or filled in during the Reformation, but many still exist. Today, stoups are mostly in use at Roman Catholic and High Anglican churches.

St Mary and St David's, Kilpeck, Herefs; St Mary Magdalene's, Caldecote, Herts (now redundant); and in Suffolk, St Mary's, Blundeston, St Mary's, Bures and St Mary's, Offton.

Stove. Stoves were installed in churches in the nineteenth and early twentieth centuries, burning coal, coke or anthracite. Sir Goldsworthy Gurney (1793–1875) patented the Gurney stove in 1856 and Charles Portway (1828–1909) made his Tortoise stove from about 1880. Nowadays, most have been replaced by other forms of heating, but some can still be seen. There are Gurney stoves in the cathedrals of Chester, Ely, Cambs, Hereford, Peterborough, Cambs, and Salisbury, Wilts, and Tewkesbury Abbey, Glos, all converted to gas, and a Tortoise stove at St Leonard's, Rodney Stoke, Som.

Super-frontal. See Altar frontal.

Tester. See Sounding board.

Tomb, chest tomb. (See also Tombs in the section on Churchyards). Strictly, 'tomb' means a grave, but nowadays means a box-like monument, raised above ground level in a church, mostly with a brass or an effigy of the deceased on top. In this sense, chest tombs date from the mid thirteenth century, possibly in imitation of the shrines to saints, and were not necessarily placed above the grave. In the thirteenth and fourteenth centuries, the sides and ends of the tomb were decorated in the prevailing architectural style, in many cases with weepers decorating the recesses. Chest tombs are mostly made of stone, with the effigy in stone, marble or alabaster (though a few are made of wood. See the tomb of Robert Curthose in Gloucester Cathedral), and mostly painted. In the late fifteenth to seventeenth centuries, tombs were often of two storeys, with an effigy on the upper and a cadaver or skeleton on the lower. About 150 of these survive in the UK.

See Lincoln Cathedral (tomb of Richard Fleming, died 1431, which is the earliest example); Canterbury Cathedral, Kent; Exeter Cathedral, Devon; Wells Cathedral, Som; Winchester Cathedral, Hants; Tewkesbury Abbey, Glos; St John's, Chester, Ches; St Andrew's, Feniton, Devon; Holy Trinity, Minchinhampton, Glos; St Nicholas's, Fyfield, Oxon; St Ethedreda's, Hatfield, Herts.

During the late nineteenth and twentieth century few chest tombs were built. They were mostly to eminent clerics in cathedrals, though see the tomb of the third Marquis of Salisbury (died 1903) in Westminster Abbey, London, and of Lord Kitchener (died 1916) in St Paul's Cathedral, London.

Tree of Jesse. Representation in glass, stone or paint of the descent of Christ from his distant ancestor, Jesse. Most were destroyed during the Puritan period.

See, for example, St Cuthbert's, Wells, Som, for the remains of a stone Tree of Jesse (fifteenth century). For windows, see Selby Abbey, N Yorks (1340); Wells Cathedral, Som (fourteenth century); St Mary's, Shrewsbury, Salop (fourteenth century); St Laurence's, Ludlow, Salop (fourteenth century); St Leonard's, Leverington, Cambs (fifteenth century), St Bridget's, Dyserth, Den (1500–33). For paintings, see St Mary's, Chalgrove, Oxon (fourteenth century); St Helen's, Abingdon, Oxon (late fourteenth century). For a unique mixture of tracery, sculpture and stained glass, see Dorchester Abbey, Dorchester, Oxon (fourteenth century).

Wall monuments, wall memorials, wall tablets. Wall monuments date from about 1550, in style following the chest tomb – kneeling or lying figures, decorative canopies and sometimes weepers. In the seventeenth and eighteenth centuries, Roman dress and allegorical figures became fashionable; and the wall tablet, perhaps with a bust and almost certainly with an extravagant

Tomb of Mary Wolryche, died 1678, St Andrew's, Quatt, Salop

Bishop Beckynton's tomb with *memento mori* underneath, c.1450, Wells Cathedral, Som

The Bardolph tomb: angels at the shoulders of Lady Bardolph, c.1445, St Mary's, Dennington, Suffolk

Detail of the Jesse window, c.1340, in St Mary's, Shrewsbury, Salop

Wall monument, 1668, St John's, Axbridge, Som

Wall monument to John Coke, died 1632, St Mary's, Ottery St Mary, Devon

Wall tablets, mostly eighteenth and nineteenth centuries, Bath Abbey, Som

Wall painting, c.1220, All Saints', Claverley, Salop

Weepers, tomb of Sir Robert Broke, died 1599, All Saints', Claverley, Salop

inscription, was introduced. Wall tablets, often of brass, became almost universal in the nineteenth century, maybe with a carving or picture of a woman mourning over an urn or an angel. Westminster Abbey, London, has the largest collection, followed by Bath Abbey, Som. See the tomb of John Gower, Southwark Cathedral, London (fifteenth century); of the Knightley family in St Mary's, Fawsley, Northants (sixteenth century); and St Stephen's, Norwich, Norfolk (mostly seventeenth and eighteenth century).

Wall paintings. Before the Reformation, practically all surfaces inside the church were covered with wall paintings (the 'Poor Man's Bible'). The walls were plastered, the plaster dampened, and simple pigments were applied. As a result of legislation in the 1540s and 1560s, and the Puritan revolution (1645–60), most paintings were covered with limewash. The greatest damage, however, was done in the nineteenth century, when plaster, sound or unsound, was stripped off to reveal the stonework. Where the plaster was not stripped off, wall paintings have often been rediscovered. See, for example St Nicolas's, Oddington, Glos (about 1340, said to be the largest in Britain); St Lawrence's, Broughton, Milton Keynes, Bucks, where paintings cover large areas of the north and south walls; St Mary's, Lakenheath, Suffolk; St Giles's, Pipe Aston, Herefs; St Peter and St Paul's, Pickering, N Yorks; St Clement's, Ashamptead, Berks.

Watching loft. A post from which to watch a shrine to prevent theft. See St Albans Cathedral, Herts; Worcester Cathedral; and Malmesbury Abbey, Wilts.

Weepers. Figures of the bereaved family, or relations, or saints, carved on the sides and ends of a tomb chest. See the tomb of John of Eltham (died 1336) at Westminster Abbey, London; Ralph Fitzherbert (died 1483) at St Mary and St Barlock's, Norbury, Derbys; and Richard Beauchamp (died 1439) at St Mary's, Warwick.

West gallery. See Gallery.

Winding sheet. A type of linen shroud, and, like shrouds, sometimes seen in pictures, sculptures and brasses.

STAINED GLASS

Stained glass – which is really painted and stained glass – was introduced into Britain from France in the seventh century. The oldest piece of stained glass in England was made in France, dates from around 675, and is from Wearmouth Monastery, near Jarrow, Tyne & W. Stained glass became common in cathedrals in the eleventh century and parish churches in the thirteenth, and reached its peak between 1250 and 1450. The oldest stained glass window is at York Minster: it dates to around 1150.

In 1134 the Cistercians forbade the use of coloured glass or figures in their buildings. This led to the development of 'grisaille' windows – windows in which the glass was monochrome, generally faint brown, grey or green, painted with foliage and flowers. The Five Sisters window at York Minster (about 1250) is a fine example. Grisaille windows initially competed with the more common highly-coloured narrative windows but rapidly spread beyond Cistercianism, and by the middle of the fourteenth century, it was a common feature of stained glass. See, for example, the east window of Gloucester Cathedral (1350–60).

Mediaeval stained glass – pot-metal glass – was made by mixing oxides of metal to the molten glass. Copper produces green, cobalt, blue and iron, red. In some cases, such as blue or red, the resulting colour was too dark to let much light through, so the glass was 'flashed': a thin layer of coloured glass was applied to clear glass.

At the beginning of the fourteenth century new colours came into use, including brown, violet, deep green and yellow. Yellow was produced by silver staining, a method of staining clear glass various shades of yellow by fusing on to it a derivative of sulphide of silver.

The design of the panel was drawn on a table, providing a pattern, and the white or coloured glass was nibbled into shape by a grozing iron, a notched metal rod. The pieces of glass were painted – inscriptions, faces, drapery – and baked in a small kiln, so that the black paint could fuse with the coloured glass. The pieces of glass were then re-assembled on the table and fastened together with H-shaped lead strips called cames. When the panels were on site, they were held together with an armature and placed in the window opening and fixed with copper wire soldered to iron saddle bars – horizontal bars set into the stonework.

Like statues, rood lofts, wall paintings, bells and other works of art in churches, stained glass windows were a victim of the Dissolution of the Monasteries (1536–40) and the Reformation. An enormous quantity was smashed. In Scotland virtually all stained glass was destroyed. Most of the rest disappeared during the Puritan Revolution (1645–60). Pre-Reformation stained glass is uncommon today. Notable examples exist at York and Canterbury Cathedrals, St Mary's, Fairford, Glos, and King's College Chapel, Cambridge. Denied religious subjects, from about 1550 to 1600, stained glass was limited to heraldic panels or pictures of flowers.

Two other factors occurring at much the same time contributed to the demise of stained glass for the next two hundred years. Around the middle of the sixteenth century, probably in the Netherlands, enamel painting was discovered. This was the art of painting in colours on clear glass and then firing the glass to fix the colours. This dispensed with the need to cut glass to shape and the need for leading: soon, all painted glass was on rectangular panels. The second was the destruction of the Lorraine glass works in 1633–6, during the wars between Louis XIII and Duke Charles IV of Lorraine. Most glass used in Britain came from this source (though some glass-makers operated in London), and following the destruction, supplies of pot-metal glass virtually dried up. Most glass windows from 1650 to 1850 are painted on clear glass, not stained.

The revival of true stained glass is due to the researcher Charles Winston (1814–64) and the chemist Dr Medlock (Christian names and dates not known), who, in 1849–50, re-created pot-metal glass and had it manufactured by James Powell and Sons. There was, from this time, an explosion in stained glass making. There are 1,873 James Powell and Sons windows listed from one year alone, 1837, in just Beds, Berks, Hants, Herts, west Kent, Greater London, Surrey, Sussex and Wilts.

This explosion was fuelled by an odd mixture of causes. There was the surge of interest in mediaeval buildings, fired by the Gothic revival. There was a population explosion and the rapid growth of cities, leading to the consequent enormous increase in church building. There was the invention of rolled glass in the 1830s, in which the molten glass is poured on to a table and rolled into a sheet by a metal cylinder or pair of cylinders. There was the later invention (about 1849, also by James Powell and Sons) of moulded and textured quarries, made by pressing molten glass into patterned moulds, so producing designs of flowers, leaves, birds and so on; glass-painting pigment was applied to the pattern, and the glass was fired in the usual way. There was the still later invention of slab glass (by E S Prior in 1899, also known as Prior's Early English glass, or Norman, or *dalles de verre*), made by blowing glass into a box-shaped mould and then cutting off the sides, which resulted slabs of uneven thickness and colour.

Designers and makers

Almquist, Carl. See Shrigley and Hunt.

An Túr Gloine ('Tower of Glass'). Irish Arts and Crafts co-operative studio founded in 1903 in Dublin by Sarah Purser (whose glass is probably all outside the UK), whose members included Evie Hone, Wilhelmina Geddes and Harry Clarke.

Arnold, Hugh (1872–1915). Arts and Crafts designer and author, and pupil of Christopher Whall. Published *Stained Glass of the Middle Ages in England and France* (1913). Killed in action at Gallipoli in 1915.

St Padarn's, Llanbadarn Fawr, Cered (1904); Wythburn Church, Cumbria (1906); St Mary's, Saxlingham Nethergate, Norfolk (1910); St Mary's, Edith Weston, Rut (1912); Holy Trinity, Millom, Cumbria (date not known).

Baillie, Thomas, and Co (1832–97). Also Baillie and Mayer, and Baillie and Lutwyche. The firm was founded in 1832 by Alexander Benjamin Baillie (1787–1864), a Scot who migrated to London. His elder son Edward (1812–56) was involved from the 1850s, and

Thomas, a younger son (1815 or 1816–83), joined the firm in 1853 and took over in 1856. George Mayer (1822–84) became a partner in 1854. William Lutwyche (1840–1908), became a partner in 1890 and between 1890 and 1893 the firm was known as Baillie and Lutwyche. The firm ceased production in 1897.

St Botolph's, Apsley Guise, Beds (1845–62); Winchester Cathedral, Hants (1852, restored); St Margaret's, Buxted, Sussex (1853); St Mary's, Brownsea Island, Dorset (1854); St James's, Fulmer, Bucks (1860); St Andrew's, West Tarring, Sussex (1860–74); St Mary's, Bepton, Sussex (1869); St Michael's, North Waltham, Hants (between 1865 and 1878); St Andrew's, Oving, Sussex (1881); St James's, Nayland, Suffolk (date not known).

Ballantine and Allen (1837–1940). Edinburgh neo-Gothic and Arts and Crafts designers and makers. James (1807 or 1808–1877), author and poet, founded the firm in 1837 with George Allan (dates not known); James's son Alexander (1841–1906) joined in c.1860 and the firm was called Ballantine and Son from 1860 to 1892; then in 1905 by Herbert Gardiner (dates not known), when it was called Ballantine and Gardiner; then by James's grandson James II (1878–1940), when the firm was called A Ballantine and Son.

Falkirk Old and St Modan's, Falkirk (1852, 1862); St Eurgain and St Peter's, Northop, Flint (c.1856); St John the Evangelist's, Edinburgh (1857–1935); Sandyford Henderson Church, Glasgow (1857); Corpus Christi, Tremeirchion, Den (1861, 1866); Freuchie Parish Church, Fife (after 1876); Emmanuel Church, Buckley, Flint (1881); St Andrew's, Tain, Highland (1887); Walkerburn Parish Church, Innerleithen, Borders (1892, 1912); Christ Church, Walmsley, Manchester (1896); St Serf's, Dunning, Perth and Kinross (1899–1910); St Stephen's, Inverness, Highland (1901–6); Corstorphine Old Parish Church, Edinburgh (1904–5).

Betton and Evans (1806–61). Sir John Betton of Shrewsbury, Salop (1765–1849) began making stained glass in 1806, and in 1815 formed a partnership with his ex-apprentice, David Evans (1793–1861). Betton retired in 1825 but Evans continued making and restoring stained glass, helped by his two sons, Charles and William. The firm ceased trading in 1861, when Evans died.

Lichfield Cathedral, Staffs (c.1815); Winchester College chapel, Hants (1822–3); St Deiniol's, Worthenbury, Wrexham (1823); Bangor Cathedral, Gwynedd (1833); St Michael's, Munslow, Salop (1835); St Chad's, Shrewsbury, Salop (1836–44); St Luke's, Ironbridge, Salop (1837); St Giles's, Wrexham (1841); Christ Church, Cressage, Salop (1843); Winchester Cathedral (1851, 1853); St Seiriol's, Penmon, Anglesey (1855); St Tysilio and St Mary's, Meifod, Powys (c.1856); St Julian's, Shrewsbury, Salop (1861).

Bossanyi, Ervin (1891–1975). Jewish-Hungarian designer, painter and sculptor. After the First World War he lived and worked in Lubeck and Hamburg, then fled to England from Nazi Germany in 1934, where he took up stained glass. Most of his glass is in museums or collections.

West End Synagogue, Bayswater, London (1937); Canterbury Cathedral, Kent (1957); St John's College and St Peter's College chapels, Oxford (dates not known).

Burlison and Grylls (1868–1945). Designers and makers. Founded in 1868 by John Burlison (1843–91) and Thomas Grylls (1845–1913), who had both trained under Clayton and Bell; later run by Thomas Henry Grylls (1873–1953). The company effectively stopped trading after it was bombed in 1945, and ceased with the death of T H Grylls.

St Mary the Virgin's, Plumtree, Notts (1870s–90s); St Cynllo, Nantmell, Powys (1875–1900); All Saints', Marlow, Bucks (1876, 1891); St Mary and St John's, Oxford (1879–92); St Mary's, Wavendon, Bucks (1888–94);

St Nicholas's, Nicholaston, Swansea, Glam (c.1894); St Etheldreda's Guilsborough, Northants (1895); Westminster Abbey, London (1902); Llandaff Cathedral, Cardiff, Glam (1909); All Saints', Brixworth, Northants (1913, 1915); St Nicholas's, Willoughby, Warwicks (1919); St Mary's, Fishguard, Pembs (1921);.St David and St Cyfelach's, Llangefelach, Swansea, Glam (1947).

Burne-Jones, Sir Edward (Coley) (1833–98). Pre-Raphaelite painter and illustrator, and designer of stained glass, tiles, tapestries and jewellery; closely associated with Dante Gabriel Rossetti and William Morris.

Christ Church Cathedral, Oxford (1858, 1870s); All Saints, Jesus Lane, Cambridge (1866); St Michael and All Angels, Waterford, Herts (1872, 1896); St Martin's, Brampton, Cumbria (1878-8); Birmingham Cathedral, W Mid (1885–91); St Deiniol's, Hawarden, Flint (1896–1911).

Chilton, Margaret (1875–1963). Arts and Crafts designer. Born in Bristol and was a student of Christopher Whall's. Moved to Edinburgh, where she established a studio in partnership with her student Marjorie Kemp (1886–1975), with whom she mostly worked. Most of her work is in Scotland.

St Andrew's, Leytonstone, London (1920s?); Chalmers Memorial Church, Port Seton, East Lothian (1924–50); Ferryhill Parish Church, Aberdeen (1925); St Leonard's, St Andrew's, Fife (1926–54); St John's Renfield, Glasgow (1929, 1933); Dirleton Parish Kirk, East Lothian (1936); St Finnian's, Lochgelly, Fife (1949, 1950); Alloa St John's Episcopal Church, Clackmannanshire (1939); Holy Trinity, Stirling (c.1951); Cumbrae Cathedral, Argyll and Bute (date not known); St Mary's, Cadogan Street, London (date not known); St Andrew's, Hampstead, London (date not known).

Clayton and Bell (1855–1993). Immensely prolific designers and makers. The firm was founded by John Richard Clayton (1827–1913) and Alfred Bell (1832–95); later it was run by Bell's son, John Clement Bell (1860–1944), then by Reginald Otto Bell (1884–1950) and finally by Michael Farrar-Bell (1911–93) until his death. Their glass was initially made by Heaton and Butler, with whom they shared a studio (1859–62). In the 1860s and 1870s they employed more than 300 people and the firm worked day and night shifts to fulfil commissions. They had considerable overseas business: their work may be seen in Australia, Canada, Ireland, New Zealand and the United States as well as the UK.

Peterborough Cathedral, Cambs (1850–65); St Llonio's, Llandinam, Powys (1857); St Mary's, Hanley Castle, Worcs (1860); St James's, Westminster, London (1861); Gloucester Cathedral (1862, designed by C E Kempe); Brecon Cathedral, Powys (1864); Reading Minster, Berks (1865, 1880); St John's College chapel, Cambridge (1866–76); All Saints', Gresford, Wrexham (1868–82), St Swithun's, Cheswardine, Salop (?1860s); Bangor Cathedral, Gwynedd (1873, c.1880); Winchester Cathedral, Hants (1875–83); St Luke's, Maidenhead, Berks (1875–93); St Peter and St Paul's, Buckingham (1876–1907); King's College Chapel, Cambridge (1878, west window); All Saints', Oving, Bucks (1882–97); All Saints', Highbrook, Sussex (1885–92); Truro Cathedral, Cornwall (1880s); Norwich Cathedral, Norfolk (1895–1910); All Saints', Hove, Sussex (1901); St Idloes's, Llanidloes, Powys (1935); St Adoenus's, Mounton, Mon (1962).

Clutterbuck, Charles Edmund senior (1806–1861) and Clutterbuck, Charles Edmund junior (1839–83). Designers. Clutterbuck senior trained as a miniature-painter, but designed glass from about 1840. He was one of the first to take thirteenth and fourteenth century glass as models. His son continued the business at Stratford, Essex until 1882.

Charterhouse Chapel, Godalming, Surrey (1844); St Ffraid's, Llansanffraid Glan Conwy, Conwy (1846); St Michael's, Aylsham, Norfolk

(1857); St Mary's, Oakley, Bucks (1860s); St Digain's, Llangernyw, Conwy (1880).

Comper, Sir (John) Ninian (1864-1960). Scottish Gothic Revival designer and architect. For his biographical details see the Architects and master craftsmen section.

Lady Chapel at St Matthew's, Westminster, London (1890s?); Lady Chapel, Downside Abbey, Som (1899–1926); St Cyprian's, Clarence Gate, London (1904); Westminster Abbey, London (1908–22); St Peter's, Huddersfield, W Yorks (c.1920); St Michael and All Angels, Inverness, Highland (c.1924); St Mary's, Wellingborough, Northants (c.1930).

Cottier, Daniel (1837 or 1838–91). Manx father, Scottish mother. Aesthetic Movement designer, art dealer and entrepreneur, who is credited with introducing the Aesthetic Movement to Scotland, Australia and the United States. Born in Glasgow, opened his first studio there in 1864, moved to London in 1869 (or 1867), where he established Cottier and Co, which eventually employed over a hundred men (and which Van Gogh visited in 1876). He opened art furnishing shops in New York, Sydney and Melbourne in 1873. He died in Florida.

St Paul's, Pilrig, Leith, Edinburgh (1863); Cottiers Theatre Glasgow (1865, built as Dowanhill Parish Church); St Machar's Cathedral, Aberdeen (1873); Paisley Abbey, Renfrewshire (c.1880); Our Lady and St Cuthbert's, Prudhoe, Northumb (1891, but incorporating windows of 1868–70 (see also windows in Prudhoe Hall, 1868–70); Kirk Christ Lezayre, IoM (1884). Lyle Community Kirk (Esplanade Building), Greenock, Inverclyde (1884).

Davis, Louis (1860–1941). Arts and Crafts designer and illustrator. Studied under Christopher Whall from 1891; worked with Lowndes and Drury; from 1906 at The Glass House, Chelsea; and from 1910 with Karl Parsons.

St Giles's, Stoke Poges, Bucks (1899); St John the Baptist's, Pinner, London (1900); St Silas's, Kentish Town, London (1900); St Mary and St Nicholas's, Littlemore, Oxon (1900); St Anselm's, Hatch End, London (1903–32); St Giles's Cathedral, Edinburgh (the Thistle Chapel, after 1911); St Laurence's, Ludlow, Salop (1912, 1928); Dunblane Abbey, Perthshire (1913); Cheltenham College chapel, Glos (1924); Abingdon School chapel, Oxon (1924); St Mary's, Rockbeare, Devon (1928); All Saints', Longstanton, Cambs (1938).

Easton, Hugh (1906–65). Designer. Born in London, worked in Guildford in the 1920s and set up his own studio in Cambridge before the Second World War. After the war he moved back to London and became well-known as a designer of stained glass war memorials.

St Nicholas's, Warwick (1930s); Durham Cathedral (1936); St Mary's, Burwell, Cambs (1936); All Saints', Southill, Beds (1936); All Saints', Hockerill, Herts (1937); Winchester Cathedral, Hants (1938, 1939); Westminster Abbey, London (1947); St Elphin's, Warrington, Ches (1947); St Cuthbert's, Philbeach Gardens, Kensington, London (1947–60); St Cybi's, Holyhead, Anglesey (c.1948); St George's RAF Chapel of Remembrance, Biggin Hill, Kent (1951); St Martin's, Roath, Cardiff, Glam (1955, 1956); Oundle School chapel, Northants (1956); Wellington College chapel, Crowthorne, Berks (1952); Holy Trinity, Coventry, W Mid (1955); St James's, Grimsby, Lincs (1957); St Luke's, Chelsea, London (1959).

Edwards, Carl (Johannes) (1914–85). Finnish designer, born in London as Kiviaho, which he changed to Edwards at the beginning of the Second World War. He joined James Powell and Sons in 1928 and became chief designer in 1948. He set up his own studio in 1952. From 1972 he worked at The Glass House in Fulham, taking over Lowndes and Drury when they liquidated.

St Mary's, Chelsea, London (1953); Liverpool Anglican Cathedral, Mersey (1954–

79); St Matthew and St James's, Liverpool, Mersey (1954); St James's, Kidbrooke, London (1955, 1959); Portsmouth Cathedral, Hants (1956, 1981); St Mary's, Denham, Bucks (1956); Temple Church, London (1957–8); St Clement Danes, Strand, London (1958);St Davids Cathedral, Pembs (1958); St Gwendoline's, Llyswen, Powys (c.1959); St John's, Hazlewood, Derbys (1963); St Mary's, Walberton, Sussex (1963). St John's, Buckhurst Hill, Essex (1964); St Wilfrid's, Church Norton, Sussex (1969).

Evans, David. See Betton and Evans.

Flower, Barnard (died 1517). Flemish (or possibly German) glazier working in Westminster. King's Glazier from about 1490. Made four of the windows in King's College Chapel, Cambridge (1515–17), and probably the windows at St Mary's, Fairford, Glos (1500–17). The windows which he made in the Lady Chapel, Westminster Abbey, London, have disappeared, and those at Our Lady of Walsingham, Norfolk (1511–12), were destroyed in the Dissolution of the Monasteries.

Forsyth, Moira (1906–91). Stained glass designer, potter and decorative painter who worked with Wilhelmina Geddes and at The Glass House.

St Thomas's, Hanwell, London (1934); St Botolph's, Chevening, Kent (1949); Emanuel School chapel, Battersea, London (1950s); St John Evangelist's, Higham, Kent (1950s?); St Mary's, Friston, Sussex (1952); St Mary's, Hampden Park, Eastbourne, Sussex (1953); Holy Family, Farnham, Surrey (1956); Aylesford Priory, Kent (1957); Norwich Cathedral, Norfolk (1964); St Mary's, Twyford, Hants (1965); and also windows, including the Rose Window, at Guildford Cathedral, Surrey.

Gauld, David (1865–1936). Scottish painter, lithographer and stained glass designer. He was loosely connected to the Glasgow Boys, a Glasgow-based group which challenged the Edinburgh-dominated art establishment and the Royal Scottish Academy from 1880s till about 1910.

Ibrox (formerly Bellahouston) Parish Church, Glasgow (?1898), Skelmorlie Parish Church, Ayrshire (1895); St David's, Upper Largo, Fife (1896).

Geddes, Wilhelmina (1887–1955). Irish Arts and Crafts designer. Joined An Túr Gloine in Dublin and in 1925 moved to The Glass House in Fulham. Perhaps her most celebrated work is the Memorial Window in St Bartholomew's, Ottawa, Canada. She also made the rose window in Ypres Cathedral, Belgium (1938).

St Luke's, Wallsend, Tyne & W (1922); All Saints', Laleham, Surrey (1926); St Michael's, Northchapel, Sussex (1930); St Peter's, Lampeter, Cered (1943); St Mildred's, Lee, London (1951); All Hallows, Greenford, London (1952); Holy Trinity, Bardsea, Cumbria (1955).

Gibbs, Alexander (1832–86). Eldest son of Isaac Alexander Gibbs (1802–51, also a stained glass maker) and brother of Charles Alexander Gibbs and Isaac Alexander Gibbs jnr (1849–99). Collaborator with the architect William Butterfield.

St Mary Magdalene's, Taunton, Som (1862); St Mary's, Battle, Sussex (1870, 1882); St Nicholas's, Arundel, Sussex (1878, 1881); and, all with Butterfield, St Peter's, Elerch, Cered (1868); All Saints', Margaret Street, London (1877); and Keble College chapel, Oxford (1878).

Gibbs, Charles (Alexander) (1825–77). Brother of Alexander Gibbs, but set up on his own in London in 1858.

St Beuno's, Aberffraw, Anglesey (c.1850); St Margaret's, Angmering, Sussex (1853); St Nicholas's, Arundel, Sussex (1856); St Luke's, Sambrook, Salop (1856); St Cattwg's, Llanspyddid, Powys (c.1856); Winchester Cathedral, Hants (1857); St Margaret and St Peter's, Pett, Sussex (1865); St Andrew's, Biggleswade, Beds (1870); St Mary's, Ruabon, Wrexham (c.1872); St Edmund's, Crickhowell, Powys (1872); St Bridget's, Liverpool, Mersey (1872).

Glass House, Fulham, London (1906–93). Arts and Crafts purpose-built studio in which Louis Davis, Moira Forsyth, Wilhelmina Geddes, Mary Lowndes, Eddie Nuttgens, Karl Parsons and Christopher Whall (among others) worked.

Glazier, Thomas (died 1427). Nothing is known of his life except that his workshop was in Oxford and that he was married. His work can be seen in New College (1380–3), All Souls College and Merton College, all in Oxford; Winchester College chapel, Hants (c.1393–1404); and probably in St Mary's, Thenford, Northants. Also in the Victoria and Albert Museum (?1393, from Winchester College Chapel).

Guthrie, J & W (c.1870–2002), later J & W Guthrie and Andrew Wells (1897–c.1960), later still Guthrie and Wells (c.1960–2002): decorators, furniture makers and stained glass manufacturers. In 1870 John and William Guthrie (dates unknown but fl. 1870–1900) inherited an established studio in Glasgow founded about 1850 by their father, John senior. From about 1890, they were the most prolific studio in Glasgow. Hired many designers including David Gauld, Christopher Whall and Charles Rennie Mackintosh. Glass from their studio is usually listed under the name of the designer.

Gyles, Henry (1645–1709). York glass painter, mostly of heraldic glass.

St Paul's, Witherslack, Cumbria (1671); St John's, Staveley, Derbys (1676); St John's, Adel, Leeds, W Yorks (1681); University College, Oxford (1687); St Helen's, Denton, W Yorks (1700); and, dates not known, Wadham College chapel, Oxford; Trinity and St Catharine's College chapels, Cambridge.

Hardman & Co (1844–2008). Birmingham firm founded by John Hardman (1811–67) in 1838 to manufacture ecclesiastical metalwork. In 1845 Hardman, urged by A W N Pugin, began making stained glass. Hardman worked to Pugin's designs until Pugin's death in 1852; thereafter Hardman's nephew John Hardman Powell (1827–95), who trained under Pugin and married Pugin's daughter Anne in 1850, was his designer. Hardman & Co created many thousands of windows throughout the United Kingdom, as well as much of the stained glass for the Houses of Parliament (and the dial for Big Ben).

St Chad's Cathedral, Birmingham W Mid (1845, 1868, 1919); St Mary's Wymeswold, Leics (1845); St Joseph's Avon Dassett, Warwicks (1854, 1857–77); St Nicolas's, Newbury, Berks (1858–84); St Mary Magdalene's, Great Alne, Warwicks (1860); Gloucester Cathedral (1860s and 1870s); St Augustine's, Edgbaston, Birmingham, W Mid (1868); St Davids Cathedral, Pembs (1870); St Nicolas's, Kings Norton, Birmingham, W Mid (1870s, 1950s); Worcester Cathedral (1874–80); All Saints' Ladbroke, Warwicks (1876); St Cyprian's Hay Mills, Birmingham, W Mid (1878); Norwich RC Cathedral, Norfolk (1878, 1890); St Eurgain and St Peter's, Northop, Flint (c.1880); Tewkesbury Abbey, Glos (1886–92); Newport Cathedral, Glam (1890); St Patrick's, Anderston, Glasgow (1898); St John the Divine's, Penrhyn-coch, Cered (1900); St David's, Swansea, Glam (1920, c.1970–80); Southwark Cathedral, London (1921); St Winifrede's, Holywell, Flint (1936).

Heaton, Butler and Bayne (1852–1953). Neo-Gothic designers and makers. Clement Heaton (1824–82) founded the firm in 1852 and was joined by James Butler (1830–1913) in 1855 and Robert Turnill Bayne (1837–1915) in 1862. One of the most prolific firms of the second half of the nineteenth century. Bayne's son Richard Cato Bayne (1870–1940), and Richard's son, Basil Richard Bayne (1897–1953) successively controlled the firm until Basil's death, when it was wound up.

Wimborne Minster, Dorset (1857); Peterborough Cathedral, Cambs (1864);

Roundel, c.1200, Trinity Chapel ambulatory, Canterbury Cathedral, Kent

Mediaeval stained glass, fourteenth century, St Mary's, Dennington, Suffolk

Head of Jesse, the Jesse window, c.1340, St Mary's, Shrewsbury, Salop

South transept window, c.1530, 'The heroes of the West Country', glass by Burlison and Grylls, late nineteenth century, Bath Abbey, Som

Great east window, c.1500, glass by Clayton and Bell, 1872, Bath Abbey, Som

Nave window, fourteenth century, 'The cleansing of the temple', glass by Hardman and Co, nineteenth century, Beverley Minster, E Yorks

West window, c. 1500, glass by Clayton and Bell, 1872–94, Bath Abbey, Som

East window, c. 1420; glass, incorporating fifteenth century fragments, by C E Kempe, 1902, St Bartholomew's, Tong, Salop

Great west window (fourteenth century) with glass by W G Taylor, 1898, Brecon Cathedral, Powys

East window, glass by Ward and Hughes, ?1870s, St Pancras's, Widecombe-in-the-Moor, Devon

East end lancet windows (about 1300) with windows by James Powell (1895), St Nicholas's, Blakeney, Norfolk

South-west nave window by Henry Payne, early twentieth century, St John's, Stokesay, Salop

Chancel window (fourteenth century) with glass, incorporating mediaeval glass, by Betton (1814), St John's, Kinlet, Salop

St Mary's, Osterley, London (1864, 1866); St Peter's, Eype, Dorset (1865, now an arts centre); St Mary's, Abbey-cym-hir, Powys (1866); Westminster Abbey, London (1868); St Luke's, Camden, London (1868, c.1880–90, 1891); Tewkesbury Abbey, Glos (1869); Christ Church, Worthing, Sussex (1871–92); St Peter and St Paul's, West Newton, Norfolk (c.1880–1910); St Mary Magdalene's, Enfield, London (1883); Chester Cathedral, Ches (1887); St Mary's, Hampton, London (c.1888); St Nicolas's, Taplow, Bucks (1891, 1898); All Saints', Orton, Cumbria (c.1892); St Barnabas's, Bexhill, Sussex (1895–1927); St Mary's, Staverton, Northants (1896); St Paul's, Slough, Bucks (1906, 1921, 1922); St Martin's, Haverfordwest, Pembs (1909); St Michael's, Cwmystwyth, Cered (1933).

Hedgeland, George (Caleb), 1825–98. Designer. Worked in London, but bad health led him to emigrate to Australia in 1860, where he died.

Jesus College chapel, Oxford (1853); Norwich Cathedral, Norfolk (1853); Lincoln Cathedral (1854); Halifax Minster, W Yorks (1856).

Holiday, Henry (1839–1927). Pre-Raphaelite designer, painter, sculptor and illustrator, perhaps more famous today as the illustrator of Lewis Carroll's *The Hunting of the Snark* (1874) and for his painting *Dante and Beatrice* (1883). Joined Powell and Sons in 1861, after Burne-Jones had left for Morris & Co, and carried out some 300 commissions there. He left Powell's in 1891 to set up his own glass company in Hampstead. His later works were made at The Glass House, Fulham.

Westminster Abbey, London (1868); St Mary Magdalene's, Paddington, London (1869); St John's, Keswick, Cumbria (c.1880); St Salvator's Chapel, St Andrew's, Fife (1880s); St Mary's, Bramshott, Hants (1897–1918); St George's, Perry Hill, London (1900, church rebuilt 2003-4); St Matthew's, Buckley, Flint (1901–10); St Deiniol's, Hawarden, Flint (c.1902); Southwark Cathedral (1903); St Hilda's, Crofton Park, London (1912); St Peter's, Bushey Heath, Herts (1918, 1919).

Hone, Evie (1894–1955). Irish designer and painter, believed to be a descendant of Gaylon Hone. A member of An Túr Gloine before setting up in Rathfarnham, Dublin. Influenced by the Cubist painters, and later by Rouault. Much of her work is in Ireland, some of it in museums.

St Mary Magdalene's, Lanercost Priory, Cumbria (c.1947); Eton College chapel, Berks (1949–52); St Michael's, Highgate, London (1954).

Hone, Gaylon (died c.1551). Flemish master glazier about whom not much is known. He worked from Southwark before 1517, when he is recorded as working at Eton, and was King's Glazier from about 1520. He created the east window and sixteen others at King's College Chapel, Cambridge (1526–31). Four were made by Barnard Flower and four by Francis Williamson and Symon Symondes: nothing appears to be known about Williamson and Symondes. The stained glass at Withcote Chapel, Oakham, Rut (c.1530–40), brought from elsewhere, is attributed to him.

Jewitt, E H. See Shrigley and Hunt.

Kempe, Charles Eamer (1838–1907). Prodigiously prolific stained glass designer and maker. His studio produced over 4,000 windows and it is said that within thirty miles of anywhere in the United Kingdom there is a Kempe window. Studied for the priesthood but because of his stammer gave the idea up and went to study architecture with C F Bodley and Clayton and Bell. In 1866 he started his own studio, supplying designs for glass to Bodley. By 1899 he had fifty employees and clients in Africa, Australia, Canada, India, Ireland, Pakistan and USA. After Kempe's death, his cousin Walter Tower took over the firm. It closed in 1934.

Gloucester Cathedral (1865, 1878–87); St Ethelburga's, Bishopgate, London (1871); St Nicholas's, Brighton, Sussex (1878–87); St Mary's Cathedral, Edinburgh (1878); St Mary's, Monmouth, (1882); St John Baptist's, Burford, Oxon (1887–1907); Holy Trinity, Stirling (1890–1906); St Peter's, Heswall, Mersey (1891); Lichfield Cathedral, Staffs (1894–1904); Southwark Cathedral, London (1895–1907); Winchester Cathedral, Hants (1897–1900); St Hilda's, Whitby, N Yorks (1902–6).

Ketelbarn, Robert (fl. 1339). Creator of the Great West Window, York Minster (1339). Nothing appears to be known of him or his other works.

Lavers, Barraud and Westlake (1855–1921). Firm of stained glass designers and makers. Nathaniel Wood Lavers (1828–1911) opened his studio in 1855 and was joined by Francis Philip Barraud (1824–1900) in 1868 and by the designer Nathaniel Westlake (1833–1921) in 1868. Both Lavers and Barraud had been employed by James Powell and Sons, and Westlake had worked with William Burges and Clayton and Bell. After the deaths of Lavers and Barraud, Westlake continued to run the firm (now called N H J Westlake) until his own death in 1921.

All Saints', Higher Walton, Lancs (1864); Worcester Cathedral (1866); St Margaret's, Angmering, Sussex (1868–88); St Michael's, Winterbourne Earls, Wilts (1868); St Margaret's, Bowers Gifford, Essex (1871); St Andrew's, Wraysbury, Bucks (1872, 1875); St Mor and St Deiniol's, Llanfor, Gwynedd (1875); St Andrew's, Worthing, Sussex (1888); St Peblig's, Caernarfon, Gwynedd (1894, 1897); St Mary's, Caernarfon, Gwynedd (c.1910).

Lee, Lawrence (1909–2011). Stained glass artist. Masterminded the creation of ten seventy-foot stained glass windows for Coventry Cathedral, W Mid (1962), with the assistance of Keith New and Geoffrey Clarke. Lee, New and Clarke designed three lights apiece, with the tenth light being a collaboration.

St Magnus the Martyr, London (1949–55); Southwark Cathedral, London (1959, 1980s); St James's, Abinger Hammer, Surrey (1967); King Charles the Martyr, Tunbridge Wells, Kent (1969); Holy Cross, Binstead, IoW (1971); Guildford Cathedral, Surrey (1988); St Martin's, Brasted, Kent (1992).

Lowndes, Mary (1857 or 1856–1929). Arts and Crafts designer and suffragette. First worked under Henry Holiday. From 1887–1902 was designer with James Powell and Sons. In 1897, with Alfred J Drury (1868–40), founded Lowndes and Drury. In 1906, they founded The Glass House in Fulham, London.

St Peter and St Paul's, Shropham, Norfolk (1890s); St George's, Altrincham, Ches (1895); St John's, Wittersham, Kent (1897); St Mary's, Bourne Street, London (1897); St Mary's, Sturminster Newton, Dorset (1901); St Peter's, Kensington, London (1904–6, now St Yeghiches); St Andrew's, Meonstoke, Hants (1906); St Mary and St Blaise's, Boxgrove, Sussex (1906); St Peter's, Great Cheverell, Wilts (1909, 1920); St Margaret's, Mountain Ash, Glam (1911, 1917); Holy Trinity, Aberaeron, Cered (1920).

Morris, Marshall, Faulkner & Co (1861–75) and Morris & Co (1875–1940). Pre-Raphaelite and Arts and Crafts companies founded by William Morris (1834–96) the author, poet, translator, painter, illustrator, illuminator, textile designer, embroiderer, publisher, mediaevalist, socialist, founder of the Society for the Protection of Ancient Buildings, and stained glass manufacturer and designer. The companies usually made stained glass windows for other members of the group, such as Burne-Jones, Ford Madox Brown and Dante Gabriel Rossetti, but Morris contributed to many and designed a few windows himself.

St Michael and All Angels, Brighton, Sussex (1860s); All Saints', Selsey, Glos (?1862); St James's, Staveley, Cumbria (?1864).

Nuttgens, Joseph Edward (Eddie) (1892–1982). Born in Aachen, Germany, of a German father and an English mother. The family moved to England in 1896. He was arrested and interned in 1914–15 (though his father, who was pure German, was not). Influenced by Christopher Whall; from 1911 used The Glass House. His son, Joseph Ambrose Nuttgens (born 1941), is also a stained glass maker.

St Giles's, Dallington, Sussex (1920); Our Lady and St Thomas of Canterbury's, Harrow, London (1921–47); St Mark's, Staplefield, Sussex (1924); Holy Trinity, Sissinghurst, Kent (1944–57); All Saints', Ebbw Vale, Glam (1948, 1953); St Etheldreda's, Holborn, London (1952); St Stephen's, Lewisham, London (1954); St Nicholas's, West Itchenor, Sussex (1954); Holy Cross, Hucknall, Nottingham (1959); Christ Church, Heald Green, Stockport, Manchester (1962); St Peter's, Gorleston-on-Sea, Norfolk (1963); St Peter's, Aberdeen (1970s); Church of Our Lady, Llandovery, Carms (1978); St Nicholas's, Newport, Salop (1978).

O'Connor, Michael (1801–67). Born in Dublin, came to London in 1823 and studied under Thomas Willement, set up his own workshop in London in 1848 and was joined by his sons Arthur (1826–73) in 1851 and William Henry (1838 or 1839–77?) in 1860. He worked with A W N Pugin and W Butterfield and seems to have retired in the 1850s. W G Taylor (1822–97) joined the firm in 1873 and took over when William Henry died. The firm closed in 1915.

St Eurgain and St Peter's, Northop, Flint (1850, 1867); St John the Baptist's, Aston Cantlow, Warwicks (1850s); Salisbury Cathedral, Wilts (1855); Chester Cathedral (1857); St Margaret's, Bodelwyddan, Den (1859-60); St Andrew's, Kingswood, Surrey (1866–7).

Parsons, Karl (Bergmann) (1884–1934). Late Arts and Crafts designer: another of Christopher Whall's pupils, later to become his principal assistant. Set up a studio in The Glass House, London.

St Alban's, Hindhead, Surrey (1912); St Bride's Episcopal Church, Glasgow (1915); St Matthew's, Oxhey, Herts (?1916); St Mary's, Tenby, Pembs (1917); All Saints', Porthcawl, Glam (1927); St Mary's, Bibury, Glos (1927); St Michael and All Angels, Waterford, Herts (1929); St James's, Pyle, Glam (1929); St Peter's, Bardon, Leics (1929); St Lawrence's, Ansley, Warwicks (1930); Christ Church, Catshill, Worcs (1931).

Payne, Henry (1868–1940). Arts and Crafts designer, maker and painter. Another pupil of Christopher Whall's, he studied, and later, from 1899, taught, at the Birmingham School of Art. In 1904 he established his own business designing and making stained glass.

St Botolph's, Carleton-in-Cleveland, N Yorks (c.1897, c.1920); St Martin's, Kensal Rise, London (1909–28); St Andrew's, Roker, Tyne & W (c.1910); St James's, Goldenacre, Edinburgh (?1921); St James's, Chipping Campden, Glos (1925); St John's, Elkestone, Glos (1929); All Saints', Hutton Rudby, N Yorks (1932); Good Shepherd's, Hook Common, Worcs (1938); St Mary's, Madresfield, Worcs (date not known); St Alban's, Bordesley, Birmingham, W Mid (date not known).

Pearson, James (c.1740–1838). Famous painter in his time, and also painter of enamelled glass, mostly heraldic. Born in Dublin, studied art in Bristol and later moved to London.

St Mary's, Glynde, Sussex (1774, attrib); Brasenose College chapel, Oxford (1776); Salisbury Cathedral, Wilts (1781); St Botolph's, Aldersgate, London (1788).

Peckitt, William (1731–95). York glass painter and, unusually for his time, stained glass maker. Apart from outside commissions, he worked on the maintenance of window glass and the creation of new windows in York Minster throughout his life. He is buried in St Martin-cum-Gregory, York (now The Stained Glass Centre), where he made two windows in memory of two of his four daughters.

Lincoln Cathedral (1761); St Mary Magdalene's, Yarm, Stockton-on-Tees, Durham (1763); chapels of Oriel College (1767) and New College (?1770), both in Oxford; St Andrew's, Boynton, E Yorks (1768); St John of Beverley's, Harpham, E Yorks (1771); St Bartholomew's, Binley, Coventry, W Mid (1772); St Michael's, Coxwold, N Yorks (?1774); York Minster (Abraham and Solomon 1780, Moses, St Peter 1793).

Piper, John (Egerton Christmas) (1903–92). Painter, printmaker and stained glass designer. Abandoned abstract art in 1938 and turned to figurative and landscape works. Turned to glass design about 1950 and was introduced to Patrick Reyntiens in 1954. From then on, Reyntiens made almost all his windows.

Oundle School chapel, Northants (1956); Christ Church, Flackwell Heath, Bucks (1961); Coventry Cathedral, W Mid (1962); Newport CathedraL, Glam (1964); St Mary's, Swansea, Glam (1966); St Peter's, Babraham, Cambs (1966); Liverpool Metropolitan Cathedral, Mersey (1967); St Paul's, Pishill, Oxon (1967); St Paul's, Bledlow Ridge, Bucks (1968); St Bartholomew's, Nettlebed, Oxon (1970); St Mary the Virgin's, Turville, Bucks (1975); St Peter's, Wolvercote, Oxon (1976); St Peter and St Paul's, Aldeburgh, Suffolk (after 1976); Robinson College chapel, Cambridge (1977); St Mary's, Fawley, Bucks (1977); St John's, Lichfield, Staffs (1984); St Mary's, Lamberhurst, Kent (1985); St Peter's, Firle, Sussex (1985); St Paul's, Jarrow, Tyne & W (1985); All Saints', Farnborough, Berks (1986); Churchill College chapel, Cambridge (1987).

Powell, James, and Sons (1834–1980). Stained glass makers and designers: probably the most long-lived and prolific of Victorian stained glass firms. In 1834 James Powell (1774–1840), a London wine merchant, bought the small London firm of Whitefriars Glass Company, which had existed since about 1680, apparently to keep his three sons – Arthur, Nathanael and John – occupied. The three ran the firm until 1875 when Nathanael's son Harry (1853–1922) took over. He ran the firm until 1919. From 1919 the firm was called Powell and Sons (Whitefriars) Ltd; from 1962 Whitefriars Glass Ltd. It was bought in 1981 by Caithness Glass. As well as designing their own glass, Powell's hired other designers, including Burne-Jones, Henry Holiday, Harry Wooldridge, Christopher Whall, Mary Lowndes, Leonard Walker, Carl Edwards and J E Nuttgens. The firm manufactured Charles Winston's recreation of mediaeval glass (1849–50) and were (with several designers) the main stained glass contractors to Liverpool Anglican Cathedral, Mersey.

St Peter's, Britford, Wilts (1852–1904); St Mary's, Amport, Hants (1866–80); St Martin's, Dorking, Surrey (1876–1945); Salisbury Cathedral, Wilts (1879–1920); St John Baptist's, Garboldisham, Diss, Norfolk (1880–1920); St Peter's, Frimley, Surrey (1880–1996); Cranleigh School chapel, Surrey (1880–86); St George's, Wolverton, Bucks (1884–1919); St Leodegar's, Hunston, Sussex (1885–92); Romsey Abbey, Hants (1889–1902); St Lawrence's, West Woodhay, Berks (1890–93); St Faith's, Havant, Hants (1890–1930); St Luke's, Bromley, London (1891–1914); St Luke's, Battersea, London (1894–1934); St Laurence's, Upton, Slough, Berks (1895–1928); St Olave's, Stoke Newington, London (1896–1938); St Martin Ludgate, London (1898); St Luke's, Kew, London (1898–1945); Holy Trinity, Kensington, London (1900–28); St Gabriel's, Cricklewood, London (1900–29); St Davids Cathedral, Pembs (1904); Winchester Cathedral, Hants (1904–17); Bangor

Cathedral, Gwynedd (1911); St Giles's, Wrexham (1911–14); Holy Trinity, Colemans Hatch, Sussex (1913–50); Rochester Cathedral, Kent (1917–27); Brecon Cathedral, Powys (1921, 1925); St Mary's, Burghfield, Berks (1945–63); St Mary's, Strata Florida, Cered (1961–7).

Powell, John Hardman (1827–95). See Hardman & Co.

Price, Joshua (c.1672–1722), Enamelled glass-painter who worked in Oxford, where he repaired the windows in Queen's College chapel, originally painted in 1518, and in 1717 repaired the windows by Van Linge there and at Christ Church.

Queen's College chapel, Oxford (1715); St Michael's, Great Witley, Worcs (1719–21); Magdalen College chapel, Oxford (c.1720?); St Andrew-by-the-Wardrobe, Victoria Street, London (c.1720).

Price, William the elder (died 1722), Brother and fellow-pupil of Joshua Price. Enamelled glass-painter who also worked in Oxford, a pupil of Henry Gyles.

Christ Church, Oxford (1696, designed by Sir James Thornhill); Merton College chapel, Oxford (1700, 1702).

Price, William the younger (1703 or 1708–56). The son of Joshua Price, also an enamelled glass-painter, also working in Oxford. At New College, Oxford, he filled the windows with Flanders glass which he had acquired.

Westminster Abbey, London (1735); Sir William Turner's almshouses chapel, Kirkleatham, Redcar, N Yorks (c.1740); Mereworth Castle chapel, Kent (1746); St Mary's, Preston-on-Stour, Warwicks (1754); 'The Genealogy of Christ' Winchester College chapel, Hants (date not known);'The Resurrection' for the bishop's palace at Gloucester Cathedral (date not known).

Prudde, John (died 1460–1). Westminster glass designer and maker, some say the pre-eminent glazier of his time. He was appointed King's Glazier in 1440, but otherwise little is known of him.

All Souls College chapel, Oxford (c.1441); Beauchamp chapel, St Mary's, Warwick (1447–50); Jesse window in St Margaret's, Margaretting, Essex (c.1460).

Reyntiens, Patrick (1925–). Stained glass maker and designer who made most of John Piper's windows, including the Baptistery windows at Coventry Cathedral, W Mid, and Liverpool Metropolitan Cathedral, Mersey (in *dalles de verre*).

On his own, he designed and made windows at All Saints', Hinton Ampner, Hants (1970); St Andrew's Much Hadham, Herts (1995); Southwell Minster, Notts (1996); Ampleforth Abbey, N Yorks (2002); and in the USA, the National Cathedral, Washington DC (1969).

Shrigley and Hunt (1878–1982). Stained glass makers. From about 1750, Shrigley's was a firm of painters and gilders in Lancaster. In 1868, Arthur Hunt, a stained glass maker from London, was hired as managing director and later took it over, focused it on stained glass and tile making, and made it one of the foremost manufacturers of stained glass in the in the north. His main designers were Edward Holmes Jewitt (1849–1929) and Carl Almquist (1848–1924), a Swede who came to London in 1870. The firm continued under Joseph Fisher (1911–82) and closed down on his death. Their premises were burnt down in 1973 and their last windows were made in 1980.

Designed by Almquist: St Barnabas's, Great Strickland, Cumbria (?1871); St Thomas's, Garstang, Lancs (1877); St Bledrws's, Betws Bledrws, Cered (1886); St Peter's, Finsthwaite, Cumbria (1894); St Olave's, York (1905); Holy Trinity, Blackpool, Lancs (1909); St Lawrence's, Crosby Ravensworth, Cumbria (date not known).

Designed by Jewitt: St Mary's, Great Ouseburn, N Yorks (1884); St Patrick's, Bampton, Cumbria (? 1885); St Mary's, Nun Monkton, N Yorks (1903); St Columba's,

Warcop, Cumbria (date not known); St Martin's, Yapham, E Yorks (date not known).

Other church windows: St James's, Gerrards Cross, Bucks (1894); St Mary's, Higham Ferrers, Northants (1897); St Mary's, Amersham, Bucks (1905); All Saints', Hovingham, N Yorks (1936); St Michael's, St Michael's on Wyre, Lancs (1936); St Oswald's, Preesall, Lancs (c.1971).

Taylor, W(illiam) G(eorge) (1822–97). London glass designer and maker, who joined Michael O'Connor in 1873, and took over when his son W H O'Connor died (1877 or 1878). The firm was then called O'Connor and Taylor; later, Taylor (1886); later still (1902) Taylor and Clifton. (Nothing appears to be known of Clifton). See Michael O'Connor.

St Mary de Haura, Shoreham, Sussex (1871, 1884, 1889); Holy Trinity, Lower Beeding, Sussex (1882); St Anne's, Lewes, Sussex (1889); Brecon Cathedral, Powys (1898).

Thomas of Oxford. See Glazier, Thomas.

Thornton, John (fl. 1405–33). Coventry glass painter and master glazier who was commissioned to create the great East Window, York Minster (1405–8, at present being restored) and maybe the St William window in the north choir aisle (c.1415).

Other attributed work includes: 'The Prick of Conscience' in All Saints', York (c.1410–20); window in All Saints', Thurcaston, Leics (c.1425); east window of Great Malvern Priory, Worcs (mid fifteenth century); the Haigh Chapel, Coventry Cathedral and St Mary's Hall, Coventry, W Mid (both first half of the fifteenth century).

Traherne, (Hazel) Margaret (1919–2006). Designer and painter. Trained at the Royal College of Art, where one of her tutors was Lawrence Lee.

St Peter's, Wootton Wawen, Warwicks (1950s); the Chapel of Unity, Coventry Cathedral, W Mid (1958); St Mary Magdalene's, Lockleaze, Bristol (1961); St Chad's, Patchway, Bristol (1964); Manchester Cathedral (1966 and 1996); Liverpool Metropolitan Cathedral, Mersey (1966–7, Chapel of Reconciliation and Lady Chapel); St Peter's, Nottingham (1976, the Baptistery); Holy Innocents', Orpington, Kent (1985).

Wailes, William (1808–81). Prolific Newcastle-upon-Tyne stained glass manufacturer, at one time one of the two largest makers in England (the other one was Hardman's). He studied stained glass in Munich from 1830, started his own company in 1838 and began producing his own glass in 1841. He made his name by making windows for local churches and by 1851 employed seventy-six craftsmen, including several designers, supplying architects like Pugin, Butterfield and Pearson. Thomas Rankine Strang (William Wailes's son-in-law) and William Thomas Wailes (his son), continued the firm after his father's death until 1910.

St Mary's Cathedral, Newcastle on Tyne, Tyne & W (1844, designed by Pugin); Chichester Cathedral, Sussex (1849); St Deiniol's, Hawarden, Flint (1854); All Saints', Hursley, Hants (1858); Gloucester Cathedral (1859); Sandyford Henderson Church, Glasgow (1859–60); St Matthias's, Richmond, London (1862); St Helen Witton's, Northwich, Ches (1863); St Mary's, Chilham, Kent (1864); St Peter and St Paul's, Great Missenden, Bucks (1865); St Edmund's, Emneth, Norfolk (1866, 1869); St Editha's, Tamworth, Staffs (1870); St Elidyr's, Crunwere, Pembs (c.1878); St Mary and St Nicholas's, Beaumaris, Anglesey (1899).

Walker, Leonard (1877–1964). Mostly Expressionist stained glass designer. He studied in London and began producing stained glass in the 1890s. Most of his windows (most of them made of slab glass) were produced by James Powell and Sons.

St Cynon, Tregynon, Powys (1922); St Dingad's, Llandovery, Carms (1924); St Ethelburga's, Bishopsgate, London (1928–47); St Mary's, North Stifford, Essex (1929); St Mary's, Burpham, Sussex (1930);

St Gwyrthwl's, Llanwyrthwyl, Powys (1934); St Andrew's, Southburgh, Norfolk (1935); All Saints', East Tuddenham, Norfolk (1950s); St Peter's, Bocking, Essex (date not known).

Ward and Hughes (1836–c.1930). Prolific stained glass makers. James (Henry) Nixon (1802–57) and Thomas Ward (1808–70) set up the firm, as Nixon and Ward, in 1836 and continued it until about 1850. When Nixon died, Henry Hughes (1822–83), a designer, took his place (1857) and this partnership (Ward and Hughes) lasted until Hughes died, when Thomas Figgis Curtis (1845–1924), a relation of his, took over (Curtis, Ward and Hughes). On the death of Curtis, Edith Kibblewhite, a cousin of his, ran the firm. It ceased trading in about 1930. Much of their work in London was destroyed in the Blitz.

St Martin's, Oswestry Ferry, Lincs (1836); St Margaret's, Angmering, Sussex (1853); Lincoln Cathedral (1855, 1869); St Oswald's, Warton, Lancs (1856–95); St Giles's, Chalfont St Giles, Bucks (1859); St Mary's, Rhuddlan, Den (1870s); St Margaret's, Bodelwyddan, Den (1880); St Mary's, Staverton, Northants (1881); St John's, Wolverhampton, W Mid (1882, 1884); St Mary's, Ruabon, Wrexham (1884–92); All Saints', Jesus Lane, Cambridge (1893); St Michael's, Wood Green, London (1894, 1901); St Mary Magdalene's, Great Hamden, Bucks (1898); St Seiniol's, Penmaermawr, Conwy (c.1901); St James's, Tebay, Cumbria (1911, 1920); St Mary's, Swansea, Glam (1914).

Warrington, William (1796–1869). Argumentative stained glass artist and author (*The history of stained glass*, 1841, illustrated with pictures of stained glass solely by himself). Worked with Thomas Willement and then with A W N Pugin, 1837–c.1841 but Pugin, always difficult, broke with him because he was 'so conceited' and also too expensive.

St Mary's College chapel, Oscott, Birmingham, W Mid (1837); St Mary's, Derby (1839); Reading Minster, Berks (1839); St Chad's Cathedral, Birmingham, W Mid (c.1841); St Peter's, Heversham, Cumbria (1844); Norwich Cathedral, Norfolk (1847); Ely Cathedral, Cambs (c.1850); St Mary's, Ottery St Mary, Devon (c.1852).

Webb, Christopher (Rahere) (1886–1966). Son of Sir Aston Webb, the architect, younger brother of Geoffrey Webb, stained glass designer, and pupil of Sir Ninian Comper.

St Michael's, Bishops Stortford, Herts (c.1928); Sherborne Abbey, Dorset (1930s); St John's, Lemsford, Herts (1935, 1961); Sheffield Cathedral, S Yorks (1935–48); St Helen's, Wheathampstead, Herts (1937); Church of the Epiphany, Gipton, Leeds, W Yorks (?1938); St Albans Cathedral, Herts (1939–55); St Nicholas's, Harpenden, Herts (1939, 1944); All Saints', Croxley Green, Herts (1940); Christ Church, Little Heath, Herts (1944); Salisbury Cathedral, Wilts (1946–53); St Lawrence Jewry, London (1946–60); Chichester Cathedral, Hants (1949–53); St Boniface's, Bunbury, Ches (1950); Portsmouth Cathedral, Hants (1952); Lincoln Cathedral (1953, 1955); St Mary's, Welwyn, Herts (?1953); St James's, Piccadilly, London (1954); St Anne's, Moseley, Birmingham, W Mid (1956); Letheringsett Church, Norfolk (1958); St Peter's, Dunstable, Beds (1962); St Mary's, Redbourne, Herts (1963).

Whall, Christopher (Whitworth) (1849–1924). Arts and Crafts designer and teacher who was trained as a painter, travelled in Italy, became a Catholic, and returned to England in 1879. During the 1890s he worked in Scotland; returned to London in 1895; from 1906 he worked out of The Glass House; and in 1907 he opened his own studio in London (which continued after his death under his daughter Veronica (1887–1970) until she retired in the 1950s). He was the most influential stained glass artist of his time, and a circle of pupils and followers formed round him, including Louis Davis and Karl Parsons. As well as the UK, his work can also be seen in Australia, France, Ireland, South Africa and the USA.

St Seiriol's, Penmaenmawr, Conwy (1889); St Mary's, Stamford, Lincs (1890); St James's, Somerton, Oxon (1893); Falkirk Old and St Modan's, Falkirk (1897); Gloucester Cathedral (Lady Chapel 1899–1913, Chapter House from 1903); St Luke's, Milland, Sussex (1899, 1904); Holy Trinity, Bracknell, Berks (1900, 1906, 1919); All Saints', Brockhampton, Herefs (after 1902); Canterbury Cathedral, Kent (1902); Holy Trinity, Chelsea, London (1905–23); All Saints', Lindfield, Sussex (1906); All Saints', Glasbury, Powys (1914); St Laurence's, Corringham, Lincs (c.1914); Winchester Cathedral, Hants (1916); St Peter's, Racton, Sussex (1918); St Mary's, Chippenham, Wilts 1919); Leicester Cathedral, (1920); St Mary's, Iwerne Minster, Dorset (1920); St George and St Martin of Tours, Caernarfon, Gwynnedd (c.1920).

Whitefriars Glass. See James Powell and Sons.

Willement, Thomas (1786–1871). Decorator, tilemaker, painter (chapter house ceiling, York Minster, 1845), author (*A Concise Account of the Principal Works in Stained Glass That Have Been Executed, 1840*) and stained glass maker. Armorial Painter to George IV; Artist in Stained Glass to Queen Victoria. An early pioneer of stained glass in the early nineteenth century, using pot-metal glass and lead lines to outline the design, instead of simply enamel painting almost universal in the eighteenth century. Worked with A W N Pugin 1840–c.1842, but Pugin broke with him, as he had with Warrington, because he was too expensive.

St Martin's, Epsom, Surrey (1824); St Peter's, Hampton Lucy, Warwicks (1837); St George's Chapel, Windsor Castle, Berks (1840–61); Holy Sepulchre, Cambridge (c.1843); St Peter and St Paul's, Thruxton, Hants (1843–51); St Mary's, Chilton Foliat, Wilts (1843, 1849); St Michael's Lambourn, Berks (1849); Temple Church, London (1840s); St Laurence's, Ludlow, Salop (c.1850); St Nicholas's, Grafton, Wilts (1856–7); St Mary's, Shrewsbury, Salop (1859–69).

Winston, Charles (1814–65). Barrister, stained glass historian, author and consultant: he rediscovered mediaeval glass. Called to the bar 1845, developed a large legal practice, and retired 1864. His fascination with stained glass began at the age of 16. He sketched mediaeval stained glass windows throughout England; and published. *An Inquiry into the difference of style observable in ancient glass paintings* in 1847. He used chemical analysis, conducted by Dr Medlock at the Royal College of Chemistry in London in 1849, to analyse fragments of mediaeval glass, and James Powell and Sons began manufacturing it in 1849–50. His glass was used in Bristol Cathedral (c.1853); Lincoln Cathedral (1855); and Gloucester Cathedral (1860).

Wooldridge, Harry (Ellis) (1845–1917). Designer, Slade Professor of Fine Arts at Oxford, and musical antiquary. Worked with Sir Edward Burne-Jones and Henry Holiday and was retained as chief designer by James Powell and Sons for over twenty years.

St Mary's, Derwen, Den (1869); St Andrew's, Thursford, Norfolk (c.1873); St Michael's, Ewenny, Glam (1876).

Younger, Alan (Christopher Wyrill) (1933–2004). Designer. For six years he worked in Carl Edwards's studio. He set up his own studio in 1966.

St Michael's, Haselbech, Northants (1966); St John's, Boldre, Hants (1967, 1980); St Michael's, Winterbourne, Glos (1970); Durham Cathedral (1973); St Editha's, Tamworth, Staffs (1975); St Mary's, Putney, London (1982); St Albans Cathedral, Herts (1989); St Paul's, Deptford, London (1992); Chester Cathedral (1992); Southwark Cathedral, London (1993); Westminster Abbey, London (2000).

FLOOR TILES

Floor tiles are found in churches in two distinct periods. The first lasted some four hundred years, from the twelfth to the sixteenth centuries, and the second, a mere sixty years, from 1840 to about 1900. However, mediaeval tiles are relatively scarce, while Victorian tiles are found in most cathedrals and half the parish churches in the United Kingdom. This is due partly to the explosion in church building in the nineteenth century, and partly to the restoration mania at the same time, which put tiles where there had never been tiles before (see, for example, the south transept of St Mary's, Ottery St Mary, Devon), or, paradoxically, threw away mediaeval tiles by the cartload in favour of new imitations.

Although some tiles have been found dating back to the late tenth or early eleventh century, floor tiles did not become common until the late twelfth century. Floors before that time were usually packed earth, sometimes covered with rushes or plaster. Tiles were first used in abbey churches and royal palaces, in time percolating downwards to parish churches and the houses of wealthy merchants and officials. In the second half of the thirteenth century, tile-making became commercial: rather than tiles being made by itinerant gangs of craftsmen, they were made in standard sizes and at tile-making centres, such as Penn in Buckinghamshire and Danbury in Essex. The names of virtually all mediaeval tile-makers are unknown. Those few that are known are recorded in written documents. Very few scratched their names on the backs of tiles.

The clay for tiles was dug in the autumn and left to weather over the winter. In spring and summer, tiles were formed, using either a template or a wooden mould, and left to dry and shrink by about 10%. The tiles were glazed with a lead glaze made by boiling up scraps of lead and then skimming off the lead oxide which formed on the surface, drying it, powdering it and mixing it with water. When the tiles were fired in a wood-burning kiln to about 1,000°C (since tile-makers had no thermometers, experience was the only guide), the glaze melted and formed a thin skin over the tile, giving a rich brown colour to the tile and, if any were used, a honey tone to the white clay inlays. The cycle of loading the kiln, firing, cooling and unloading took six days.

Tiles were of three types, apart from the plain tile. The relief tile, the earliest, had the pattern stamped on the tile so that the pattern stands proud of its background. Variants were the counter-relief tile, in which the pattern was recessed into the background, and the line-impressed tile, in which the design was made up of single lines. Mosaic tiles, as the name implies, were shaped tiles which formed a pattern when laid. The inlaid tile was a tile in which a design was hammered into the body of the tile with a stamp and the indentation was then filled up with white clay.

Tiles went out of fashion towards the end of the sixteenth century. This was due to the Dissolution of the Monasteries (1536–40), which removed at a blow the tile-makers' biggest and wealthiest customers; and to the import of painted polychrome majolica tiles from Flanders, starting in about 1580, which the wealthy found far more fashionable than inlaid tiles. But the majolica tiles proved to have a short floor life, and the fashion died quite quickly, and with it the fashion for tiled floors, for around 250 years.

Mediaeval tiles can be seen in the ruins of Byland, Fountains and Rievaulx Abbeys, N Yorks; Cleeve Abbey, Washford, Som; Melrose Abbey, Borders; and at Ely Cathedral, Cambs; Gloucester Cathedral; Winchester Cathedral, Hants; Westminster Abbey, London (in the chapter house); St Davids Cathedral, Pembs; St Peter and St Paul's, Leominster, Herefs; St Michael's, Croft, Herefs; Shrewsbury Abbey, Salop; St Mary's, Acton Burnell, Salop; Great Malvern Priory, Worcs; St Stephen's, Old Radnor, Powys; Strata Florida Abbey, Cered; St Mary's, Monmouth.

In 1830 Samuel Wright (1783–1849), of Shelton, Staffs, patented a process for making inlaid – 'encaustic', ie 'burnt in' – floor tiles. Bizarrely, he aimed at the domestic market, in spite of the enormous increase in the number of churches being built, and, disappointed by the sales, he sold his equipment in 1835 (though he hung on to the patent), to Herbert Minton (1793–1858) and Walter Chamberlain (1795–1868). (The only Wright tiles existing are at Kilmory Castle, Argyll and Bute, laid by Minton from Wright's stock in about 1837).

Manufacturers are mostly easy to identify, since they stamped their names, or other devices, on the back of the tile.

In 1841 Minton & Co won a sizeable commission to supply tiles to re-floor the Temple Church, London (since damaged in the Second World War), and never looked back. Minton & Co had the virtual monopoly of floor tiles until Herbert Minton's death in 1858. In 1840 Herbert took Michael Daintry Hollins (1840–1901, Herbert's nephew) and in 1849, Colin Minton Campbell (1827–85: perhaps another nephew?) into partnership. In 1859, the firm split into a tile company, Minton Hollins & Co, run by Hollins (who acquired a partner, Robert Minton Taylor (yet another nephew?) in 1863), and a china company, Mintons Ltd, run by Campbell. Thereafter the story gets acrimonious. All partnerships were dissolved in 1868, there were law suits in 1871 and 1875, and there were at one time seven firms competing to use the Minton name. (All now belong to Waterford Wedgwood).

Minton tiles can be seen at York Minster (the chapter house); Lincoln Cathedral; Wells Cathedral, Som; Ely Cathedral, Cambs; Gloucester Cathedral; Salisbury Cathedral, Wilts (the chapter house); Lichfield Cathedral, Staffs; St Albans Cathedral, Herts; Wimborne Minster, Dorset; St Giles's, Cheadle, Staffs; St Mary's, Battlefield, Salop; St Mary's, Shrewsbury, Salop; St James's, Louth, Lincs; Holy Trinity, Skipton, N Yorks; Christ Church, Doncaster, S Yorks; St Edward's, Knighton, Powys.

Chamberlain & Co of Worcester, on the other hand, were not altogether successful as tilemakers. In 1848 they ceased tile production, and on Walter Chamberlain's retirement in 1851 they sold the factory, designs, moulds and stock to Maw and Co.

Chamberlain tiles may be seen at Great Malvern Priory, Worcs; St John's, Slebech, Pembs (now redundant); St Mary's, New Radnor, Powys; St Mary de Crypt, Gloucester; St James's, Wigmore, Herefs; St John's, Redhill, Surrey; St Nicholas's, East Grafton, Wilts.

Mediaeval floor tiles, late fifteenth century, St Stephen's, Old Radnor, Powys

Floor tiles by Maw and Co, 1888, St Mary's, Shrewsbury, Salop. The church also has floors by Minton (1864-5) and Godwin (1868)

Tiles by William Godwin of Lugwardine, c.1870, St Davids Cathedral, Pembs

Maw & Co was established in 1850 by John Hornby Maw (who invented the baby's glass feeding bottle and was an enthusiast for mediaeval tiles) for his sons, George (1832–1912) and Arthur (1835–1912), at Worcester in the old works of Chamberlain & Co. The firm moved to Benthall, near Broseley, Salop, in 1852 for better clays, and in 1883 to nearby Jackfield. By 1880 they were the largest tile company in the world. For the first ten years, they made only encaustic tiles for churches, but after 1860 they developed a wide range of tiles of all types. In 1968 they were absorbed into H & R Johnson, but in 2001 were re-established as a private company.

See Chester Cathedral, Ches; Carlisle Cathedral, Cumbria; St Asaph Cathedral, Den; Bangor Cathedral, Gwynedd; St Mary's, Jackfield, Salop; St Mary's, Battlefield, Salop; St Mary's, Princes Risborough, Bucks.

Godwin of Lugwardine, Herefs, was founded by two brothers, William (1813–83) and Henry (1828–1910) Godwin in 1852. Henry had worked at Maws for a couple of years and provided the technical expertise. Godwin supplied the tiles for hundreds of churches in Herefordshire, Gloucestershire, the Welsh borders and further afield. A sampler floor in Lugwardine Chapel, Herefs, contains 5,000 Godwin tiles. The business went into liquidation in 1906

Worcester Cathedral; Hereford Cathedral, St James's, and St Peter's, all three in Hereford; Gloucester Cathedral; Tewkesbury Abbey, Glos; St John's, Cirencester, Glos; St Mary's, Frampton on Severn, Glos; Holy Cross, Owlpen, Glos; St Giles's, Downton, Herefs; Exeter Cathedral, Devon; Chichester Cathedral, Sussex (the Lady Chapel); St Stephen's, Old Radnor, Powys; St John's, Cardiff, Glam; St Davids Cathedral, Pembs; St Cuthbert's, Darwen, Lancs; Holy Trinity, Hull, E Yorks. .

Henry Godwin left the partnership in 1876. He was joined in 1884 by William Hewitt (dates not known), with whom he set up Godwin and Hewitt. His firm was always outperformed by his brother's, and Henry sold his share to Hewitt in 1894 and went in for cider-making instead. A good example of their work is in All Saints', Hereford. The firm went into liquidation in 1907.

Craven Dunnill grew out of Hawes and Denny (forenames and dates not known), who were active tilemakers at Jackfield, Salop, in the 1860s. Hawes left, and James Craven (dates not known), a builder from Manchester, and James Hargreaves (dates not known) put money into the firm. The firm was known as Hargreaves and Craven from 1867. Then Hargreaves and Denny left and Henry Powell Dunnill (1821–95) joined the firm in 1872. Thereafter it was called Craven Dunnill. The Jackfield works (now the Jackfield Tile Museum) were built in 1875. Craven Dunnill stopped producing tiles in 1951 and became a tile distributor in Bridgnorth, Salop, but Craven Dunnill Jackfield Ltd returned to the Jackfield site in 2001, reviving the manufacture of commercial tiles there.

See Chester Cathedral, Ches; Bangor Cathedral, Gwynedd; Shrewsbury Cathedral, Salop; St Magnus's Cathedral, Kirkwall, Orkney; St Andrew and St John's, Kemberton, Salop; St John's, Burslem, Staffs; Christ Church, Tunstall, Staffs; St Peter's, Anlaby, E Yorks; All Saints', Thorpe Basset, N Yorks; St Peter's, Willerby, N Yorks.

The end came quite quickly. Tiles became too expensive to make, due to the unavoidable amount of hand-work involved; and fashions changed, just as they had three hundred years earlier. As the long Gothic Revival drew to a close, architects preferred plain wooden or slabbed floors to tiles. In its restoration of 2011–12, St Peter's, Hereford, laid a complete floating floor of oak over its Victorian tiles, in contrast to its neighbour, All Saints'.

CHURCH PLATE

Though many of these objects may be made of non-precious metals, all are also made of silver or gold or some kind of plate. Silver-gilt is silver covered with a thin layer of gold; silver plate is stainless steel with a thin layer of silver; and Sheffield plate is copper with a thin layer of silver.

There is not much mediaeval work around, since an enormous quantity was melted down during the Reformation, and much of the rest during the Civil War. These days, few churches care to keep their plate on display unless it is very well protected, and so church plate which is not in daily or weekly use is usually on long-term loan to the diocesan cathedral, to be shown in its treasury, or kept in a museum, or stored in the local bank. Most cathedrals have interesting treasuries: for example, see the treasuries of Gloucester Cathedral, Durham Cathedral, Norwich Cathedral, Norfolk and St Davids Cathedral, Pembs.

Alms dish. A tray for collecting offerings from the congregation; a collection plate.

Altar bell, mass bell, saints' bell, sanctus bell. A small, hand-held bell (or bells), rung at mass and communion when the bread and wine are being shown. Mostly a Roman Catholic custom, but sometimes used in High Church Anglican, Lutheran and Methodist churches.

Altar cross. See Cross.

Aspergillum. See Sprinkler.

Aspersorium. See Church bucket.

Baptismal shell, christening shell. A shell-shaped container used at baptisms to pour water over the head.

Bread plate. A plate for holding bread or wafers during mass or communion: a paten.

Candlestick. Used frequently in most rites. Their most common use is to hold the candles on the altar.

Censer, thurible. An incense burner suspended from chains and carried by an altar server (thurifer). Burning charcoal is placed inside the censer, and incense scattered over the top of the charcoal. Use of censers is mainly a Catholic practise, but is not uncommon in High Anglican churches.

Chalice. Cup containing the consecrated wine at mass or communion.

Chrismatory, chrismarium. Vessel for containing holy oil or oils, for use at baptism, confirmation, ordination etc.

Christening shell. See Baptismal shell.

Church bucket, holy water bucket, aspersorium. A container holding holy water for censing the congregation.

Ciborium. A goblet-shaped container, sometimes veiled, for holding the consecrated bread or wafers for mass or communion

Communion plate. In mass or communion, a plate held under the communicant's chin to catch any fragments of the Host.

Communion tray. Tray with holes for holding many glasses of wine, for mass or communion. It sometimes has a cover.

Cross. *Altar cross*: cross placed on the altar, not widely used before the nineteenth century.

Pectoral cross: a cross suspended by a chain round the neck and worn on the breast, usually by a bishop.

Processional cross: a cross on a staff carried before a liturgical procession, such as the entry of the priest and choir into the church.

Crozier, crosier. A staff of office, usually with a silver head consisting of a stylised shepherd's crook or, more rarely, a cross, carried by bishops. Funerary croziers were also made. See the example in the Treasury of St Davids Cathedral, Pembs, recovered from the grave of Bishop Gower (fourteenth century).

Crucifix. An image of Christ crucified. Since the Reformation, the plain cross is mostly used in Anglican churches where the Roman Catholic church uses crucifixes. During the Reformation, using the crucifix (or indeed crosses) was regarded as idolatrous, by Calvin among others, and from about 1600 to the Restoration it virtually disappeared.

Cruet, cruet tray. A pair of cruets, each with a stopper (phoedelia), is used to contain wine and water for mass and communion, which are mixed for the ceremony. A cruet tray is used for putting the cruets on.

Ewer. A flagon or jug, used at baptisms (when it contains holy water), or during mass or communion (when it contains wine or wine mixed with water).

Flagon. See Ewer.

Goblet. See Chalice.

Hanging pyx. See Pyx.

Holy water bucket. See Church bucket.

Incense burner. See Censer.

Incense boat. A small metal jug, with a spoon, holding a supply of incense. It is carried by the boat boy or boat bearer, who accompanies the altar server and replenishes the thurible.

Lunette box. A box holding the Host inside a monstrance.

Mass bell. See Altar bell.

Monstrance, ostensorium. A vessel holding the Host (or sometimes a relic) for displaying to the congregation.

Paten. A plate or shallow dish, to hold the bread before it is consecrated.

Pectoral cross. See Cross.

Phoedelia. See Cruet.

Pome. A hand-warmer, filled with charcoal, for the priest when he is administering the Host and the wine.

Processional cross. See Cross.

Pyx. A small round vessel in which the priest carries consecrated bread on his visits to the sick; sometimes, simply a ciborium.

A *hanging pyx* is a pyx suspended above the altar by a pulley, surmounted by a canopy and covered by a pyx cloth. It is used for holding the reserved sacrament. One mediaeval example of a pyx cloth survives, found in St Ethelbert's, Hessett, Suffolk and now in the British Museum; a mediaeval wooden canopy (c.1500) still hangs in St Mary's, Dennington, Suffolk.

Reliquary. A container holding a relic.

Ring. Conferred on a bishop when he is consecrated, and often buried with him. See examples in the Treasury of St Davids Cathedral, Pembs.

Sanctus bell, saints' bell. See Altar bell.

Spoon. 1 For measuring the water to be mixed with the wine, at mass or communion. 2 For spooning out incense from the incense boat. 3 *Straining spoon*: perforated spoon for straining impurities from the communion wine.

Sprinkler, aspergillum. An implement used to sprinkle (cense) the congregation with holy water before mass ('asperges'). It can be a perforated ball, sometimes containing a sponge for retaining the holy water for longer and sometimes needing to be dipped in a bucket of holy water; or simply a brush dipped in holy water.

Straining spoon. See Spoon 3.

Thurible. See Censer.

Viaticum. The receptacle in which the consecrated bread and wine are carried to a sick person.

Wafer box. A small box in which the consecrated wafers are kept.

The Treasury, Lincoln Cathedral

SCRATCHDIALS AND SUNDIALS

From early Saxon times to the eighteenth century, the local church was the sole timekeeper in most towns and villages throughout Great Britain.

Scratchdials or mass dials were scratched or cut on the south walls of churches (usually by the local priest), about four or five feet from the ground, from the earliest times until about 1600. They were used by priests to tell the times for masses. They are often inside a later-built porch, and some churches have several scratchdials. The dial is roughly nine inches across, and may consist of dots, semi-circles, complete circles, circles with radii, circles with numbers, multi-ringed: in general, the simpler, the earlier. In the middle, a wooden peg or gnomon (now, almost always missing) stuck out. There are thought to be between two thousand and five thousand examples, though it often takes a trained eye to spot them.

St Peter's, Hanwell, Banbury, Oxon (where there are twelve); St Mary's, Berkeley, Glos; St Mary's, Burnham on Crouch, Essex; Romsey Abbey, Hants; St Mary and St David, Kilpeck, Herefs; St Peter's, Ketteringham, Norfolk; St Peter's, Englishcombe, Som; St Peter and St Paul's, Lavenham, Suffolk; St Helen's, Clifford Chambers, Warwicks; St Andrew's, Cleeve Prior, Worcs; All Saints', Driffield, E Yorks.

Sundials were once commonly found on the walls of churches throughout the country. Just under 2,000 vertically-fixed sundials have been so far recorded by the British Sundial Society, of which 60% are fixed to churches. Sundials in churchyards, on the other hand, are generally horizontally fixed.

The earliest sundial in the United Kingdom — by some margin — is carved on the south face of an Anglo-Saxon cross standing in St Cuthbert's churchyard, Bewcastle, near Carlisle, Cumbria. It is thought to date from the seventh or early eighth century. It is divided into four 'tides' (three-hour periods) into which the working day was then divided, following four of the canonical hours: Terce (9am), Sext (12 noon), None (3 pm) and Vespers (6 pm). The Saxon church at Corhampton, Hants (probably before 1020), has a sundial with the four tides each divided into two. Other Saxon sundials can be seen at St Gregory's Minster, Kirkdale, N Yorks; St John's, Escomb, Durham (still in its original position. There is another one, seventeenth century, over the south porch); Holy Rood, Daglingworth, Glos; St Michael's, Winchester, Hants; St Mary's, North Stoke, Oxon; All Saints', Old Byland, N Yorks. Plenty of old sundials still survive.

See, for example, St Lawrence's, Alton, Hants (? fourteenth century); St Mary's, Wisbech, Cambs; Norton Priory, Runcorn, Ches; St Mary's, Dymock, Glos; St Peter and St Paul's, Weobley, Herefs; St Margaret's, Westminster, London; St Laurence's, Stanwick, Northants; St Mary's, Thame, Oxon; St Andrew's, Bishopstone, Sussex; All Saints', Bingley, W Yorks.

Scratchdial, undated, St Lawrence's, Ingworth, Norfolk

Scratchdial, undated, St Mary's, Bexley, London

Sundial, 1718, St Mary's, Longnor, Salop

Hanging pyx, canopy c 1500, St Mary's, Dennington, Suffolk

Clock mechanism, c.1675, removed from the tower in 1948, on display at St Mary's, Dennington, Suffolk

CLOCKS

For some reason not yet understood, in the twenty years between 1280 and 1300, the clock suddenly appeared in a number of cathedrals and abbeys through Britain. Of these, only the clock in Salisbury Cathedral, Wilts (or an early replacement) survives. This has been dated to 1386 from an entry in Cathedral accounts, though whether that entry refers to this clock has been disputed. It has no face: dials only became common in the eighteenth century, and were frequently added to older clocks. It strikes bells every hour. Wells Cathedral, Som is claimed to be the second oldest working clock in the world (1392), though now without its original mechanism. This was removed in 1837 and transferred in 1884 to the Science Museum in London, where it continues to work. There is a clock face on the outside face of the north transept which is operated by the same mechanism, probably originally mediaeval but restored in the seventeenth century. Wells Cathedral is also believed to have the earliest set of clock jacks in the United Kingdom. Clock jacks are carved and painted figures which strike bells at quarter-hourly or hourly intervals. Other clock jacks may be seen at St Mary Steps, Exeter, Devon; St Thomas's, Salisbury, Wilts; and St Mary's, Rye, Sussex.

Wells Cathedral's clock is an astronomical clock. In addition to showing the time, it has dials showing astronomical information, such as the position of the sun and moon, signs of the zodiac, and the planets. Astronomical clocks are not uncommon in the west of England: other examples may be seen at Exeter Cathedral and St Mary's, Ottery St Mary (both in Devon) and Wimborne Minster, Dorset. There is a modern astronomical clock (1955) in the north transept of York Minster, a memorial to the airmen from bases in Yorkshire, Durham and Northumberland who were killed in the Second World War.

The oldest working tower or turret clocks (ie a clock placed within a tower) in the United Kingdom are at St Augustine's of Canterbury, East Hendred, Oxon (1525), St Mary's, Rye, Sussex (1561–2), and St Bride's, Douglas, South Lanarkshire, which probably dates from sometime before 1562.

Gradually clocks replaced sundials, though the process was a long one, and for three hundred years clocks and sundials existed side by side. Clocks changed remarkably little until about 1670, when the pendulum, which had been patented in 1656 by Christian Huygens, started appearing in churches. Probably the longest pendulum in the United Kingdom is at St Giles's Cathedral, Edinburgh, which is nearly sixty feet long and was installed in 1912.

The Wells Cathedral clock, c.1390

Clock mechanism, c.1698, by Nicholas Paris, on display at St Mary's, Warwick

Clock by John Smith of Derby, installed in 1901, Beverley Minster, E Yorks

Of an estimated 12,000 clocks in British churches, most are Victorian. With the industrial revolution, there was a wholesale destruction of earlier clocks and their replacement by more accurate, modern, mass-produced clocks. In most cases, the clockmaker is not noticed in church leaflets, and in many, the church does not even know his name. This is why some of the following entries have so few identified clocks. Nonetheless, many church clocks still conform to Henry VIII's decree (following Exodus 39, 21–22) that the dials should be 'blew with the signs upon them gilt'.

Church clock designers and clockmakers

James Benson of Ludgate Hill (1849–1973). James William Benson (1826–78) and his older brother (or maybe cousin) Samuel Suckley Benson (born 1822) founded the firm in 1849, but they parted in 1855 and James continued on his own. On his death his sons Alfred and Arthur took charge. Their premises were bombed in 1915 (or maybe 1914) and they stopped making clocks or watches: they bought them in and had their own name put on them. The company name was sold in 1973.

Christ Church, Tintwistle, Derbys (1866); St Mary's, Gamlingay, Beds (1869); St Peter's, Cleethorpes, Lincs (1872); St Peter's, Church Lawford, Warwicks (1872); St Peter's, Wrestlingworth, Beds (1874); St Peter and St Paul's, Skendlesby, Lincs (1877); St Martin's, South Willingham, Lincs (1878); St Andrew's, Abbots Ripton, Cambs (1881); St Mary's, Abbots Ann, Andover, Hants (1882); St Lawrence's, Alton, Hants (1890); St Mary's, Painswick, Glos (1899); St Mary's, St Mary in the Marsh, Kent (1919).

G and F Cope of Nottingham (1845–1984). George and Francis Cope, bachelor brothers, established their factory in Nottingham in 1845. In 1877, they were joined by their nephew William Cope I (1870–1922), still a child, who succeeded to the business on the deaths of his uncles (c.1900). William II (1902–?) succeeded his father and was succeeded by his sons Richard and David. The firm gave up making tower clocks in about 1970 and maintaining them in 1975. It was taken over by Smith of Derby in 1984.

St Peter's, Nottingham (1850s, movement replaced by Smith of Derby, 1970s); St Helen's, Trowell, Notts (1881, taken from the old Nottingham Exchange in 1927); St Andrew's, Maghull, Sefton, Mersey (?1880s); Holy Trinity, Lenton, Nottingham (1950); St Michael and All Angels, Averham, Notts (late 1960s).

E Dent and Co (1840–1975). Edward John Dent (1790–1853) worked for Vulliamy and Son from 1815 to 1829 and was a partner with John Roger Arnold (1769–?) from 1830 to 1840. He founded his own firm in 1840, and is most famous for building the Great Clock at the Houses of Parliament, Westminster, London in 1852, but died before completing it. His stepson, Frederick Rippon Dent (died of alcoholism, 1860) finished the job. Dent chronometers accompanied Darwin (1831), Livingstone (1850) and Stanley (before 1890) on their expeditions. F R Dent and his brother Richard Rippon Dent (both sons of his cousin and mentor, Richard Rippon), divided the business between them. It remained a family firm until 1975; it is now owned by Smith of Derby. Dent made the Standard Clock for the Royal Observatory at Greenwich, London (1871) and also many turret clocks: Holy Trinity, Meanwood, Leeds, W Yorks (1850); St Osmund's, Evershot, Dorset (1853).

Gillett and Bland, later Gillett and Johnston, of Croydon (1844–present). The firm was started in 1844 by William Gillett (1800–83). He was joined in 1854 by

Charles Bland (died 1884), who introduced turret and public clocks to the business, and, in 1877, Arthur Johnston (died 1916), who added a bell foundry. Cyril Johnston joined his father in 1902 and became a partner in 1907. He resigned in 1948 (died 1950) and in 1958 the business was sold. Between 1844 and 1950 more than 14,000 tower clocks were made at the Croydon factory. In 1960 the firm was acquired by Cecil Coombes (died 1972), an old employee, followed by his wife Doris (retired 1976) and his son, Stephen. See also under the section Bells.

St George's, Toddington, Beds (1875); St Mary's, Shrewsbury, Salop (1879); St Anne's, Soho, London (1884); St Mary's, Tenby, Pembs (1889); St Mary's, Wargrave, Berks (1915); All Saints', Wickhambrook, Suffolk (1947); St Bartholomew's, Wednesbury, W Mid (date not known); St John's, Bethnal Green, London (date not known).

Grimthorpe, Lord (1816–1905). Edmund Beckett (Denison) was created first baron Grimthorpe in 1886 for his services to churches. Most famous for designing the Great Clock in the Houses of Parliament (1859), and, to some, more famous as the inventor of the gravity escapement (1851), with which this clock was fitted. An amateur and argumentative horologist, as he was architect (see the Architects and master craftsmen section), theologian and mathematician.

He designed (but did not make) clocks for St Andrew's, Helion Bumstead, Essex (1838); All Saints', Ilkley, W Yorks (1848); Holy Trinity, Meanwood, Leeds, W Yorks (1850); Lincoln Cathedral (1880); St Paul's Cathedral, London (1893).

J B Joyce of Whitchurch, Salop (1690–1965). The firm claims to be the oldest tower clockmaking company in the world – but see Thwaites and Reed. William Joyce began making clocks in Cockshutt, Salop in 1690. In 1790, the firm moved to Whitchurch. In 1834 Thomas Joyce diversified into the manufacture of large clocks for public buildings; in 1849 it was making clocks with the then new gravity escapement. In 1965, Norman Joyce, the last member of the Joyce family, retired and sold the company to Smith of Derby. The last turret clock made by Joyce's was installed in 1964 in St Andrew's, Hope Bowdler, Salop.

St Alkmund's, Whitchurch, Salop (1849); Pershore Abbey, Worcs (1872); Lichfield Cathedral, Staffs (1891); St John's, Hughley, Salop (1893); Southwell Minster, Notts (1898); St Laurence's, Ludlow, Salop (1931, removed 1988, mechanism on display); Worcester Cathedral (date not known).

John Moore of Clerkenwell (c.1791–1899). Major nineteenth century clockmaker, who also made anemometers (wind dials) and weather vanes. His clocks were celebrated for their solidity rather than their adventurousness. George Handley (died 1824) and John Moore (dates not known), two ex-apprentices of Thwaites started the firm in c.1791 as Handley and Moore. After 1821, the firm was known as John Moore; after 1829, John Moore and Sons; after about 1887, B R and J Moore (probably John Moore's sons: names and dates not known). George, third son of John Moore, continued the business until 1838. When Henry James Moore (1839–99, probably John Moore's grandson) died, the firm was acquired by Thwaites and Reed.

St Katharine and St Peter's, Milford Haven, Pembs (1803); Crimond Church, Aberdeenshire (1817, displayed in the church); St Mark's, Kennington, London (1824); St George's, Ivychurch, Kent (1826); St Mary's, Cropredy, Oxon (1831); St John's, Hoxton, London (1833); St Anne's, Limehouse, London (1839); St Helen's, Abingdon, Oxon (1845); St Margaret's, Kings Lynn, Norfolk (1845); St Andrew's, Kingswood, Surrey

(1854); St Alfege's, Greenwich, London (1865); All Saints', Milton Keynes, Bucks (1869); St Michael's, Wood Green, London (1874).

Potts of Leeds (1833–1935). William Potts (1809–87) set up the business in 1833. His sons, (Thomas) Robert (1842–1917), James (1847–1910) and Joseph 1859–1937) joined the firm and it was known as William Potts and Sons until 1930. The next generation, William (1870–1957), Tom (1875–1947) and Charles (1889–1958), joined the firm after 1918, but Tom left the firm in 1928 and Charles in 1930, both to set up their own clockmaking firms. Charles H Potts & Co, later run by Anthony Potts, existed until the 1950s. Potts merged with Smith of Derby in 1933, but preserved its corporate identity. There are 1,600 Potts clocks around Britain.

Holy Trinity, Queensbury, W Yorks (after 1843); All Saints', Ilkley, W Yorks (1848); Christ Church, Hartlepool, Durham (after 1854, now an art gallery); Saltaire Congregational Church, W Yorks (after 1859); Pudsey Parish Church, Leeds, W Yorks (1864); St Chad's, Far Headingley, Leeds, W Yorks (1872); St John's, Clayton, W Yorks (1879, second dial by Charles Potts, 1933); Lincoln Cathedral (1880); St Mary's, Boston Spa, W Yorks (1884); St Mary's, Tadcaster, N Yorks (1887); Newcastle Cathedral, Tyne & W (1895); St Mary's, Staindrop, Durham (1896); Holy Trinity, Wensley, N Yorks (1899, church now redundant); St Andrew's, Aysgarth, N Yorks (1903); St Mary's, Myton-on-Swale, N Yorks (1920); St Cuthbert's, Amble, Northumb (1925).

James Ritchie and Son of Edinburgh (1809–present). James Ritchie (c.1771–1850) opened a shop selling and repairing watches in 1809. In 1819 he took over Joseph Durward's clockmaking business which had been established since 1775. In 1836/7 James's son, Frederick James (1828–1906), became a partner. He pioneered the 'master and slave' system of synchronised clocks, setting up such a system in Edinburgh, linked to the Royal Observatory. After Frederick's death, his sons James (born c 1859) and Leone (born c 1871) ran the firm. The last member of the Ritchie family retired in 1953. The firm is now partly owned by Smith of Derby.

St Giles's Cathedral, Edinburgh (1912).

John Smith & Sons of Clerkenwell (1780–present). The firm started in 1780 and by 1850 had become one of the largest clock makers in England. The firm had its own brass foundry, timber store, dial shop, clock case workshop, assembly areas and showrooms, and also supplied parts to other makers. World War I saw a sharp decline in the demand for the large clocks that the company specialised in, and the last clock was made by Smith and Sons in 1938. Now the firm concentrates on stockholding and supply of non-ferrous metals.

All Saints', Bourton, Oxon (1883).

John Smith & Sons of Derby (1856–present). John Smith (1813–66), who founded the firm in 1849, was trained by John Whitehurst III (1788–1855). Though not Whitehurst's formal successor, John Smith took over much of the business when John III died. His sons Frank (died 1913) and John (1857–1910) succeeded him; Frank's son Alan succeeded his father, and was succeeded by his son Howard and his grandson Nicholas. Smith's took over Potts of Leeds in 1933 and J B Joyce in 1965.

St Lawrence's, Heanor, Derbys (1870, their first turret clock); St Paul's Cathedral, London (1893), Beverley Minster, E Yorks (1901); St Bartholomew's, Hognaston, Derbys (1911); St Mary's, Ilminster, Som (1926 or 1946).

Thwaites and Reed (1740–present). This firm, like J B Joyce, claims to be the oldest clockmaking firm in the world, citing documentary evidence back to 1610. (The documents have unfortunately disappeared). The present company was founded in 1740 by Aynsworth (or Ainsworth) Thwaites (dates not known) in Clerkenwell, London and continued there until 1780. The firm moved to Sussex in 1975. Its earliest commission was the clock at Horse Guards Parade, Whitehall, London. In 1780, Aynsworth was succeeded by John (1757–1826), who ran the firm from 1780 to 1816, when he took into partnership George Jeremiah Reed, a relative, and the firm became Thwaites and Reed. In the 1900s the business was sold to the Buggins family. From the 1960s to the 1980s it had a somewhat chequered history, but still makes and maintains clocks.

St Helen's, Benson, Oxon (1795); All Saints', Wokingham, Berks (1817); Balliol College chapel, Oxford (1838); St Michael's, Aughton, Lancs (date not known).

Vulliamy family (c.1740–1854). The Swiss clockmaker, Justin Vulliamy (1712–97), moved to England in the late 1730s and became, with his partner and father-in-law Benjamin Gray, King's Clockmaker to George II. The Vulliamy family held the post until the death of Benjamin Lewis Vulliamy in 1854. His son, Benjamin Vulliamy (1747–1811), in about 1780, built London's Regulator Clock at Kew, which was responsible for the official London time until 1884, when Greenwich Observatory took over. Benjamin's son, Benjamin Lewis Vulliamy (1780–1854), was perhaps the most famous of the family.

His church clocks include St Luke's, West Norwood, London (1825); St John's, Stratford, London (1834); St Michael's, Basingstoke, Hants (1843); St Peter's, Bushley, Worcs (1843).

Whitehurst and Son of Derby (c.1736–1855). The firm was founded by John Whitehurst I (1687–c.1731) at Congleton, Ches. His elder son, John Whitehurst II (1713–88) moved to Derby in 1736 and London in about 1780: he was an eminent scientist and philosopher as well as a clockmaker. His second son, James, stayed with his father's business in Congleton. John Whitehurst III (1788–1855), John II's nephew, took over the firm on reaching his majority. One of his apprentices was John Smith of Derby. On John Whitehurst III's death, the firm was taken over by W & R Roskell of Liverpool, a clock- and watchmaker: it closed in 1862.

St Peter's, Stockport, Manchester (1769).

CHURCHYARDS

Churchyards and graveyards are not necessarily (though mostly) the same thing, since graveyards (apart from municipal cemeteries) may exist without a church and, much more rarely, churchyards may exist without a grave.

In 597, when Pope Gregory sent Augustine to convert Britain to Christianity, he ordered that pagan temples should be used as churches; and in c.650 St Cuthbert was authorised by the Pope to establish churchyards around churches. Ancient churchyards were often taken over from pagan sites. They are often circular, especially in Wales. See St Stephen's, Old Radnor, Powys; St Tudius's, St Tudys, Cornwall, St Mary's, Wirksworth, Derbys, All Saints', Rudstone, E Yorks, and St Michael and All Angels, Winwick, Northants; or on a mound, such as St Michael's, Winwick again, St Tysilio's, Llandysilio, Powys and St Peter's, Maxey, Cambs; or contain large standing stones, such as All Saints', Rudstone again, and St John's, Pewsey, Wilts.

Whether the church or the churchyard came first, the church was normally situated to the north of the churchyard. This was because in the north part of the churchyard the sun shines briefly and evil spirits live there; 'devil's doors' were in the north side of the church and were left open at baptisms so that evils spirits could leave. So, until the nineteenth century, the godly were buried in the larger, southern, part of the churchyard, and the godless were buried to the north – suicides, criminals, stillborn and unbaptised babies, and strangers. Until the middle of the seventeenth century, almost everyone was buried without a coffin in an unmarked grave.

Churchyards were at first unenclosed, though their boundaries may have been marked by wooden crosses. Slowly, during the course of the Middle Ages, churchyard fences or walls were built, probably at first to keep out cattle.

In the Middle Ages and long after, the churchyard was a hive of activities, as was the church. Legal business was transacted and oaths were sworn in the church porch. Feast days were celebrated, fairs and markets were held, games were played (including football, cockfighting, single-stick, archery, fencing, wrestling and fives), and plays and music entertained the crowds. Animals grazed there (and sometimes still do) or were tied up there. Sometimes bells were cast in the churchyard, due to the dangers of transporting them from a distance.

In the nineteenth and twentieth centuries, many town churches lost all or part of their churchyards, sometimes because of new buildings, new railways or new roads; sometimes because they were full, and sometimes because they were too small for the enormous expansion of urban populations. If new building was planned, the remains were often exhumed and reburied. This was done in 1866–7, when the new Midland Railway clipped off a large corner of St Pancras churchyard, near Euston, London, and again in the 2000s. If the graveyard was simply closed, the gravestones were often removed and set against the graveyard walls.

Altar tomb. See Table tomb.

Bale tomb, barrel tomb. See Table tomb.

Bier. A four-wheeled carriage on which the body was placed at the lych gate for transport to the church and, usually, from there to the grave. Survivals are not uncommon these days, usually kept inside the church or cathedral. See for example Chester Cathedral, Ches; St Mary's, Grendon, Northants; St Kyneburgha's, Castor, Cambs; St Michael's, Great Wolford, Warwicks. The modern version is called a church truck.

Chest tomb. See Table tomb.

Churchyard cross. A stone cross erected to the south of most pre-Reformation churches to denote consecrated ground. Between the thirteenth century and the Reformation, they were commonly used as a preaching place by wandering friars. Many were destroyed in the sixteenth and seventeenth centuries, but many examples of crosses, or parts of crosses, survive.

St Mary's, Plympton, Devon (fourteenth century, the shaft); St Mary's, Cricklade, Wilts (fourteenth century); St Cuthbert's, Holme Lacy, Herefs (fourteenth century); Holy Rood, Ampney Crucis and St James the Less, Iron Acton (both in Glos and both fifteenth century); St Mary's, Derwen, Den (fifteenth century).

Lantern cross, tabernacle cross: churchyard cross with a lantern-shaped top. The top usually contains sculptures or other decorations.

Coffin. Stone coffins, or their lids, are occasionally found in churchyards, sometimes converted to other uses. Probably, but not always, these had come from inside the church or indeed somewhere else, and were the coffins of the rich and eminent. Until the mid seventeenth century, most people were buried in shrouds without coffins, tied head and foot and, by law from 1667, made of wool, though they might have used the parish coffin during the funeral service (as a re-usable coffin is today for cremations). See the parish coffin at St John and All Saints', Easingwold, N Yorks.

Coffin table, corpse stone, lych stone. A wooden or stone block for resting coffins on, usually under the lychgate. The clergyman used to meet the procession here, at the entrance to the churchyard, and often still does. Few survive. See St Mary Magdalene's, Bolney, Sussex; St Mary's, Chiddingfold, Surrey; and St David's, Ashprington, Devon.

Columbarium. See Dovecote.

Cremation. Most churches today have a Garden of Remembrance, in which the ashes of those who have been cremated are buried and marked with a small slab. Christian churches have historically discouraged (though they have never forbidden) cremation, and burial was practically universal until the eighteenth century. Protestant churches approved cremation earliest: The Cremation Society of Great Britain was founded in 1874; the first Protestant crematorium was built at Woking, Surrey in 1878, and by the early 1900s churches whose space was limited could insist on cremation before the remains were buried, as Westminster Abbey did in 1908. The Roman Catholic church still prefers burial: it was not until 1966 that Catholic priests were allowed to officiate at cremations. In the United

Bier, maybe nineteenth century, inside St Gregory's, Heckingham, Norfolk

Churchyard cross, undated but probably fifteenth century, All Saints', Claverley, Salop

Ruins of the churchyard cross, undated, Holy Trinity, Holdgate, Salop

Stone coffins, undated, Lincoln Cathedral

Coffin table, nineteenth century, St Andrew's, Hope Bowdler, Salop

The canons' graveyard: graves marked by kerbstones, from thirteenth century, Wells Cathedral, Som

Graveboard, 1859, St Margaret's, Darenth, Kent

Graveside shelter or hudd, eighteenth century, St Augustine's, Brookland, Kent, displayed inside the church

Cast iron ledger stone, 1813, St Michael's, Madeley, Salop

Tea-caddy tomb, ? 1817, St Andrew and St Mary's, Condover, Salop

Lychgate, thirteenth century, reputed to be the oldest in England, St George's, Beckenham, London

Kingdom today, seventy per cent of deaths are followed by cremation.

Culvery. See Dovecote.

Dovecote, columbarium, culvery. Breeding place for doves, which, in the Middle Ages, provided meat, eggs and manure and so were an important part of the economy. Two church types survive. The free-standing dovecote – square, circular, polygonal – normally belonged to a monastery in pre-Reformation days. See St Mary's, Broughton, Hants (c.1340); St George's, Dunster, Som (fourteenth century); St Mary's, Stoke-sub-Hamdon, Som (fifteenth century). The dovecote built into the fabric of the church, either the tower or the roof, may have been for the use of the vicar. See St Michael's, Compton Martin, Som (seventeenth century, above the ceiling of the Bickfield Chapel); St John's, Elkestone, Glos (? thirteenth century, in a room above the altar); St Faith's, Overbury, Worcs (? fourteenth century, above the chancel); St Nicholas's, Buckenham, Norfolk (seventeenth century, in the octagonal tower).

Footstone. See Graves.

Graves. Congestion is now, and has been since the mid-nineteenth century, the great problem with graves. Opening municipal cemeteries has done something to help. Glasgow Necropolis was opened in 1832, Kensal Green, London, cemetery in 1833, St Woolos cemetery in Newport, Glam in 1854, and Belfast City cemetery and Milltown cemetery, Belfast in 1869. So has the growing popularity of cremation. In England and Wales today, a graveyard burial plot is leased from the church for a set period of time: the maximum period is a hundred years. Five years before the end of the lease, the descendant or executor is asked whether he wants to renew it. If no option to renew is exercised, the plot may be sold again, or it may be kept vacant: graveyards may therefore be cleared of graves a hundred years after the last burial, and be sold or put to other uses. In Scotland, titles to burial plots ('lairs') are in perpetuity and therefore can never be closed. Given the acute congestion problem, a change in the law to permit the re-use of graves is now (2012) under review.

Graveboard. Piece of wood with a short post at each end, usually placed lengthways over the grave, used in place of a headstone: most common in the southeast and the Chilterns. Graveboards were used either for those who were too poor to afford a headstone, or in places where stone is scarce. They are unlikely to last much more than a hundred years: dates here (where given) are approximate.

St Mary's, Lower Dicker, Sussex (1840); St Margaret's, Darenth, Kent (1859); St Mary in the Marsh, Kent (?1924); St Peter and St Paul's, Peasmarsh, Sussex (date unknown); St Mary's, East Barnet, and St Peter and St Paul's, Little Gaddesden, both in Herts and of unknown date; St Peter's, Twineham, Sussex. Also, St Giles's, Codicote, Herts (a replacement) and Chiddingly Parish Church, Sussex (restored).

Graveside shelter, watch-box, hudd. Portable shelter shaped like a sentry-box, often without a base, to protect the priest conducting the funeral if the weather was bad. It was used from the eighteenth century to the beginning of the twentieth, and few survive. See examples at St Mary's, Beaumaris, Anglesey; St Mary's, Bucklebury, Berks; St James's, Deeping, Lincs; St Augustine's, Brookland, Kent; St Mary's, Silverton, Devon.

Gravestone, headstone, tombstone. A slab marking a grave, usually with the name of the deceased, some details, and an epitaph written on it. Gravestones in the churchyard came into relatively common use in the middle of the seventeenth century. They were normally made of stone, but sometimes wood (see Graveboard), sometimes slate (such as at St Tysul's, Llandysul, Cered), and sometimes, especially in the nineteenth century, of cast iron.

For cast iron gravestones see: St Margaret's, West Hoathly, Sussex (1619 and 1624); St Mary's and St Leonard's, both in Bilston, W Mid (1850s); St Leonard's, Bridgnorth (1692–1707), and St Michael's, Madeley (1785–1850s, gravestones, ledgers and chest-tombs), both in Salop; St Mary's, Climping, Sussex (?1875, chest tomb); St John's, Corby Glen, Lincs (1885); St Barnabas's, Great Tey, Essex (1908, 1932).

Graves originally were marked with footstones, and sometimes with kerbs as well, but these have mostly been removed to make grass-cutting easier. Gravestones were occasionally re-used: see St Thomas's, Heptonstall, W Yorks.

Hearse. A metal cage over a bier designed to carry a pall (a cloth protecting the coffin) and maybe candles; sometimes hearse refers to the bier itself. See also Hearse in the Church furnishings section.

Hogback tomb. Thought to be a Viking grave marker, dating, probably, from the beginning of the tenth century. It is a low, tomb-shaped, elongated rectangle of stone, with curved sides rising to a ridge that runs the length of the tomb. It is mostly carved. There are only about a hundred left, mainly, but not always, in Scotland and the north of England.

St Blane's, Bute, Argyll and Bute; Dalserf Church, South Lanarkshire; St Thomas's, Brompton, N Yorks; St Mary's, Gosforth, Cumbria (inside the church); St Peter's, Heysham, Lancs (inside the church); St Nevet's, Lanivet, Cornwall.

Hudd. See Graveside shelter.

Kerb. Stone edging round the sides of a grave.

Lantern cross. See Churchyard cross.

Ledger tomb. See Table tomb.

Ledger, ledger stone. A flat slab of stone marking a grave, usually with the name of the occupant carved on it.

Lychgate, lichgate. A roofed gateway to a churchyard ('lic' or 'lich' is Anglo-Saxon for corpse), roofed in case of bad weather. This was where the body was transferred to a bier. The oldest is claimed to be at St George's, Beckenham, London, thirteenth century.

Lych stone. See Coffin table.

Mausoleum. A monument, usually detached from the church, built to receive a tomb or tombs. Most date from the eighteenth and nineteenth centuries. The Mausolea and Monuments Trust lists 460 mausolea in England and ninety-five in County Down and County Antrim.

De Grey mausoleum (begun 1615) at St John the Baptist's, Flitton, Beds; the Allen mausoleum (c.1765) at St Mary's, Claverton, Som; the Hoare mausoleum (1819), at St Peter's, Stourton, Wilts; the Sandys mausoleum (c.1830), at St Andrew's, Ombersley, Worcs; the Greenwood mausoleum (c.1850), at Addington Methodist Church, W Yorks; the Macquarie mausoleum (1851), near St Columba's, Gruline, Isle of Mull, Argyll and Bute; the Boileau mausoleum (c.1854), at St Peter's, Ketterhingham, Norfolk; the Moody mausoleum (c.1870), at Saintfield C of I Church, Co Down.

Mortsafe, morthouse A device invented in the early nineteenth century, probably in Scotland, to keep a body safe from bodysnatchers, who provided bodies for dissection and were rife near every medical school. It consisted of an exceptionally heavy framework of iron, or iron and stone, padlocked over a coffin for six weeks (or permanently), until the body was sufficiently decayed to be of no interest to medical schools. Some were owned and leased out by churches; others

Cast iron chest tomb, 1800, St Michael's, Madeley, Salop

Bier with a hearse, nineteenth century, Chester Cathedral, Ches

Mortsafe, nineteenth century, St Michael's, Aylsham, Norfolk.

Table tombs, seventeenth/eighteenth centuries, St Mary's, Fairford, Glos

Pedestal tombs, 1850s, St Michael's, Madeley, Salop

Tomb of Antony Wingfield (died 1714), St Mary and St Lambert's, Stonham Aspal, Suffolk. Figure carvings are rare in churchyard tombs.

were owned and leased by self-help societies. They were more common in Scotland than in England.

Examples in Scotland can be seen at Skene Parish Church, Aberdeenshire; Logierait Church, Perth and Kinross; Greyfriars Kirkyard, Edinburgh; in England at St Michael's, Aylsham, Norfolk; St Mary's, Holystone, Nothumb; St Mary's, Henham, Essex.

Pedestal tomb. See Table tomb.

Tabernacle cross. See Churchyard cross.

Table tomb, altar tomb, chest tomb. Chest-shaped tomb in a churchyard, often carved on all five sides. (For tombs inside the church, see Tombs in the Church furnishings section). The body was buried in the earth beneath the table tomb. The oldest in the United Kingdom is the Perceval Monument, St Peter and St Paul's, Weston in Gordano, Som (sometime after 1202); there are two fourteenth century survivors, at All Saints', Necton, Norfolk and at St Katherine's, Loversall, W Yorks; and a few more of the fifteenth century. Most table tombs date from the seventeenth and eighteenth centuries, and, though they are country-wide, the most elaborate of them are in Glos, Wilts and the Cotswolds. Significant collections are at St Mary's, Painswick and St Mary's, Berkeley, both in Glos; and at Holy Cross, Sherston, Wilts. A bale tomb or barrel tomb is a variant, having a semi-cylindrical top, thought to resemble a bale of wool. It is exclusively from the Costwolds and from the seventeenth and eighteenth centuries. A pedestal tomb is higher and largely square in plan; a tea-caddy tomb is still higher, circular or hexagonal in plan, and topped with an ornament, such as an urn.

Tapsel gate. A kind of lychgate unique to Sussex, said to have been invented by John Tapsel in the early eighteenth century. It is mounted on a central pivot and swings through ninety degrees, stopped by pegs. Only six examples survive: original gates are at St Mary's, Friston; St Simon and St Jude's, East Dean; Coombes Church; twentieth century replicas are at St Andrew's, Jevington (restored 1933); Church of the Transfiguration, Pyecombe; and St Pancras's, Kingston.

Tea caddy tomb. See Table tomb.

Tombstone. See Gravestone.

Watch-box. See Graveside shelter.

Yew. Long-living evergreen hardwood tree (*taxus baccata*) which, since pagan times, has been associated with burials. In some graveyards, there is a circle of yews surrounding the church (such as St Aelhaiarn's, Guilsfield, Powys). St Mary's, Painswick, Glos, has a hundred yew trees (or perhaps a hundred and one, or maybe ninety-nine). There is unlikely to be any truth that yew trees in churchyards were grown in order to make the wood into bows: Spanish yew was always used for preference.

MUSIC AND SINGING

Church music grew up with monasteries. Plainsong (or plainchant, or Gregorian chant), which is a single line of melody, unaccompanied by instruments, was introduced to Britain (they say) by St Augustine on his arrival in 597. Between the twelfth and sixteenth centuries, it slowly gave way to polyphonic music, which has different parts sung simultaneously. Plainsong was retained (as it is today) for prayers, the officiant singing the versicle (the first part of the verse) and the choir, or the choir and congregation, the response.

At the time of the Reformation at least fifty monasteries maintained choirs. These, like the monasteries, were dissolved with the Dissolution of the Monasteries (1536–40). Some musicians were taken into the service of the five abbey churches which became new cathedrals, but, as part of the Reformation, services were greatly simplified and sung in English, though usually accompanied by an organ. Strangely, this was the age of the great English church music composers: Thomas Tallis (c.1505–85), a Catholic; William Byrd (1542–1623), another Catholic; Thomas Morley (1557–c.1603); Thomas Tomkins (1562–1656), who wrote, during the Commonwealth, musical tributes to Strafford and Laud (royalists executed in 1641 and 1645 respectively); Thomas Weelkes (c.1575–1623), who was fined for 'urinating on the Dean from the organ loft during Evensong'; and Orlando Gibbons (1583–1625).

The Civil War and the Commonwealth (1642–60) saw the temporary cessation of cathedral music, which was seen, like many other things, as idolatrous. Organs were destroyed, cathedrals were desecrated and choirs disbanded. The only music allowed was the singing of psalms. However, it was only in churches that music was banned: Cromwell himself, in spite of his aversion to organs in churches, appropriated the organ of Magdalen College, Oxford, and had it rebuilt at his own house at Hampton Court, where (strangely) John Milton played it. It was later moved to Tewkesbury Abbey, Glos.

Until about 1700, music in parish churches played very much the second fiddle. There were few choirs, and the singing of the congregation was accompanied sometimes by a small, simple organ. After the Restoration (1660) things hardly altered. Few of the organs that had been destroyed were restored, and the singing, usually led by the parish clerk, attracted genial contempt.

Things changed in the early years of the eighteenth century. Choirs of men and boys began to be formed to lead the singing during services, singing mostly in three or four parts. Choir members came from the local community. Some of them were musically literate, while others learnt their parts by ear. As the eighteenth century progressed, instrumentalists joined the choir, so that by the end of the century, the choir consisted of singers and a small band. Instruments included flute, oboe, clarinet, bassoon, violin and cello (or bass viol). All Saints', Winterton, Lincs, has a unique collection of instruments (as well as a collection of contemporary sheet music) played in church before the church got its first organ in 1840: three flutes (c.1790), bassoon (c.1800), clarinet (c.1800), and tenor oboe (late eighteenth century). The choir and musicians usually occupied a gallery at the west end of the church (at All Saints', it was erected in 1754 and pulled down in 1872), and so their music, which has recently undergone something of a revival, is known as West Gallery music.

There was often friction between the clergy and the players, especially as the players commonly played at village festivities and dances as well, which led to efforts being made by the clergy and gentry to reform the music, usually by installing an organ or harmonium to replace the instrumentalists. Many west galleries were pulled down. These attempts were chronicled in Thomas Hardy's *Under the Greenwood Tree* (1872: Hardy's father and grandfather had both played the violin in St Michael's, Stinsford, Dorset). The efforts were ultimately successful, though nonconformist chapels were the last to go. See Samuel Butler's *The Way of All Flesh* (1903, but written 1873–84). Today, practically all churches have organs and most have choirs.

Meanwhile, during the eighteenth and early nineteenth century, cathedral music had fallen into a deplorable state. It was ignored and under-funded, musical endowments were raided, choirs were undermanned (some consisted of only one chorister) and choristers were boarded out cheaply and used for menial jobs. It is strange that the Three Choirs Festival, probably the oldest music festival in the world, first took place at Gloucester Cathedral in 1715 in this dreary period.

The improvement in the condition of choristers was due largely to Maria Hackett (?–1876), 'the choristers' friend', who, starting with St Paul's Cathedral, London in about 1810, eventually visited all the cathedrals in England and Wales, and wrote *A Brief Account of Cathedral and Collegiate Schools, with an Abstract of their Statutes and Endowments* in 1827. Samuel Sebastian Wesley (1810–76) also fought to reform cathedral music, with some success, but the tide was eventually turned by the Oxford (or Tractarian) Movement (1833–45), a high church splinter group which advocated ritual and ceremony. Many clergymen came under the Movement's influence, including the Rev Walter Kerr Hamilton (1808–69), who became Precentor at Salisbury Cathedral, Wilts in 1841 and immediately began to raise the standard of music there. (He became Bishop of Salisbury in 1854). Other cathedrals slowly followed. They have never looked back.

Today, cathedral, abbey and college chapel choirs consist of boys (and, increasingly, girls) who sing the treble part and sometimes the alto part, and men (lay clerks, lay vicars or vicars choral) who sing the alto, tenor and bass parts. Choirs are traditionally divided into two parts: the Decani (the Dean's side) which sits on the south side of the choir, and the Cantoris (the Precentor's side) which sits on the north. Most cathedrals have a choir school nearby.

West gallery, late seventeenth or early eighteenth century, St John's, Stokesay, Salop

Outside staircase to west gallery, eighteenth century, St Mary's, Longnor, Salop

Musician, fourteenth century, Beverley Minster, E Yorks

Musician, fourteenth century, Beverley Minster, E Yorks

Musician, fourteenth century, Beverley Minster, E Yorks

Musician, fourteenth century, Beverley Minster, E Yorks

Musician, fourteenth century, Beverley Minster, E Yorks

THE ORGAN

The pipe organ, which produces sounds by driving air through pipes (one note per pipe), has existed since the fourteenth century. Until the late nineteenth century, the air was driven by a man (the blower) operating a bellows, but now the bellows are usually operated electro-pneumatically. (A long handle with which the blower used to pump air is still often seen sticking out beside the organ). From the bellows, the air is passed to a reservoir or reservoirs, then trunked to the soundboard on which the pipes stand, and admitted to the pallet box. The pallets are valves, one for each pipe, which are opened by pressing the corresponding key on the keyboard and closed by releasing the key. The pipes, of different materials and of widely different sizes, from thirty-two feet to a fraction of an inch, are arranged into ranks (divisions), each division being controlled by stops above the keyboard console and combination pistons (which in turn control stops in pre-arranged combinations), usually on the console but sometimes on the pedal board.

The console contains from one to five keyboards or manuals, each usually containing five octaves, and one pedal board containing two and a half octaves. In a five-manual organ the manuals are the great, swell, choir, solo and echo. The manuals are linked to the pipes by a mechanical, electrical or pneumatic tracker action. The manuals and pedal board have no expressive value: they simply switch the sound on and off. A swell pedal, or two swell pedals, above or slightly to one side of the pedal board, are the only means of increasing or decreasing volume: they operate the flaps of swell boxes in which some divisions of pipes are enclosed.

Little is known about organs in churches in the UK until the sixteenth century. It is a reasonable to assume that most cathedrals and larger churches, and many smaller ones, possessed organs, but almost nothing survives. The oldest organ case in the UK is in St Stephen's Church, Old Radnor, Powys. This dates from about 1500–30, and now contains an organ by J W Walker and Sons, installed in 1872. During the Commonwealth (1649–60) practically all church and cathedral organs were removed or destroyed, and organ builders fled to the Continent. Organ building was slow to resume at the Restoration, and only got into its stride with the beginning of the eighteenth century, The oldest church organ in the UK, ie the oldest collection of pipes in their original positions on their original soundboards, is in St Botolph's, Aldgate, London. The organ was built by Renatus Harris between 1702 and 1704 and added to by Harris's son-in-law, John Byfield, in 1740. It was enlarged several times in the nineteenth century and again in the 1960s. It was restored to its 1744 specification by Goetze and Gwynn in 2005–6.

Very few church organs are in the condition in which they left their original builder. This is partly because of technical development, partly because of changing fashions, partly because of the Puritan revolution, partly because of the closure of so many churches in the twentieth century, and partly because the organ, as a large and complex instrument with many moving parts, needs parts replacing, repairing or restoring. Usually, the whole instrument may need rebuilding several times.

The largest church organ in the UK is the Willis organ in Liverpool Anglican Cathedral, Mersey (1923–6), which has two five-manual consoles (one is a mobile recital console) and 10,268 pipes. The organ also has a trompette militaire stop, which has a very loud brassy sound, added in 1998, one of only three in UK churches. The others are in St Paul's Cathedral, London (1930) and Exeter Cathedral, Devon (1968).

Organ builders

J(ames) J(epson) Binns (1855–1928). Organ restorer and builder of Leeds, N Yorks, nicknamed 'Battleship' Binns because of the robustness of his organs. Founded his own firm in 1880, later known as Bramley Organ Works. His finest achievement, the organ at St Nicholas's, Great Yarmouth, Norfolk, was destroyed in the Second World War.

Surviving organs include Old Independent Church, Haverhill, Suffolk (1901); St Nicholas Buccleuch, Dalkeith, Midlothian (c.1905, re-located from West Church, Dalkeith, Midlothian, 1991); Christ Church, Watford, Herts (1907); Trinity Church, Hawick, Borders (1911); St Mary's, Shrewsbury, Salop (1911); Jesmond Parish Church, Newcastle on Tyne, Tyne & W (1913); St Mary's, Wombwell, S Yorks (c.1920, moved from St George's, Barnsley, S Yorks 1980–2).

Bishop and Son (c.1795–present). Organ builders and (mostly at present) restorers. Presently working from Ipswich and London. James Chapman Bishop (1782 or 1783–1854) set up the firm in London in 1807. His sons, Charles and George, and afterwards Charles's son, Charles Kenwrick Kenelm, ran the business until it was bought out in 1880 by an employee, Edward Hadlow Suggate, who moved it to Ipswich in the late 1890s.

St James's, Bermondsey, London (1829); St James's, Hampton Hill, London (1830s, transported from St Peter's, Eaton Square, London); St Mary's, Hampton, London (1831); St Bartholomew's, Great Gransden, Beds (1888); St Peter's, Ealing, London (1894); St Matthew's, Buckley, Flint (1905); St Peter's, Sheringham, Norfolk (1907); St Peter and St Paul's, Bardwell, Suffolk (1909); St Michael's, Brantham, Suffolk (1970). Modern restorations include organs at the United Reformed Church, Caterham, Surrey (1971), Sherborne Abbey, Dorset (1986–7), and (all in London) St James's, Spanish Place (1982), Hinde Street Methodist Church (1984), The Immaculate Conception, Farm Street (1988), and The Annunciation, Bryanston Street (1989).

Richard Bridge (?–1758). Trained under Renatus Harris (or perhaps under his son John); contemporary, ally and competitor of the younger Abraham Jordan and John Byfield II. Only one of his organs survives in anything like complete form: Christ Church, Spitalfields, London (1735; the largest organ in England for a hundred years), which is currently (2012) being restored. The organ at St Giles's, Cripplegate, London, is partly his (1733: it was relocated from St Luke's, Old Street, London). His organ case (1753) survives at St Andrew's, Enfield, London.

Brindley and Foster (1854–1939). Sheffield, S Yorks, firm founded by Charles Brindley (c.1830–93) in 1854. He was joined by Albert Healey Foster (?–1919) in 1871. His son Charles Frederick Brindley (died 1925) took over in 1887 and his grandson in 1919. The business went bankrupt and was bought by Willis in 1939. The firm exported organs to Australia, New Zealand and South Africa.

St Mary's, Arnold, Notts (1876); St John's, Ranmoor, Sheffield, S Yorks (1888); Lesmahagow Old Parish Church, South Lanarkshire (1889); St Mark's, Mansfield, Notts (1900); St John's, Worksop, Notts (1896); Holy Trinity, Lenton, Nottingham (1906); Christ Church, Chester, Ches (1909); St Paul and St John's, Monklands, Airdrie, North Lanarkshire (1911).

John Byfield II (?–1774). Son of the organ builder John Byfield I (?–1757). None of John Byfield I's organs survive except the choir division in the Main Organ of Chichester Cathedral. Byfield II built organs at Truro Cathedral, Cornwall (1750, saved from St Mary's Church, which was demolished in 1888 to create the site of the cathedral); St Silas's, Pentonville, London (c.1750, bought from St Thomas's, Regent Street, London in 1966; greatly altered); St Botolph-without-Bishopsgate, London (1764); St Mary's, Rotherhithe, London (1765). Took Samuel Green (1740–96) into partnership in 1768. They built the organs of St Nicolas's, Newbury, Berks (1770, greatly altered) and Holy Trinity, Berwick-on-Tweed, Northumb (1773, greatly altered). Byfield retired in 1772.

Peter Collins Ltd (1964–present). Organ builders and restorers, first at Redbourn, Herts, and then, from 1989, at Melton Mowbray, Leics.

Sacred Heart, Henley, Oxon (1976); St Mary's, Paddington Green, London (1978); St Oswald's, Durham (1980s); St Peter Mancroft, Norwich, Norfolk (1984); St George's, Walthamstow, London (1997); Leighton Buzzard RC Church, Beds (2002).

John Compton Organ Company (1902–65). John Compton (1865–1957) set up business in 1902 in Nottingham in partnership with J F Musson, but the partnership was dissolved in 1904. He moved to London in 1919 and set up a factory in Willesden in 1930. He specialised in electronic organs (his were the main cinema organs of the mid twentieth century) and electronic action pipe organs. The firm was wound up in 1965 and the pipe organ business was sold to Rushworth and Dreaper.

St Luke's, Chelsea, London (1932); St Mary Magdalene's, Paddington, London (1933); All Saints', Weston-super-Mare, Som (1935); Emmanuel United Reformed Church, Worthing, Sussex (1937); Downside Abbey, Stratton-on-the-Fosse, Som (1937); Derby Cathedral (1939); Wakefield Cathedral, W Yorks (1951); St Eugene's Cathedral, Derry, Co Londonderry (1955); St Bride's, London (1957).

Thomas Elliot (?–1832). Took over Snetzler's business and trained Hill, who married his daughter and became his partner in 1825.

Ashridge chapel, Berkhamsted, Herts (1818); St Margaret's, Crick, Northants (1819, originally built for the Chapel Royal, St James's Palace, London); St Michael's, Ledbury, Worcs (c.1820).

(Martin) Goetze and (Dominic) Gwynn Ltd (1980–present). Organ restorers and builders, first based at Nottinghasm and now at Welbeck, Notts.

New organs include St John the Baptist's, Marldon, Devon (1990); St Michael and All Angels, South Shields, Tyne & W (1991); St Matthew's, Sheffield, S Yorks (1992); St Lawrence Whitchurch, Edgeware, London (1994); St Helen's, Bishopsgate, London (2000); St Endelienta's, Endellion, Cornwall (2001).

Gray and Davison (1772–1973). Firm founded in London 1772 by Robert Gray (died 1796) and later passed to his son William (died 1821: he built the organ in St Botolph's, Trunch, Norfolk (1808) and St Nicolas's, South Kilworth, Leics) and grandson John (died 1849). John Gray went into partnership (1842) with Frederick Davison, previously a partner of William Hill, and Gray and Davison became the first great Victorian organ-builders,.

St Mary's, Osterley, London (1857); St James's, Hunstansworth, Durham (c.1865); Christ the King, Gordon Square, London (1870); St Barnabas's, Burnmoor, Durham (1874); St Philip and St James's, Rock, Northumb (1881); St Katherine's, Regent's Park, London (1886); Clumber Park chapel, Worksop, Notts (1889); St Mary's, Stapleford Abbots, Essex (1901).

Samuel Green (1740–96). London organ builder. Trained under John Byfield I, went into partnership with John Byfield II in 1768 and carried on Byfield's business, under his own name, when Byfield retired in 1772.

St Peter and St Paul's, Appleford, Oxon (1777, originally in the Abbey House, Sutton Courtenay, Oxon); Holy Angels, Hoar Cross, Staffs (1779, moved from Bangor Cathedral, Gwynedd, 1877); All Saints', High Wycombe, Bucks (1783); St Mary's, Edith Weston, Rut (1787); St John the Baptist's, Armitage, Staffs (1789, moved from Lichfield Cathedral, Staffs, in 1869); Royal Naval College chapel, Greenwich, London (1789); Kensington Palace chapel, London (1790, originally at Sandbeck Hall, Maltby, S Yorks); St George's Chapel, Windsor Castle, Berks (1790); St John's, Lacey Green, Bucks (1792).

Renatus Harris (c.1652–1724). Son of an organ builder; born in France (possibly at Quimper) during the Commonwealth, when music was forbidden in churches, and returned to England at the Restoration. Very few of his organs survive. The organ at St Botolph's, Aldgate, London (1702–4) is the most complete. Others, surviving in parts, are at St John's, Wolverhampton, W Mid (1684, sold by Christ Church Cathedral, Dublin to St John's, 1762); Bristol Cathedral (1685; much altered, though the case and some of the pipes survive); and All Hallows, Twickenham, London (1695, transported from St Dionis Backchurch, Lombard Street, London which was demolished in 1878).

Harrison and Harrison (1861–present). Organ builders and rebuilders. Thomas Harrison founded the firm in 1861, first in Rochdale and then, in 1872, in Durham. It had only moderate success until his sons Arthur (1868–1936) and Harry (1871–1957) took over in 1896 and secured the commission to rebuild Durham Cathedral's organ (1905). Between 1904 and 1939, Harrison and Harrison rebuilt nineteen of England's cathedral organs including Ely, Cambs (1908), Leicester (1930) and Exeter, Devon (1933).

King's College chapel, Cambridge (1934 and 2009), Westminster Abbey, London (1937), and the cathedrals of Winchester, Hants (1938), Lincoln (1960), Salisbury, Wilts (1978–93), Hereford (1978), Peterborough, Cambs (1981, 2004) Glasgow, (1996), Lichfield, Staffs (2000), St Davids, Pembs (2000), followed, all rebuilds of Willis organs. Wells Cathedral, Som (1910) and St Albans Cathedral, Herts (1962), were largely new and Coventry Cathedral, W Mid, was completely new (1959), as were many college and parish church organs.

William Hill & Son (1832–1998). William Hill (1789–1871) trained with Thomas Elliot, married his daughter, became his partner in 1825, and on Elliot's death in 1832, set up as William Hill & Son. The firm passed to his son and grandson, finally amalgamating with Norman & Beard in 1916 to become Hill, Norman & Beard. The firm closed in 1998.

Binns organ, believed to be his largest, 1911, St Mary's, Shrewsbury, Salop

Gray and Davison organ, with dummy display pipes and a blower lever, 1854, St Peter's, Stanton Long, Salop

Hill's organ, 1909, at Selby Abbey, N Yorks

Norman and Beard's organ, 1910, St Nicholas's, Blakeney, Norfolk

Organ by Casson's Positive Organ Company, 1912, All Saints, Kettlestone, Norfolk

Snetzler's organ, 1764, St Laurence's, Ludlow, Salop

Snetzler's organ, 1769, rebuilt by Hill in 1884 and by Hill, Norman and Beard in 1963, Beverley MInster, E Yorks

Organ case built for Thomas Swarbrick, eighteenth century, St Mary's, Warwick

Sweetland's organ, 1849, St Michael's, Bath, Som

Thomas Thamar's organ, 1674, St Michael's, Framlingham, Suffolk, moved from Pembroke College, Cambridge in 1707

'Father' Henry Willis's organ, 1898, moved to St Mary's, Dennington, Suffolk from St Katherine's College, Tottenham (now demolished) in 1967 by Bishop and Son

King's College chapel, Cambridge; (1834, 1859, 1889 and 1911); Westminster Abbey, London (1848); Ely Cathedral, Cambs (1850); Chelmsford Cathedral, Essex (1864); Beverley Minster, E Yorks (1884); Lichfield Cathedral, Staffs (1884, rebuilt 1974); Eton College chapel, Berks (1885); Peterborough Cathedral, Cambs (1894); Norwich Cathedral, Norfolk (1899, rebuilt 1940–2); Selby Abbey, N Yorks (1909); St Andrew's Cathedral, Aberdeen (1917); Southwell Minster, Notts (1934).

Lewis and Company (c.1860–1919). Firm founded in London by Thomas Christopher Lewis (1833–1915) with John Tunstall and John Whittacker. Lewis left the firm in about 1900 and in 1919 the firm merged with Henry Willis and Son, trading as Henry Willis and Son and Lewis and Company. Lewis's name was dropped in 1925.

St Mary's RC Cathedral, Newcastle, Tyne & W (1869); St Mary's, Plympton, Devon (1879); Newcastle Cathedral, Tyne & W (1880); St John the Evangelist's, Upper Norwood, London (c.1882); St Barnabas's, Tunbridge Wells, Kent (1884); St Giles's, Shipbourne, Kent (1880s); Southwark Cathedral, London (1897); the apse organ, Westminster Cathedral, London (1910); St Mary's, Bourne Street, London (1913, much altered); St Luke's, Battersea, London (1914); St Ninian's, Nairn, Highland (1924).

Mander Organs (1936–present). Founded by Noel Mander (1912–2005) in 1936. The firm initially rebuilt or restored organs damaged in the Second World War.

Restorations are at St Paul's Cathedral, London (1972–6), Chichester Cathedral, Sussex (1985), Chelmsford Cathedral, Essex (1994, 1995), and church organs including St James's, Clerkenwell, London (1978), Great St Mary's, Cambridge (1995), All Saints', Marlow, Bucks (1997). New organs at St Andrew's, Holborn, London (1989), Gray's Inn chapel, London (1993), St Peter's, St Albans, Herts (2006), and St Giles without Cripplegate, London (2008).

Nicholson and Co (Worcester) Ltd (1841–present). Organ builders and restorers. The firm was founded by John Nicholson of Rochdale, Lancs, who moved to Worcester in 1841, first to Palace Yard and in 2003 to Malvern.

St John the Baptist's, Fladbury, Worcs (1838); St Michael and All Angels, Great Witley, Worcs (c.1860); Portsmouth Cathedral, Hants (1861, 1994, 2001); St Hilary's, Spridlington, Lincs (1878); St Mary's, Dymock, Glos (1884); Holy Trinity, Stratford-on-Avon, Warwicks (1991, rebuild); St Clement's, Sandwich, Kent (1995, rebuild); Southwell Minster, Notts (1996); Christchurch Priory, Dorset (1998); Gloucester Cathedral (1999, full restoration); Great Malvern Priory, Worcs (2004, rebuild); Bridlington Priory, E Yorks (2006, complete rebuild); Llandaff Cathedral, Cardiff, Glam (2010).

Norman and Beard (1868–1916). E W Norman founded the firm in Diss, Norfolk, in 1868, and was joined by his brother Herbert and George Wales Beard. The firm later moved to Norwich, adopting, in its new factory, a mass production technique for building instruments parts. Many of their organs survive in Norfolk. Norman and Beard amalgamated with William Hill of London in 1916 and moved into Hill's factory in London. The firm of Hill, Norman and Beard closed in 1998.

All Saints', Huntingdon, Cambs (1890); St Margaret's, Paston, Norfolk (1890); Holy Trinity, Formby, Lancs (1896); St Chad's, Shrewsbury, Salop (1904); St Nicholas's, Blakeney, Norfolk (1910); All Saints', Carleton Rode, Norfolk (1913); St Paul's, Herne Hill, London (1914).

Positive Organ Company (1887–1910). Thomas Casson (1842–1910), father of Sir Lewis Casson, the actor, was a banker turned organ builder who founded the company in 1887. Its aim was to make small, good quality organs that small churches could afford. They were cheap, solidly built, and ideal for the pianist who had to play the organ.

St Mary's, Bodney, All Saints', Kettlestone (1912) and All Saints', Freethorpe, all in Norfolk; Holy Trinity, Melbecks, N Yorks (1911); St George's, Bicknolter, Som (1922).

Samuel Renn (1786–1845). Born in Derbyshire, trained in London, moved to Stockport in 1823 and to Manchester in 1825. Built over a hundred organs in a conservative, eighteenth century style, many of which have been destroyed.

St Philip with St Stephen, Salford, Manchester (1829); St George's, Nailsworth, Glos (c.1830, bought from St John's, Bollington, Ches); St George's, New Mills, Derbys (1835); St Mary's, Disley, Ches (1836, much restored); St Mary and All Saints', Great Budworth, Ches (1839).

Rushworth and Dreaper (1828–2002). Liverpool firm of organ builders, founded by William Rushworth in 1828, run by the same family for five generations and went into voluntary liquidation in 2002. Dreaper (Christian names not known) is said to have been in business separately until 1905, when he joined Rushworth. The firm's archives, covering much of the nineteenth century, were shredded when the firm went bankrupt.

St Oswald's, Winwick, Ches (1838); St Mary's, Knowsley, Mersey (1913); St Barnabas's, Bromborough, Mersey (1923); Christ's Hospital chapel, Horsham, Sussex (1931); St Michael and All Angels, Bassett, Southampton, Hants (1937); St Peter's, Heswall, Mersey (1947); Royal Memorial Chapel, Sandhurst, Berks (1950); St Andrew's, Plymouth, Devon (1957); Guildford Cathedral, Surrey (1961).

'Father' Bernard Smith (c.1630–1708). Born in Germany as Bernhardt Schmidt and was apprenticed there. He emigrated to England in 1667, and in 1681 became the King's Organ-maker in Ordinary. He was a rival of Renatus Harris. Very few of his organs survive, even in part.

Christ Church Cathedral, Oxford (1680, case only); Durham Cathedral (1683, remaining parts in Tunstall Chapel, Durham Castle); Emmanuel College chapel, Cambridge (c.1690, case and some pipes); Trinity College chapel, Cambridge (1694, 1708, greatly altered); St Paul's Cathedral, London (1695: greatly altered); Great St Mary's, Cambridge (1698); the Chapel Royal (1699, first at the Banqueting House, Whitehall, London and then (1890) at St Peter's ad Vincula, Tower of London. Only the case survives); Christ's College chapel, Cambridge (1705; attributed); St Mary's, Barnsley, S Yorks (undated, only the case survives).

John Snetzler (1710–85). Swiss organ builder who was born and died in Schaffhausen, who worked mostly in England.

All Saints', Wingerworth, Derbys (1755, transported from St Paul's, Sheffield, S Yorks, in 1936 (this church was demolished) via St Paul's, Arbourthorne, S Yorks, in 1975 (church also demolished)); Holy Trinity, Hull, E Yorks (1756, 1758); St Leonard's, Swithland, Leics (1756); Eton College chapel, Berks (a chamber organ of 1760, at Buckingham Palace until 1820, then in the possession of Lord Egremont, then presented to Eton College, 1926); St Laurence's, Ludlow, Salop (1764); Peterhouse chapel, Cambridge (1765); St Margaret's, Whaddon, Glos (1768, from Brookthorpe, Glos); Beverley Minster, E Yorks (1769); Rotherham Minster, S Yorks (1777).

Thomas Swarbrick (1679–1752). Said to have been a German, said to have been trained by Renatus Harris and may have lived in Warwick. Very little of his work survives, though his name crops up many times.

Holy Trinity, Coventry, W Mid (1732, pipes only); Birmingham Cathedral, W Mid (before 1733, organ case only, attributed); St Mary's, Warwick (undated, case only).

William Sweetland, later the **Sweetland Organ Building Company** (?1847–1962). William Sweetland (1822–1910), an organ builder based in Bath, Som, who set up the firm in the late 1840s and retired in 1902. He handed over the business to the Sweetland Organ Building Company, which lasted until 1962, when it was taken over by **Rushworth and Dreaper**.

St Michael's, Bath, Som (1849); Ewenny Priory Church, Bridgend, Glam (1850, originally built for the Theological College, Wells); St Mary's, Devizes, Wilts (1855); Bridgeyate Methodist Church, Bristol (1860, transported from Cock Road Methodist Church, Bristol); St Cuthbert's, Wells, Som (1864); Bath Central United Reformed Church, Som (1888); Gillingham Methodist Church, Dorset (1890); Holy Trinity, Kingwood, Bristol (1903); St Michael and All Angels, Lyneham, Wilts (1909); Holy Trinity, Nailsea, Som (undated).

Thomas Thamar (fl. 1660–80). Cambridge organ builder. His most complete surviving organ is at St Michael's, Framlingham, Suffolk (1678; from Pembroke College, Cambridge in 1708).

Parts of his organs survive at St Michael and All Angels, Brownsover, Warwicks (attributed; after 1660, from St John's College chapel, Cambridge); St Mark's, Bilton, Rugby, Warwicks (1660s, case only, attributed); St Peter's, Southsea, Hants (1665, originally built for Winchester Cathedral, Hants, much altered); Gloucester Cathedral (undated); and St Nicholas's, Stanford on Avon, Northants (undated);.

J W Walker and Sons Ltd (1828–present). Joseph William Walker (1802–70) originally made small church organs in London, but in 1858 he was commissioned to build an organ at Romsey Abbey, Hants. His son John James and his grandson Reginald ran the firm until Reginald died in 1975. It was then restructured and moved to Brandon, Suffolk.

All Saints', Maidenhead, Berks (1879); St James's, Stretham, Cambs (1886); Holy Trinity, Sloane Street, London (1890); Wimborne Minster, Dorset (1899); Good Shepherd's, Lake, IoW (1901); Bristol Cathedral (1907); St Mary's, Wollaton Park, Nottingham (1938); Brompton Oratory, London (1954); Liverpool Metropolitan Cathedral, Mersey (1967); St Chad's Cathedral, Birmingham, W Mid (1993).

Henry Willis and Sons (1845–present). 'Father' Henry Willis (1821–1901) founded the firm in 1845 and received an early commission at Gloucester Cathedral (1847). Willis's shortly became the best known and largest organ builders in Britain, building organs in town halls, schools and other secular buildings (such as the Albert Hall, London, Blenheim Palace, Oxon, and Windsor Castle, Berks) as well as in cathedrals and churches.

The most famous cathedral organs are probably those in St Paul's, London (1872), Salisbury, Wilts (1877) and Truro, Cornwall (1887). Others include the cathedrals of Durham (1876–7), St Mary's, Edinburgh (1879), Canterbury, Kent (1886), Hereford (1892) and Lincoln (1898: this was 'Father' Willis's last cathedral organ. The organ in St Bees Priory Church, Cumbria (1899) was the last he supervised personally).

His son, grandson and great-grandson, (Henrys II, III and IV) continued to run the firm after Henry I's death. Liverpool Anglican Cathedral, Mersey, has an organ built by Henry II and Henry III (1923–6: the largest church organ in the United Kingdom); Henry II built the organ of Christ Church, Port Sunlight, Mersey (1904). Henry III built the organ of Westminster Cathedral, London (1932). Henry IV (retired 1997) specialised in 'Junior Development Plan' organs, which were cheap but could be expanded as funds became available (such as that in St Anne's, East Wittering, Sussex (c.1960).

LIBRARIES

All religious houses had libraries, but the Dissolution of the Monasteries (1536–40) was responsible for the destruction of almost all of them. At Worcester Priory (now Worcester Cathedral) only six books are known to have survived out of 600; at York Abbey, three out of 650. Many libraries were sold off by the cartload. Some books were destroyed for the sake of their precious bindings. Some books survived: Henry VIII himself rescued some important historical manuscripts, and other private collectors saved many; about half of the collection at Buildwas Abbey, Salop, is known to have survived in other museums and libraries. Some partly survived: Durham Cathedral's library (now one of the largest cathedral libraries in the United Kingdom) contains some 300 manuscripts and sixty printed books from the monastic collection. Some eventually found their way into church collections. Thirty years later, the Elizabethan Injunctions of 1559 commanded every church to keep a bible and a copy of Erasmus's *Paraphrases*. This may have been the start of church libraries.

Chained libraries. Chaining was a security measure, common from about the fifteenth century to the seventeenth. Libraries were progressively un-chained in the course of the seventeenth and eighteenth centuries. The books were shelved with their spines to the back (ie the wrong way round), so that they could be read without the chain becoming tangled. The chains ran from a hole in the bottom of the front cover to a rod on the bookcase, which was locked in position. In front of the bookcase was a shelf for putting the book on while reading. The oldest chained library in a church was created in 1598: Francis Trigge's library in St Wulfram's, Grantham, Lincs. Eighty-two books remain chained. Hereford Cathedral has the largest, with about 2,000 books, 1,500 of which are chained. It also has 225 manuscripts. The bookcases date from 1611, though the beginnings of the library date from about 1100. Wimborne Minster, Dorset, has the second largest: it is in the old Treasury and dates from 1686.

Cathedral libraries. Most cathedrals have libraries, some of them of special interest.

York Minster library is the biggest cathedral library in the United Kingdom (in spite of its misfortunes during the Reformation), with 120,000 volumes.

Wells Cathedral library, Som, lost its mediaeval books at the Reformation and is partly chained. The library is housed above the east cloister and dates from the mid fifteenth century.

The Wren Library at Lincoln Cathedral was built in 1674 on the instructions of Michael Honywood, the Dean, by Sir Christopher Wren, and contains

Honywood's own collection of 5,000 books. Next to it is the mediaeval library, built in 1422, containing three bookcases and a bench, housing for about a hundred manuscripts.

St Edmundsbury Cathedral's Ancient Library, Bury St Edmunds, was founded in 1595 by Dr Miles Mosse and contains some 550 books, mostly printed during the sixteenth and seventeenth centuries.

Exeter Cathedral library, Devon, has existed since at least 1072, when Leofric, Bishop of Exeter, died and bequeathed sixty-six books to the cathedral library. Only one is thought to be still at Exeter. A catalogue made in 1506 lists 530 titles. The library has changed premises many times. It has been in the Lady Chapel, the Chapter House, the Pearson building and the Bishop's Palace.

Old St Paul's Cathedral lost almost all its books in the Great Fire of London. The present cathedral library is housed in a specially designed room, and was completely re-stocked by the commissioners for rebuilding St Paul's. They bought complete collections: in 1712 they accepted a bequest by Henry Compton, Bishop of London, and in 1783 the library of John Mangey, vicar of Dunmow.

St Davids Cathedral library, Pembs, lost all its contents during the Reformation and the Civil War, and, when it was re-stocked, lost its books in a flood, but it has collections dating back to the sixteenth century. It is now housed in the fourteenth century chapter house built by Bishop Gower.

Church libraries. The following churches have interesting libraries. Some of them have chained books.

The Kedermister (or Kederminster) Library, at St Mary's, Langley Marish, Berks, was presented to the parish in perpetuity around 1613 by Sir John Kedermister (?–1631). A catalogue compiled in 1638, and still existing, lists 307 volumes.

St Peter's, Wootton Wawen, Warwicks, has a small chained library of seventeenth century theological books.

St Botolph's, Boston, Lincs, has a library in a room above the porch, built in 1634. Some of the seventeenth century books are believed to be the gift of the vicar, Anthony Tuckney, at the time the library was created. The bookcases are from 1766. It is one of the biggest church libraries in the United Kingdom.

St Mary Magdalene's, Newark, Notts has a library in the parvis over the south porch. It contains the library bequeathed to the church by Thomas White (1628–98), vicar between 1660 and 1666, and Bishop of Peterborough from 1685. (He was deprived of his see in 1690).

St Mary's, Hatfield Broad Oak, Essex, was presented with a library in 1708 by Sir Charles Barrington (c.1671–1715). It occupies one of the vestries.

Chained books, fifteenth century, Wells Cathedral, Som

Campanile at Chester Cathedral, Ches, 1975

Bell tower adjoining the Gatehouse, thirteenth century, St Davids Cathedral, Pembs

Detached wooden bell tower, c.1260, St Augustine's, Brookland, Kent

Carillon, 1890, on display at St Laurence's, Ludlow, Salop

BELLS

From the earliest times, church bells hung in towers were used as a way of announcing important local or national events – births, deaths, celebrations, fires, or military attacks. A parish church had maybe two or three bells; a cathedral more. The Dissolution of the Monasteries (1536–40) led to the destruction of bells in monasteries and abbeys, and often churches, and during the Commonwealth (1649–60) all bells were silenced. Few bells exist earlier than the Reformation. The earliest dated bell in the United Kingdom is that at St James's, Lissett, E Yorks, dated 1254. The oldest bell hung for change ringing – see below – and still in regular use, is thought to be the fifth bell at St Dunstan's, Canterbury, Kent. It was cast in about 1325.

After the Restoration (1660), most churches and cathedrals re-hung their bells, though there are still three cathedrals without bells – Ely, Norwich and Salisbury – and Roman Catholic churches were forbidden to have any bells until 1829.

Bells are sometimes rung singly – tolled – to call people to church or to announce a death. The Sanctus bell or altar bell, hung on the outside of a Roman Catholic church, is rung when the Host is raised. Sometimes bells play a simple tune, sounded by moving the clappers or moving the bells slightly. Nowadays the bells are mostly played electrically, but until recently they were played by a carillon, a kind of giant musical box cylinder with pegs inserted on the outside which operated levers which in turn operated the bells. Several superannuated carillons are displayed in churches. See St Laurence's, 1890, Ludlow, Salop, for example.

A far more sophisticated musical instrument is also known as a carillon. This is played by a carillonneur by means of a keyboard and pedalboard. Carillons have existed in the United Kingdom since at least 1698, when one was recorded at St Giles's, Edinburgh. Ten churches in the United Kingdom (and six secular locations in England) have this kind of carillon: four in England, five in Scotland and one in Northern Ireland. There are never fewer than twenty-three bells, a two-octave carillon, and mostly much more. The concert or standard carillon is a set of forty-seven bells, a four-octave carillon. (The largest set of bells is seventy-seven, in Kirk in the Hills, Bloomfield Hills, Michigan, USA, and Hyechon College, Daejoen, South Korea. The South Korean carillon has seventy-eight bells, but one is only used to strike the hours).

Change ringing dates from the Restoration. The first book on the subject, *Tintinnalogia: or, The Art of Ringing* was written by Fabian Stedman (or Steadman) in 1668. Change ringing is a system of ringing in which the bells do not play tunes but change places in their sequence according to mathematical permutations. It is a peculiarly English phenomenon: there were, at the beginning of 2012, 5,773 rings (ie sets) of ringable bells in cathedrals and churches in England, 182 in Wales, twenty in Scotland and sixteen in Northern Ireland. In the rest of the world there were only 149, 100 of them in Australia and the USA.

Not all bells are kept in church towers, though the vast majority are. Some are kept in campaniles, towers standing apart form the church. See, for example, Chester Cathedral; Chichester Cathedral, Sussex, St Davids Cathedral, Pembs; All Saints', Evesham, Worcs; St Mary's, Pembridge, Herefs; and St Michael and All Angels, Ledbury, Herefs. One ring, and perhaps it is the only one, at St Mary's, East Bergholt, Suffolk, is kept in a bell cage, a single-storey building set, like a campanile, apart from the church.

Bells are cast from bell-metal, an alloy composed of roughly 4:1 copper and tin. There are several sizes of rings, all tuned to a normal (diatonic) scale, or part of one. Some churches have three-, four- or five-bell rings, most churches have six or eight (a 'minor' or a 'major'), many have ten (a 'royal' ring), some twelve (a 'maximus'). Only one has fourteen (Winchester Cathedral, Hants) and one sixteen (St Martin's, The Bullring, Birmingham, W Mid. There is another ring of sixteen at Christ Church Cathedral, Dublin). Sometimes, extra semitone bells are added to a ring: they are occasionally used and are not counted in the size of the rings: for example, the ring of sixteen at Christ Church Cathedral, Dublin, has in fact nineteen bells.

The bells are hung from a frame in the belfry, at a high level in the tower, with louvred openings to let the sound out.

They are numbered from the lightest, the treble, to the heaviest, the tenor, so that an eight-bell ring is numbered 1 (the treble), 2, 3, 4, 5, 6, 7, 8 (the tenor). The bells are mounted on bearings and fixed to a wheel which allows them to be swung through 360°: a simple mechanism (the slider) prevents them turning the complete full circle. There is a clapper inside each bell which strikes the lip each time the bell is swung. Ropes attached to the wheels descend to bell-ringers (one for each bell) who stand in the ringing chamber, which is sometimes at ground level but more often one or two levels up. The leader of a band of ringers is called the Tower Captain.

When all the bells have rung once in their correct order, this is called a round. Everything else is called a change. A surprising number of different changes is possible. For an eight-bell ring, you can ring 40,320 changes without repetition. For a twelve-bell ring, 479,001,600 changes are possible, which would take over thirty years to ring. Any ring of five thousand or more changes is called a 'peal'. Anything less is a 'touch'. A full peal on an eight-bell ring (an 'extent') was rung at Taylor's Foundry campanile in Loughborough, Leics, on 27 July, 1963. It took the ringers just under eighteen hours.

Bell founders

There are only two bell foundries in the United Kingdom at present.

John Taylor & Co, Loughborough, Leics (fourteenth century – present). The largest bell foundry in the world. The Taylor family became involved in 1784 and the present site was established in 1839. The site contains its own ten-bell bell tower, its own carillon and its own museum. In 1881 Taylors cast the largest bell in the United Kingdom, Great Paul, for St Paul's Cathedral in London, weighing 36,960 lbs (sixteen and a half tons), and in 1940 Great George, at Liverpool Anglican Cathedral, Mersey, the second heaviest bell in the United Kingdom, weighing 32,480 lbs (fourteen and a half tons). In 2009 the company went into administration but was rescued by Bellfounders Holdings Ltd, a consortium of investors and people working in the bell industry. It re-opened later the same year.

Whitechapel Bell Foundry, London (?1420– present). The oldest manufacturing company of any kind in the United Kingdom. For a long time the firm bore the names or initials of its master founders, of whom Robert Chamberlain was the first in 1420. From 1574–1606 it was Robert Mot; from 1616–1700 the Bartlett family; from 1700–38 by Richard Phelps; from 1738–69 Thomas Lester; from 1769–81 William Chapman; from 1781–1865 the Mears family; from 1865–1904 Mears and Stainbank; from 1904 until the present day, the Hughes family. The name 'Whitechapel Bell Foundry' was adopted in 1968. In 1858 the firm cast Big Ben, the third largest bell in the United Kingdom, weighing 30,240 lbs (thirteen and a half tons).

Other bell founders

A substantial number of bells cast by the following founders still exist. The family history is in many cases very tangled.

Bagley family, from Chacombe, Northants (1605–1785). The firm was founded by Henry Bagley I (active 1630–83, died 1683). It was continued by his son (or nephew), Matthew Bagley I (1653–1716), who, with his own son, also Matthew, was killed by an explosion while re-casting a captured cannon. There was also James Bagley (fl. 1712), perhaps another son of Matthew's; William (born 1663), perhaps yet another son of Matthew's; and Matthew's brother (or cousin) Henry Bagley II (active 1679–1703, died perhaps 1703), who also ran a foundry at Ecton, Staffs, from about 1687 to 1703. They were followed by William Bagley (active 1687–1712); Henry Bagley III (active 1706–46), who also ran a foundry at Witney, Oxon; and Matthew Bagley III (active 1740–82, died 1785).

Bilbie family (1698–1814). Eminent family of West Country clockmakers and bell founders, based in Chew Stoke, Som, and later both at Chew Stoke and (in 1746) Cullompton, Devon. The firm was founded by Edward Bilbie I (1666–1724) and was continued by his children until his grandson, Thomas Castleman Bilbie (1769–?1813), who cast bells from 1781 to 1814, sold the business in (perhaps) 1815 to William Pannell. It was continued at Cullompton by Pannell and his son, Charles T Pannell, until the latter moved the firm to Exeter in 1850 (or maybe 1855).

John Briant, Hertford (1748–1829). Clockmaker and bell founder, active from 1790 to 1816. Most of his bells are in Hertfordshire and adjoining counties, though he did make bells for Devon, Kent, Montgomeryshire and Salop. He carried out a consultancy for Lincoln Cathedral (1827–8) at the age of seventy-nine. He sold his business to Thomas Mears (see Whitechapel Bell Foundry above) in 1825. He died in Marlborough Almshouses (though he was not poor and probably simply wanted comfort and privacy) in St Albans, Herts.

Eayre family, Kettering, Northants, and St Neots, Cambs (1710–84). Thomas Eayre I (1691–1757) was a clockmaker who set up a bell founding business in c.1710. His brother Joseph (1707–72) and son Thomas II (died 1768) went into partnership about 1717. Thomas II remained at Kettering: the Kettering foundry closed in 1762. Joseph moved to St Neots, Cambs, and cast bells there at least from 1735, and in 1770 took his cousin (or possibly nephew), Edward

Arnold, as partner. After Joseph's death the St Neots foundry was briefly held by Edward Arnold and Joseph's foreman, Thomas Osborn: they cast their first bells in 1784. When they dissolved their partnership, Osborn moved to Leicester and Arnold stayed in St Neots until 1784, when he moved to Leicester.

Gillett and Johnston, Croydon, London (1844–1958). William Gillett founded his clockmaking firm in 1844 and took Charles Bland as partner in about 1854 and Arthur Johnston in 1877. At the end of the 1870s the firm added bell founding to clockmaking and cast bells for distribution all over the world. In 1958 the bell founding business was sold and the bell foundry was demolished in 1997. The clockmaking and bell-hanging business still survives.

Lester and Pack. See Whitechapel Bell Foundry.

Llewellins and James, Bristol (1832–1972). In 1832 Peter Llewellin took over a small foundry and machinists business. It became Llewellins and James in 1850. It was not until 1874 that the firm started bell-founding, though they had been involved with bellhanging before that, and other foundries had cast bells with the name of Llewellins & James on them. At its peak, bell-founding contributed only 25% of the firm's turnover. Business curtailed dramatically in the 1930s, and their last bell was cast in 1940. They were taken over by Braby Ltd in 1972.

Mears and Mears and Stainbank. See Whitechapel Bell Foundry.

Norris family, Stamford, Lincs (1575–1708). Matthew Norris, a bell founder originating in Leicester (fl. 1575–97), probably started the foundry in Stamford. His second son, Tobias (or Tobie) Norris I (1585–1626), was casting bells from at least 1606 until his death. Tobias's son, Thomas (fl. 1629–76), expanded the business, possibly with the co-operation of his brother, another Tobias. Thomas's son, Tobias II (1634–99) was the last Norris to run the business. Tobias II was succeeded by Alexander Rigby, perhaps Tobias II's foreman, who died in 1708, when the foundry closed. Most of their bells are in Lincolnshire and other eastern counties, but they extend to Warwickshire and Leicestershire.

Thomas Osborn, Downham Market, Norfolk (1779–1832). Thomas Osborn (1743–1806) was a foreman and later partner to Thomas Eayre, bell-founder of St Neots, and his successor, Edward Arnold, and in 1779 started casting bells on his own account. He was joined by his grandson, William (1779–1842), in the 1790s. William succeeded Thomas in 1806. William sold the foundry and the business to Thomas Mears (see Whitechapel Bell Foundry above) on his retirement in 1832.

Rudhalls, Gloucester (1684–1835). Abraham Rudhall (1657–1736) founded the firm in 1684, and the business was continued by his eldest son, also called Abraham (1680–1735), Abraham's son Abel (1714–60), and three of Abel's sons, Thomas (?1740–83), Charles (1746–1815) and John (1760–1835). John Rudhall was declared bankrupt in 1815. The business formally closed in 1828 and was bought by Mears and Stainbank (see Whitechapel Bell Foundry above) in 1830. They kept John on as a manager and bells bearing John's name were made until his death in 1835. The business continued until 1848, when all the equipment was transferred to London.

Joseph Smith, Edgbaston, Birmingham, W Mid (before 1701 to 1736). Operated in the Midlands. He cast his first bells at Handsworth, Staffs and his last at Pershore, Worcs in 1735. Ninety-three currently survive.

John Warner and Sons, Cripplegate, London (1788–c.1924). The business was founded in 1739 (or maybe 1763) in Cripplegate,

London, but did not begin making bells until 1788. There were also foundries in at Tendring, Essex and at Stockton-on-Tees, Durham, where the original Big Ben (of 1856, not the present one by Mears of 1858) was cast. The firm remained in the same family until at least 1896. The firm was finally closed, not having made bells for some twenty years, in 1949.

Hugh Watts, Leicester. (c.1583–1643). Son of the bell founder Francis Watts (died 1600) and father of Hugh (died 1656) and Francis, also bell founders. He became mayor of Leicester in 1634 (and, as alderman, contributed to a 'gift' of £500 to Prince Rupert who had demanded £2,000, in 1638). He cast bells from 1600 to his death, mostly in Leicestershire, where there are still nearly two hundred. His bells are sometimes known as 'Watts's Nazarenes' from the inscription 'IHS Nazarenvs rex ivdeorvm' ('Jesus of Nazareth king of the Jews') which he often commonly used.

The ten heaviest church bells

None of these bells is hung for change ringing.
1 Great Paul, St Paul's Cathedral, London. 37,483 lbs, in the south-west tower, cast by Taylor, 1881.
2 Great George, Liverpool Anglican Cathedral, Mersey, 33,098 lbs, cast by Whitechapel in 1940, installation completed 1951.
3 Great Peter, York Minster, 24,270 lbs, cast by Taylor in 1927.
4 Hosanna, Buckfast Abbey, Devon. 16,706 lbs, cast by Taylor 1936.
5 Great John, Beverley Minster, E Yorks. 15,765 lbs, cast by Taylor, 1901.
6 Major, Newcastle Cathedral, Tyne & W. 13,272 lbs, cast by Taylor, 1891.
7 Great Tom, Lincoln Cathedral. 12,096 lbs, cast by Thomas Mears (Whitechapel), 1835.
8 Great Bede, Downside Abbey, Stratton-on-the-Fosse, Bath, Som. 11,956 lbs, cast by Taylor, 1900.
9 Great Tom, St Paul's Cathedral, London. 11,474 lbs, cast by Richard Phelps, 1716.
10 Gregory John, Ampleforth Abbey, N Yorks, 10,368 lbs, cast by Mears and Stainbank, 1961.

Largest bell in the world hung for change ringing

Great Emmanuel, the tenor, Liverpool Anglican Cathedral, Mersey, 9,195 lbs, cast by Mears and Stainbank (Whitechapel) in 1939.

The heaviest rings

The weights of these rings, and the weight of St Christopher's, Warden Hill, Cheltenham, Glos, are taken from Dove's *Guide for Church Ringers*, converted into pounds.

Heaviest rings of twelve: Liverpool Anglican Cathedral, Mersey (9,195 lbs; not only the heaviest ring of twelve in the world but also the highest, at 220 ft above ground level); Exeter Cathedral, Devon (8,122 lbs); St Paul's Cathedral, London (6,900 lbs); York Minster (6,659 lbs).

Heaviest rings of ten: Wells Cathedral, Som. Its ring of ten is the heaviest in the world (6,314 lbs); All Saints' Episcopal Church, Inverary, Argyll and Bute; (4,656 lbs, second heaviest in the world), Beverley Minster, E Yorks (4,640 lbs); St Giles's Cathedral, Edinburgh (4,635 lbs)

Heaviest rings of eight: Sherborne Abbey, Dorset (5,157 lbs); All Saints', Westbury, Wilts (3,934 lbs); St Andrew's, Congresbury, Som (3,812 lbs).

Heaviest rings of six: St Buryan's, St Buryan, Cornwall (4,209 lbs); St Barnabas's, Queen Camel, Som (4,123 lbs); St George's, Brailes, Warwicks (3,267 lbs); Holy Angels, Hoar Cross, Staffs (3,181 lbs).

Heaviest rings of five: All Saints', East Pennard, Som (2,781 lbs); St Mary's, Leighton Bromswold, Cambs (2,383 lbs); St Peter's, Mancetter, Warwicks (2,295 lbs); St Mary's, Hickling, Norfolk (2,295 lbs). St Mary's, East Bergholt, Suffolk, at 2,920 lbs, is heavier than All Saints', East Pennard, but the bells are rung by hand, not by rope, and live in a bell cage because the tower was never built.

The lightest ring of bells in a church
The ring of six at St Christopher's, Warden Hill, Cheltenham, Glos, weighing 63 lbs.

The Jubilee Ring
A ring of eight, cast by the Whitechapel Bell Foundry in 2012, rung at the Queen's Diamond Jubilee Pageant from a floating belfry on a boat by eight ringers from The Ancient Society of College Youths. (The Society is the oldest bell-ringing association in the country, founded in 1637, and provides ringers for Westminster Abbey and St Paul's Cathedral). Elizabeth, the tenor bell, weighs 1,120 lbs. They are now hung in St James Garlickhythe, London.

Statues and symbols of Matthew, Mark, Luke and John, designed by Nicholas Hawksmoor, c.1725, Beverley Minster, E Yorks

SYMBOLS OF THE APOSTLES

Thirteen apostles are listed, St Matthias replacing Judas Iscariot. All except two (or perhaps three) were martyred. St John died in his bed, and so perhaps did St Matthew, and Judas Iscariot committed suicide. The symbols of all of them except St John allude to the manner of their deaths.

St Andrew. X-shaped cross. Crucified.
St Bartholomew. Flaying knives. Flayed? Beheaded? Crucified upside down?
St James the Great. Scallop shell, pilgrim's hat. Stabbed to death.
St James the Less. A saw or a club. Thrown from the Temple in Jerusalem, but the fall failed to kill him. Stoned and sawn in two? Clubbed to death?
St John. Eagle, serpent, cup, book. Not martyred.
Judas Iscariot. Rope, thirty pieces of silver. Hung himself.
St Jude (St Thaddeus, St Lebbaeus). Ship, letter, club, book. Clubbed to death.
St Matthew. Money bags, book. Stabbed to death? Speared to death? Died of old age?
St Matthias. Axe. Stoned and beheaded.
St Peter. Inverted cross, crossed keys. Crucified upside down.
St Philip. Loaves of bread. Crucified.
St Simon. Fish, boat, saw, lance. Crucified? Head sawn off?
St Thomas. Carpenter's set square, spear. Speared to death.

CALENDAR AND COLOURS

The church calendar sometimes causes bewilderment, and rightly so, since it is a mixture of the solar calendar, based on 365 days to a year, and the lunar calendar, based on roughly 354 days to the year. The solar calendar gives the fixed feasts, such as All Souls' Day, always on 2 November, Christmas Day, always on 25 December, and the saints' days: there are from ten to twenty saints for every day of the year. The lunar calendar gives the liturgical seasons and some feast days, all of them calculated from the date Easter Day falls for the current year. The date of Easter Day may vary from anywhere between 22 March to 25 April.

The liturgical year contains several seasons, which are listed below, and it begins with the season of Advent. The seasons account for roughly half of the year. The remaining time is called 'ordinary time', though ordinary time, like the seasons, is punctuated by feasts.

The colour of the altar cloth and the priest's vestments change according to the liturgical season. Not all churches observe all of these colours. Which to observe, if any, may even be solely up to the parish priest. In the western church, full observance is often a mark of Anglican High Church or Roman Catholicism.

Although there is general agreement on the colours, there are often alternatives. A few of the principal alternatives are listed here. In addition, whatever the season, the colour changes for a christening (white), confirmation (red), a wedding (white), and a funeral (purple, black, white or gold).

Advent. The period of preparation for the birth of Christ. Advent Sunday falls on the fourth Sunday before Christmas Day and the following Sundays are called the second, third (Gaudete Sunday: Rose) and fourth Sundays in Advent. Purple or Blue.

Immaculate Conception. Celebrates the conception of the Virgin Mary,. 8 December. White.

Christmas, Christmastide. Starts on Christmas Day and finishes on Twelfth Night (the night of 5/6 January). White.

Christmas Day. Christ's birthday. 25 December.

Innocents' Day, Holy Innocents' Day, Childermas. Commemorates Herod's killing all the new-born babies in Bethlehem and its neighbourhood (Matthew 2.16–18). 28 December.

Epiphany season. A continuation of Christmastide, which starts on 6 January, or sometimes the nearest Sunday to it, and finishes on Candlemas. White.

Epiphany. Celebrates the coming of the Magi to Bethlehem to honour the infant Christ, and thus the manifestation of Christ to the Gentiles. Also, Christ's baptism in the River Jordan. 6 January.

Candlemas. Celebrates Mary's ritual purification forty days after the birth of

Jesus (Luke 2.22); the ritual presentation of Jesus to God in the temple in Jerusalem on the same day (Luke 2.22–39); and the day when the all church's candles are blessed. 2 February, forty days after 25 December.
Ordinary time. Green.
Shrove Tuesday, Mardi Gras. The day before Ash Wednesday. Forty-seven days before Easter Day.
Lent. A period of fasting, penitence and self-denial, for forty days from Ash Wednesday to either Maundy Thursday or Easter Sunday. (Sundays during Lent are often excluded from the calculation). It thus excludes Passiontide. Purple or, in the Anglican church, Lenten Array (unbleached linen).
Ash Wednesday. The first day of Lent.
Quadragesima Sunday. The first Sunday in Lent ('quadragesima' = fortieth).
Mothering Sunday. Holiday when everybody – even servants – visited their mother church. Mother's Day, a twentieth century invention honouring mothers, was placed on the same day, causing no end of confusion. Also called Laetare Sunday. Fourth Sunday in Lent. Sometimes Rose.
Passiontide. The two weeks from Passion Sunday till Holy Saturday.
Feast of the Annunciation, Lady Day. When Mary learned that she was to bear Christ. (Luke 1.26–38) 25 March. White.
Passion Sunday or First Sunday of the Passion. Passiontide begins. Fifth Sunday in Lent. Red.
Holy Week. The last week in Lent, from Palm Sunday to Holy Saturday. Holy Week thus includes Palm Sunday, Maundy Thursday, Good Friday and Holy Saturday.
Palm Sunday. Celebrates Christ's triumphal entry into Jerusalem. The Sunday before Easter Day. Red.

Maundy Thursday, Holy Thursday. The day before Good Friday: to some, the last day of Lent. White.
Good Friday. Christ's crucifixion. The Friday before Easter Day. Red or Black.
Holy Saturday. The Saturday between Good Friday and Easter Day. Purple.
Easter, Eastertide. The period of fifty days from Easter Day until Pentecost. White.
Easter Day. Christ's resurrection. Held on the first Sunday following the full moon after the spring equinox, which is said to be 21 March (even when it is really 20 March). Easter Day is a moveable feast from which all other moveable feasts are calculated.
Ascension Day, Ascension Thursday, Holy Thursday. Commemorates Christ's ascension into heaven. Forty days after Easter Day, usually celebrated on a Thursday, though often celebrated on the following Sunday.
Pentecost, Whit Sunday. Commemorates the Holy Spirit descending on the first Christians – the eleven apostles and some 110 followers – and giving them the power to 'speak with other tongues'. Fifty days after Easter Sunday. Red.
Ordinary time. Green.
Trinity Sunday. Celebrates the Holy Trinity. The first Sunday after Pentecost. White.
Corpus Christi. Celebrates the presence of Christ in the Eucharist. The Thursday after Trinity Sunday. White.
Lammas Day, Feast of St Peter in Chains. To celebrate the wheat harvest, the first of the harvest festivals. 1 August. White.
Assumption. Commemorates the assumption of the Virgin Mary into heaven. 15 August. White or gold.
All Saints' Day. 1 November. White.
All Souls' Day. 2 November. Purple or black.

CROSSES

The cross was not used as a Christian symbol until sometime in the second century. Earlier symbols were the anchor, the ichthys (the fish) and the chi-rho ('CH' and 'R' in the Greek alphabet). However, by the very early third century the cross had begun to acquire the significance which it has never since lost. Several of the crosses described below, such as the ankh and the swastika, were religious symbols long before the Christian era.

Ankh. A 'T' with a circle or oval above it.
Archiepiscopal, patriarchal. A cross with two crossbars, the lower one longer than the upper.
Canterbury cross. A square cross with its arms widening to a hammer at the outside ends. Each arm has a triangular panel inscribed and there is a small square panel in the centre of the cross.
Celtic cross. A Latin cross with a circle enclosing the intersection of upright and crossbar.
Cross anchor. An anchor in which the upper part forms a cross.
Cross crosslet. Four crosses arranged at right angles.
Crucifix. A cross with Christ's body on it.
Crux ansata. See ankh.

Empty cross. A cross without the body of Christ.
Greek cross. Cross with arms of equal length.
Latin cross. Cross with a longer descender to the upright.
Maltese cross. A cross with four arms the same length, and tapering towards the middle. Sometimes the end of each arm is flared.
Papal cross. Cross with three crossbars, each longer that the one above
Patriarchal. See Archiepiscopal.
Russian cross, Slavic cross, suppedaneum cross. Cross with three crossbars, the lowest one sloping.
St Andrew's. An X-shaped cross, a saltire: the cross on which St Andrew was said to have been crucified.
St Anthony's Cross, tau. A 'T'-shaped cross: the cross on which St Anthony was said to have been crucified.
St Peter's cross. An inverted Latin cross: the cross on which St Peter was said to have been crucified.
Swastika, hook cross, hakenkreuz. Greek cross with the ends of its arms bent at right angles.
Triumphal cross, Christus rex cross. Cross with a figure of Christ the King on it.

FIVE PAGAN SYMBOLS?

Many pagan images have been pressed into the service of Christianity, and this is what these five items feel like, though the origin and meaning of all of them has been, and is still being, disputed. Two of them – the green man and the wodehouse – are quite common in churches and cathedrals, and the other three are quite rare: in fact in the UK there is only one mediaeval example of a sciapod in existence in a church.

The Green Man is by far the most common. It is the name given to a face almost hidden by leaves, growing out of his mouth, nose, ears, eyes or all of them. He appears in many, perhaps most, mediaeval cathedrals and churches, and is seen in many nineteenth century restorations. He can be quite hard to spot. He was named the Green Man as recently as 1939, by Lady Raglan, in an article in *The Folklore Journal*. He did not appear in churches until the end of the eleventh century, but he had a long history beforehand, Europe-wide. Good examples from each century are: Canterbury Cathedral, Kent (end of the eleventh century, pillar capitals in the crypt, and also, c.1350, roof bosses in the Black Prince's chantry); St Mary and St David's, Kilpeck, Herefs (mid twelfth century, doorway); Wells Cathedral, Som (thirteenth century, roof bosses in the undercroft, and also in the Chapter House); Rochester Cathedral, Kent (mid fourteenth century, on four ceiling bosses above the crossing); St Laurence's, Ludlow, Salop (fourteenth or fifteenth century, misericord); Rosslyn Chapel, Roslin, Midlothian (fifteenth century, more than a hundred examples all over the chapel); Holy Ghost, Crowcombe, Som (sixteenth century, bench-end); All Saints', Daresbury, Ches (seventeenth century, on the rood screen behind the altar); Tewkesbury Abbey, Glos (1734, the Gage gates).

The wodehouse or wodewose is quite common. A wild man of the woods, hairy all over except his face, hands, elbows, knees and feet. The hair is sometimes green and he sometimes carries a club. Some say he is friendly. St Bartholomew's, Orford, Suffolk (fifteenth century, on the font); St Andrew's, Kettleburgh, Suffolk (fifteenth century, on a bench-end); St Michael's, Peasenhall, Suffolk (fifteenth century, above the entrance); St Helen's, Norwich, Norfolk (late fifteenth century, on a roof boss); St Mary's, Burwell, Cambs (fifteenth century, in the porch); All Saints', East Budleigh, Devon (sixteenth century, on a bench-end); St John's, Aldbury, Herts (on the tomb of Sir Robert Whittingham, killed 1471).

The Three Hares is a circular design showing three hares chasing one another, in a clockwise or anticlockwise direction. Their ears meet in a triangle so that each hare apparently has two ears, but only three are actually shown. The meaning is, of course, disputed. The hare in said to represent virginity (it was thought that the hare was hermaphroditic), the Trinity, or (though this is now doubted) the emblem of Devon tin-miners (the 'tinners' rabbits'). This motif, which is frequently found in association with green men, is especially common in Devon, where about thirty examples are known from the roof bosses in churches. See St Pancras's, Widecombe-in-the-Moor; St Eustachius's, Tavistock; St Michael's, Chagford; St Michael's, Spreyton (1451). Other examples can be found in roof bosses in St Hubert's, Corfe Mullen, Dorset (wooden); Cotehele Chapel, Calstock, Cornwall (wooden, late 1480s), Selby Abbey, N Yorks (wooden); St Davids Cathedral, Pembs (Lady Chapel, stone); and St Aidan's, Llawhaden, Pembs. In Holy Trinity, Long Melford, Suffolk the design appears in a medieval stained glass window (above the north door) and in Chester Cathedral, Ches, it appears in a floor tile, excavated from the nave (c.1400). The design is not uncommon in France, Germany and Switzerland, and has been found as far away as China (Buddhist cave paintings, sixth to ninth centuries, at Duhuang), Iran (a coin, 1281–2, at Urmiya), and Russia (a casket, late thirteenth or early fourteenth century, now in Trier Cathedral, Rheinland-Pfalz, Germany).

The number of sheela na gigs is not known, because they were almost always placed in an exposed position on the outside of a church, are often badly weathered and so may have become undecipherable. There may be some four or five dozen in Britain and about a hundred in Ireland. The sheela na gig is a primitive sculpture of a grinning, squatting woman with her legs wide apart, displaying a huge vulva. The name dates from 1840; it is evidently Irish, though the meaning is disputed. The British examples seem to date from the twelfth century, many are badly worn, and many have been moved at some time in the past. The best known is the sheela na gig at St Mary and St David's, Kilpeck, Herefs (on a chancel corbel on the south side). Salop has five or possibly six, at St Laurence's, Church Stretton (above the Norman door on the north side), St Catherine's, Tugford (two, above the main entrance), Holy Trinity, Holdgate (on the south outside wall of the chancel), St Mary's, Cleobury Mortimer (in the churchyard retaining wall), and, dubiously, at St Peter's, Diddlebury (on a corbel). There are others as far north as Iona (on the south wall of the ruined nunnery), as far south as St Nicholas's, Studland, Dorset (on a corbel), as far west as St Seiriol's, Penmon, Anglesey (inside south transept) and as far east as St Mary's, Wroxham, Norfolk (on the doorway).

The sciapod is the rarest. A dwarfish creature with one leg and a huge foot, with which it used to shelter itself from the sun when lying down during the heat of the day. It is (perhaps) first mentioned by Aristophanes in *The Birds* (414 BC). Although there is only one mediaeval example in a church, on a bench-end in St Mary's, Dennington, Suffolk, there is an early twentieth century example on a bench-end in All Saints', Hollesley, Suffolk.

Three hares, late fifteenth century, St Pancras's, Widecombe-in-the-Moor, Devon

Sheela na gig, c.1140, St Mary and St David's, Kilpeck, Herefs

Wodewose, fifteenth century, St Mary's, Cratfield, Suffolk

Sciapod carved on a fifteenth century bench end at St Mary's, Dennington, Suffolk

Green man, c.1140, St Mary and St David's, Kilpeck, Herefs

Green man, nineteenth century, St Nicholas and St Cyriac's, South Pool, Devon

LARGEST, SMALLEST, TALLEST, SHORTEST

Largest Anglican cathedral
Liverpool Anglican Cathedral, Mersey, which has a floor area of 104,270 sq ft (9,687 sq m). A long way second is St Paul's Cathedral, London, at 84,562 sq ft (7,8756 sq m). The largest Gothic cathedral in the United Kingdom is York Minster.

Largest Anglican parish churches
Which is the largest parish church by floor area is arguable. The Guinness Book of Records gives Holy Trinity, Hull, E Yorks, at 20,056 sq ft (1,863 sq m). But St Botolph's, Boston, Lincs (which is also the widest), claims a floor area of 20,070 sq ft (1,864 sq m), and St Nicholas's, Great Yarmouth, Norfolk, even more, at 23,265 sq ft (2,161 sq m).

Smallest Anglican cathedral
The smallest cathedral in the United Kingdom is the Cathedral of the Isles, Millport, Cumbrae, Argyll and Bute. The smallest in England is Derby Cathedral (though the smallest pre-Reformation cathedral is Christ Church Cathedral, Oxford). The smallest cathedral in Wales is St Asaph Cathedral, Den.

Smallest Anglican churches
The smallest church in the United Kingdom is St Gobban's, Portbradden, Co Antrim, which measures 8' by 4'. The smallest church in England is Bremilham Church, on a farm at Foxley-cum-Bremilham near Malmesbury, Wilts, which measures 110 sq ft (11' by 10'). It was built about 1850, and is used only on Rogation Sunday. St Trillo's Chapel, Rhos on Sea, Conwy (seventeenth century), which holds weekly services, has a floor area of 142 sq ft (13' by 10'6"). St Andrew's old church, Upleatham, N Yorks (? twelfth century) has a floor area of 241 sq ft (17'6" x 13'9") and is ruinous. The smallest church still holding regular services is Culbone Church near Porlock Weir, Som (twelfth century). Its floor area is 403 sq ft (chancel, 13'6" by 10', nave 21'6" by 12'4).

Tallest
The fifteen tallest churches in the UK, measured to the top of the spire, dome or tower, are:
1 Salisbury Cathedral 404 ft (123.1m)
2 St Paul's Cathedral 366 ft (111.3m)
3 Liverpool Anglican Cathedral 331 ft (101m)
4 Norwich Cathedral 315 ft (96m)
5 St Walburge's, Preston, Lancs 309 ft (94.1m)
6 St Mary's Cathedral, Edinburgh 300 ft (90m)
7 St James's, Louth, Lincs (after repairs in 1844) 295 ft (89.9m)
8 St Mary Redcliffe's, Bristol 292 ft (89.3m)
9= Liverpool Metropolitan Cathedral, Mersey 85 ft (87m)

Largest cloisters: c.1270, Salisbury Cathedral, Wilts

9= Westminster Cathedral, London 285 ft (87m)
11= St Wulfram's, Grantham, Lincs 282 ft (86.2m)
11= St Elphin's, Warrington, Ches 282 ft (86.2m)
13 St Mary Abbots, Kensington, London 279 ft (89m)
14 Chichester Cathedral, Sussex 277 ft (84.5m)
15= Lincoln Cathedral 272 ft (83m)
15= St Botolph's, Boston, Lincs 272 ft (83m).

Longest
Liverpool Anglican Cathedral, Mersey, at 620 ft (189 m). It is also the second longest in the world. The longest mediaeval cathedral in the world is Winchester Cathedral, Hants, at 558 ft (170.1 m).

Three spires
Three cathedrals have three spires: Lichfield Cathedral, Staffs, Truro Cathedral, Cornwall and St Mary's Cathedral, Edinburgh.

Four transepts
Four cathedrals have four transepts: Canterbury, Kent; Lincoln; Salisbury, Wilts; and Worcester. Beverley Minster, E Yorks, also has four transepts.

Largest cloisters
Salisbury Cathedral, Wilts.

Largest cathedral close
This is also Salisbury Cathedral's, extending over some 80 acres.

Oldest church crypt
Ripon Cathedral's, N Yorks, dating from about 672.

First iron church
St George's, Everton, Mersey, designed by Thomas Rickman and consecrated in 1814. Although the outer skin is local sandstone, the skeleton and interior are of cast iron.

Oldest pulpit
St Thomas's, Mellor, Manchester, dating from c.1330–50. It is octagonal in shape and said to have been carved out a single block of wood.

Oldest lecterns
The oldest dates from about 1180. It was found in the ruins of Much Wenlock Priory, Salop, and is made of sandstone ('Much Wenlock marble'). It is now in the Victoria and Albert Museum. Two ancient stone lecterns are still in churches, though not the churches they were built for. They are both from about 1200. One is now in St James's, Norton, Worcs and was in Evesham Abbey, Worcs, and the other is now in St John the Baptist's, Crowle, Worcs, and was in Pershore Abbey, Worcs.

Oldest church door
is said to be in St Botolph's, Hadstock, Essex. It dates from about 1060.

Oldest bells
St Lawrence's, Ipswich, Suffolk, now used as a community centre and restaurant, has the oldest set of bells in the world. They are a ring of five, the first four cast in about 1450 and the fifth about 1480. The next oldest, also a set of five, are in St Bartholomew the Great's, West Smithfield, London, cast by Thomas Bulliston and date from about 1510. The oldest individual bell hung for change ringing and still in regular use is thought to be the fifth bell at St Dunstan's, Canterbury, Kent. It was cast in about 1325.

COUNTY ABBREVIATIONS

Anglesey	Anglesey	Leics	Leicestershire
Beds	Bedfordshire	Lincs	Lincolnshire
Berks	Berkshire	London	Greater London
Bristol	Bristol	Manchester	Greater Manchester
Bucks	Buckinghamshire	Mersey	Merseyside
Cambs	Cambridgeshire	Mon	Monmouthsire
Carms	Carmarthanshire	Norfolk	Norfolk
Ches	Cheshire	Northants	Northamptonshire
Conwy	Conwy	Northumb	Northumberland
Cornwall	Cornwall	Notts	Nottinghamshire
Cumb	Cumbria	Oxon	Oxfordshire
Den	Denbighshire	Pembs	Pembrokeshire
Derbys	Derbyshire	Powys	Powys
Devon	Devonshire	Rut	Rutland
Dorset	Dorset	Salop	Shropshire
Durham	County Durham	Som	Somerset
Essex	Essex	Staffs	Staffordshire
Flint	Flintshire	Suffolk	Suffolk
Glam	Glamorganshire*	Surrey	Surrey
Glos	Gloucestershire	Sussex	Sussex
Gwynedd	Gwynedd	Tyne & W	Tyne & Wear
Hants	Hampshire	Warwicks	Warwickshire
Herefs	Herefordshire	W Mid	West Midlands
Herts	Hertfordshire	Wilts	Wiltshire
IoM	Isle of Man	Worcs	Worcestershire
IoW	Isle of Wight	Wrexham	Wrexham
Kent	Kent	Yorks	Yorkshire
Lancs	Lancashire		

*Includes Blaenau Gwent, Bridgend, Caerphilly, Cardiff, Merthyr Tydfil, Neath Port Talbot, Newport, Rhondda Cynon Taff, Swansea, Torfaen and Vale of Glamorgan. In Scotland and Northern Island county names are given in full.

STYLES AND PERIODS

Dates vary slightly from one style list to another. Sometimes the names vary too: some of the most common alternatives are given here.

Saxon	600-1066
Norman, Romanesque	1066-1200
Early English, First Pointed	1170-1300
Decorated, Second Pointed, Curvilinear	1270-1350
Perpendicular, Third Pointed, Rectilinear	1350-1540
Late Perpendicular, Tudor	1485-1600
Renaissance	1485-1690
Elizabethan	1560-1600
Jacobean	1600-1645
Commonwealth	1645-1660
Baroque	1660-1720
Queen Anne, Georgian	1700-1770
Neo-classical, Greek revival	1750-1840
Neo-Gothic, Gothic revival	1750-1900
Italianate	1805-1850
Neo-Romanesque, neo-Norman	1820-1850
Jacobethan	1835-1885
Neo-Tudor, Black-and-white revival	1870-1920
Arts and Crafts, Art Nouveau	1880-1920
Tudorbethan	1880-1920
Neo-Byzantine	1880-1920

SHORT BIBLIOGRAPHY

The bibliography on cathedrals and churches is enormous and increasing every year. Added to this are the resources online: practically every church has a website, and there is a website covering, or touching on, almost everything in this book. This booklist is therefore highly selective and most of the books are readily available.

General
Fewins, Clive, *The church explorer's handbook,* Canterbury Press, 2005.
Friar, Stephen, *The Sutton companion to churches*, Sutton Publishing, 2003.
Friar, Stephen, *The companion to cathedrals and abbeys*, The History Press, 2010.
Harbison, Robert, *Daily Telegraph Guide to England's parish churches*, Aurum, 2006.
Jenkins, Simon, *England's thousand best churches*, Allen Lane, 1999.
Taylor, Richard, *How to read a church*, Rider, 2003.

The rise and fall of church buildings
Cooper, Trevor (ed), *The Journal of William Dowsing*, Boydell and Brewer, 2001.
National Churches Trust, *The National Churches Trust Survey*, 2011.
Port, M H, *600 new churches: the Church Building Commission 1818-1856*, Spire Books, 2006.
Woodward, W E O, with additions by John McIlwain and Brian Williams, *The dissolution of the monasteries*, Pitkin Publishing, 2012.

The cathedrals
Fitchen, John, *The construction of Gothic cathedrals*, University of Chicago, 1981.
Hislop, Malcolm, *How to build a cathedral,* Bloomsbury, 2012.

Church buildings
Curl, James Stevens, *Oxford dictionary of architecture and landscape architecture*, Oxford, 2000.
Child, Mark, *Discovering church architecture,* Shire Publications, 1976.
Hislop, Malcolm, *Medieval masons*, Shire Publications, 2010.
Sladen, Teresa and Saint, Andrew (eds), *Churches 1870-1914*, Victorian Society, 2011.
Websites:
www.britishlisted buildings.co.uk, which lists all listed buildings in England, Scotland and Wales. Listed buildings in England and Scotland are also available on www.english-heritage.org.uk and www.historic-scotland.gov.uk respectively.
www.doeni.gov.ukwhich lists the listed buildings in Northern Ireland.

Architects and master craftsmen
Brodie, Antonia, and others (eds), *Directory of British architects, 1834-1914*, Continuum, 2001.
Colvin, Howard, *A biographical dictionary of British architects*, Yale, 1995.
Harvey, John, *English mediaeval architects,* Alan Sutton, 1984.
Harvey, John, *Henry Yevele*, Batsford, 1944.
Websites:
www.scottisharchitects.org.uk. which gives biographies of Scottish architects with lists of their works.
www.dia.ie, which does the same for Irish architects.
www.newulsterbiography.co.uk, which gives biographies of eminent Ulster people.

Church furnishings
Badham, Sally, *Medieval church and churchyard monuments,* Shire Publications, 2011.
Badham, Sally, with Martin Stuchfield, *Monumental brasses,* Shire Publications, 2009.
Hayman, Richard, *Misericords and bench ends*, Shire Publications, 2011.
NADFAS, *Inside churches: a guide to church furnishings*, Capability Publishing, 2001.
Rosewell, Roger, *Medieval wallpaintings in English and Welsh churches*, The Boydell Press, 2008.
Rouse, E Clive, *Medieval wall paintings*, Shire Publications, 2004.

Stained glass
Archer, Michael, ed Ann Lockhart, *Stained glass*, Pitkin, 1994.
Cowen, Painton, *English stained glass,* Thames and Hudson, 2008.
Websites:
www.stainedglassrecords.org.uk, which records (at the moment) church stained glass in Beds, Berks, Greater London, Hants, Herts, Kent Surrey, Sussex and Wilts.
www.stainedglass.llgc.org.uk, which records church stained glass in Wales.
www.cvma.ac.uk, which records mediaeval stained glass in the UK.

Floor tiles
Beaulah, Kenneth, and Hans van Lemmen, *Church tiles of the nineteenth century*, Shire Publications, 2001.
Lemmen, Hans van, *Medieval tiles*, Shire Publications, 2008.

Scratchdials and sundials
Daniel, Christopher St J H, *Sundials*, Shire Publications, 2000.

Church clocks
Beeson, C F C, *English church clocks, 1280-1850*, Antiquarian Horological Society, 1971.
Rock, Hugh, *Church clocks*, Shire Publications, 2008.

Churchyards
Badham, Sally, *Medieval church and churchyard monuments,* Shire Publications, 2011.
Child, Mark, *Discovering churchyards*, Shire Publications, 1989.
Delaney, Fred, ed Ian Godfrey, *Who's buried where?* Abson Books, 2010.

Music and singing
Brett, Vivien, *Cathedral music,* Pitkin, 2003.
Temperley, Nicholas, *Music in the English parish church,* CUP, 1979.

The organ
Baker, David, *The Organ,* Shire Publications, 2011.
Bicknell, Stephen, *History of the English organ,* Cambridge, 1996.

Bells
Camp, John, *Discovering bells and bellringing,* Shire Publications, 1997.
Dove, R H, *A bellringer's guide to the church bells of Britain,* 9th edn, 2000.

Five pagan symbols?
Harte, Jeremy, *The Green Man,* Pitkin, 2001.
Websites:
www.shellanagig.org.uk.
www.chrischapmanphotography.co.uk/hares. The three hares.

MAIN INDEX

A
Abbey 50
Act of Annexation 3
Advent 186
Aesthetic Movement 116
Africa 123
Albert Memorial, Kensington, London 74
All Souls College, Oxford 67, 118
Almery 20
Alms box 85, 99
Alms dish 136
Altar 1, 3, 20, 25, 26, 32, 37, 38, 43, 69, 79, 82, 85, 87, 93, 100, 136, 137
Altar bell 136, 137, 179
Altar cross 136, 137
Altar frontal 85, 106
Altar rails 85, 87
Altar stone 85, 86, 99
Altar tomb 150, 160
Ambulatory 20
Ancient Society of College Youths 184
Angel roof 20, 21, 32, 38
Angle 1
Angle buttress 24, 25
Anglican 4, 5, 6, 8, 9, 11, 13, 71, 136, 137, 186, 187, 193
Anglo-Saxon 32, 85, 139, 156
Ankh 188
An Túr Gloine 113, 117, 123
Apostles 185, 187
Apostolic Exarchate for Ukrainians 8
Apse 20
Arcade 20, 25, 26, 38, 43, 46
Archbishop of Canterbury 6
Archbishop of Westminster 8

Archbishop of York 6
Archdeacon 6, 7
Archdeaconry 6, 7, 8
Arches 20, 25, 31, 32, 37, 43, 49, 68
Area dean 7
Arles, Council of 1
Arts and Crafts 68, 70, 113, 114, 115, 116, 117, 118, 124, 125, 129
Aspergillum 136, 137
Aspersorium 136
Assistant Bishop 6
Astronomical clock 142
Augustinians 52
Aumbry 20, 23, 88
Austin Friars 52
Australia 58, 71, 74, 115, 116, 123, 130, 167, 180
Axial tower 20

B
Baldacchino 69, 85
Bale tomb 150, 160
Band 93, 162
Baptismal shell 136
Baptistery 20, 128
Baptists 9
Baptist Union 9
Bargeboard 20
Baroque 53, 62, 65, 67, 83
Barrel roof 25, 49
Barrel tomb 150, 160
Barrel vault 49
Bar tracery 20, 44
Basilica 25
Bay 25

Belfry 25, 43, 180, 184
Belgium 94, 117
Bell cage 180, 184
Bell-cote 25
Bell flèche 25, 31
Bell founder 180, 181, 182, 183
Bellfounders Holdings Ltd 181
Bell-gable 25
Bell Harry tower 54, 84
Bell-metal 180
Bells 3, 25, 44, 112, 179, 195
Bell tower 25, 43, 50, 177, 178, 180
Bench-end 87, 97, 99, 189
Benedictine 1, 52
Bequest board 86, 87, 88
Bible box 87
Bier 150, 151, 156, 157
Big Ben, Houses of Parliament, London 118, 181, 183
Birmingham School of Art 125
Bishop 5, 6, 8, 9, 11, 12, 50
Bishopric of the Forces 8
Bishop's Palace 50, 51, 93, 127, 176
Black Death 2, 50, 83
Black Friars 52
Blenheim Palace, Oxon 65, 174
Blind arcade 25
Blind clerestorey 25
Blind tracery 25
Blind triforium 25
Bloody Tower, London 84
Boneyard 25, 28
Bosses 23, 25, 49, 189, 190
Box pew 88, 99
Brass 86, 87, 106
Bread plate 136
Bread shelf 87, 88, 90
Britain 1, 2, 4, 8, 10, 44, 112, 113, 161, 190
British Museum, London 76
Broach spire 41, 43
Builder, The 64
Burial vault 25, 49
Buttress 25

C

Calendar, church 85, 186
Calendar, lunar 186
Calendar, solar 186
Cames 112
Campanile 25, 50, 177, 180
Canada 115, 117, 123
Candle-snuffer spire 41, 43
Candlestick 136
Canon 8
Canon chancellor 11
Canonical hours 139
Cantoris 162
Capital 25, 27, 32, 62, 189
Capuchines 52
Carillon 178, 179, 180
Carmelites 52
Carrel 25
Cartouche 87
Carthusian 1, 52
Caryatid 25
Cast iron 76, 154, 156, 157, 195
Castle Howard, N Yorks 65
Cathedral 2, 11, 13, 26, 32, 37, 52, 112, 142, 161, 162
Cathedrals Act (1840) 50
Cemetery 43, 155
Censer 136, 137, 138
Chained library 175, 176, 177
Chalice 136, 137
Chancel 3, 7, 8, 12, 20, 25, 26, 28, 31, 37, 38, 40, 43, 69, 72, 85, 87, 100, 122, 190, 193
Chancel arch 27, 88, 94, 99, 100
Change ringing 179, 180
Chantry 3, 26
Chapel 4, 5, 26, 32, 58, 61, 66, 67, 74, 78, 85, 126, 162
Chapel house 52
Chapel of ease 50
Chapter 8, 9, 26
Chapter house 24, 26, 43, 53, 72, 76, 78, 79, 130, 132, 176
Charnel house 25, 26, 37
Chelsea Hospital, London 65
Chest tomb 87, 106, 150, 156, 157, 160
China 190
Chirk aqueduct 79

Choir 26, 48, 53, 63, 67, 68, 82, 94, 165
Choir stalls 62, 87
Chrismarium 136
Chrismatory 136
Christ Church, Oxford 2
Christening shell 136
Christmas 186
Church bucket 136, 137
Church Building Acts, 1818, 1824 4
Church Building Commission 4
Churches Conservation Trust 5
Church in Wales 5, 6, 7, 8, 17
Church of England 4, 5, 6, 8, 10, 12, 13
Church of Ireland 5, 6, 7, 8, 17
Church truck 150
Churchwarden 11
Churchyard 11, 12, 31, 37, 88, 93, 94, 106, 139, 149, 150, 156, 160, 190
Churchyard cross 99, 150, 151, 156, 160
Ciborium 136, 137
Circuit 10
Cirencester 1
Cistercian 1, 52, 69
Civil War 50, 79, 136, 161, 176
Clamp buttress 25
Clasping buttress 24, 25
Clerestorey 25, 26, 44, 46
Clock 63, 141, 142, 143, 144, 145
Clock jacks 142
Cloister 25, 26, 28, 32, 43, 49, 56, 59, 68, 69, 72, 78, 79, 80, 82, 84, 175, 194, 195
Closed Churches Division, Church of England 5
Cluniac 1, 52
Coffin 150, 152
Coffin table 150, 152, 156
Collar 87, 89
Collar-beam 43, 45
College of Consultors 9
Collegiate church 3, 25, 50, 74
Columbarium 150, 155
Commissioners' churches 4, 53, 54, 69, 72, 76, 77, 79, 80
Commissioners for the Church Building Act (1818) 77

Commission for Building Fifty New Churches (1716) 67
Commonwealth 3, 53, 87, 88, 100, 161, 165, 168, 179
Communion 136, 137
Communion plate 136
Communion rails 85, 87
Communion table 85, 87
Communion tray 137
Concrete 38, 70, 76
Congregationalist 10
Congregation of Bishops 8
Consecration cross 29, 31
Consistory court 11
Console 165, 166
Convent 50, 52
Conventual priory 52
Conwy Suspension Bridge 79
Cope 87, 99
Cope chest 87, 88, 89
Corbel 29, 31, 190
Corpse stone 150
Counter-relief tile 131
Cove 31
Cradle roof 31, 49
Cradle vault 31, 49
Credence table, credence shelf 88
Cremation 150
Cremation Society of Great Britain 150
Cresset stone 88, 90
Crocket 29, 31
Cross 136, 137, 188
Crossing 31, 44, 67, 78, 79, 189
Crossing tower 32, 44, 53, 73, 81
Cross vaulting 31, 49
Crown Nominations Commission 6, 8
Crown spire 43
Crozier, crosier 137
Crucifix 94, 100, 137
Cruciform churches 26, 31
Cruet, cruet tray 137
Crypt 31, 49, 72, 189, 195
Culvery 155
Cupola 31
Curate 6, 8

Custom House, London 3
Cylindrical vaulting 31
D
Dalles de verre 113, 127
Daughter church 50
Deacon 8
Deaconess 8
Dean 8, 161, 162
Deanery 6, 7
Deanery synod 7, 11, 12
Decani 162
Decorated 22, 73
Detached tower 31, 44, 46, 178
Devil's door 29, 31, 149
Diagonal buttress 24, 25
Diagonal ribbed vaulting 31, 49
Diocesan Advisory Committee for the care of churches 11
Diocesan Chancellor 11
Diocese 1, 6, 7, 8, 9, 11, 12, 52
Dissolution of Collegiate Churches and Chantries Act (1547) 50
Dissolution of the Monasteries 2, 11, 25, 52, 81, 88, 94, 112, 117, 132, 161, 175, 179
Dole cupboard, dole shelf, dole table 88, 90
Dominicans 52
Donations board 87, 88
Doom painting 88, 91
Doors 20, 32, 37, 44, 49
Double-decker pulpit 99, 100
Double hammerbeam 31, 32, 33
Double monastery 50, 52
Dovecote 31, 150, 155
Dripstone 31, 32
E
Early English 22, 73, 77
East Anglia 20, 25, 32, 44, 88, 99
Easter 186, 187
Easter sepulchre 30, 31
Ecclesiastical Commission 4
Elders 9, 10
Electoral roll 11, 12
Ellesmere Canal 79
Enamel painting 113, 125, 127, 130
Encaustic tile 132, 135

England 1, 2, 4, 5, 7, 10, 13, 18, 20, 25, 43, 60, 62, 64, 73, 74, 79, 94, 112, 114, 155, 160, 162, 173, 179, 180, 193
Epiphany 186
Episcopal Electoral College 6
Ewer 137
Expressionism 128
F
Family pew 88, 91, 99
Fan vaulting 31, 47, 49, 59, 78, 79, 80, 84
Feretory 88
Finial 31
First World War 5, 114
Flagon 137
Flanders 87, 127, 132
Flèche 25, 31
Flemish 87, 117, 123
Flying buttress 24, 25, 80
Flying rib 30, 31
Font 20, 62, 88, 92, 189
Font canopy 88
Font cover 88
Footstone 155, 156
Foramina 93
France 72, 82, 94, 112, 130, 168, 190
French buttress 25
Friar 50, 99, 150
Friary 50
Friends of Friendless Churches 5
Funeral hatchment 93
G
Galilee chapel 31, 53
Galilee porch 31
Gallery 32, 44, 93, 111
Garden of Remembrance 150
Gargoyle 30, 32
Garth 26, 32
General Assembly 10
General Letter Office, London 3
General Synod 12
General Trustees, Church of Scotland 5
Germany 75, 94, 114, 125, 173, 190
Glass House, Fulham, London 116, 117, 118, 123, 124, 125, 129
Glastonbury chair 93

Glebe 52
Gnomon 139
Goblet 137
Gothic Revival 116, 135
Gradine 93
Graffiti 30, 32
Grave 26, 106, 150, 155
Graveboard 153, 155, 156
Graveside shelter 154, 155, 156, 160
Grave slab 94, 95
Gravestone 155, 160
Graveyard 26, 149, 150, 153, 155, 160
Greater Tithes 7
Great Famine (1315–17) 2, 50
Great Famine (1845–9) 4
Great Fire of London 3, 53, 83, 176
Greek Revival 64, 68, 77
Green Man 189, 192
Greenwich Hospital, London 65, 67
Gregorian chant 161
Gregory I, Pope 149
Gresham's College, London 83
Grey Friars 52
Grisaille 112
Groined vaulting 32
Grosvenor Bridge, Chester 80
Guinness Book of Records 193
H
Hagioscope 32, 43
Hakenkreuz 188
Hammerbeam 20, 31, 32, 38
Hampton Court, London 161
Hampton Court Palace, London 52, 65, 72
Hanging pyx 137, 141
Hansom cab 64
Harmonium 162
Hatchment 93
Headstone 155
Hearse, herse 93, 95, 156, 157
Heart burial 93
Hexagonal tower 32, 44
Highlands and Islands, Scotland 4
Historic Chapels Trust 5
Historic Churches Preservation Trust 4
Hogback tomb 156

Holy communion 85
Holy water bucket 136, 137
Holy Week 187
Hood moulding 32
Horse Guards Parade, Whitehall, London 148
Hour glass 94
House of Bishops 6, 12
House of Clergy 12
House of Laity 12
Houses of Parliament, London 54, 62, 63, 71, 118, 145
Hudd 154, 155, 156
Hyechon College, Daejoen, South Korea 179
I
Ichthys 188
Incense boat 137
Incense burner 137
Incorporated Church Building Society 4, 66
India 75, 123
Industrial revolution 145
Inlaid tile 132
Iona 66, 190
Iran 190
Ireland 1, 4, 7, 94, 115, 123, 130, 190
Irish Episcopal Conference 8
Italianate 64, 77, 80, 82
J
Jackfield Tile Museum 135
Jacobethan 77
Jesse window 94, 108, 119, 127
Jube 32
Jute 1
K
Kedermister (Kederminster) Library 176
Kensington Palace 65
Kent 84
Kerbstones 153, 156
Keystone 32
King's Glazier 117, 123, 127
Kneeler 94
L
Label 32
Lady chapel 32, 53, 54, 63, 67, 79, 116, 117,

128, 130, 135, 176, 190
Lair 155
Lambeth Palace 4
Lancet 20, 22, 32, 122
Lantern cross 150, 156
Lantern tower 32, 34
Lavatorium 32, 34
Lay rector 8, 11
Lead glaze 131
Leaning Tower of Pisa 80
Lectern 94, 195
Ledger 94
Ledger stone 94, 154, 156
Ledger tomb 156
Legal Department, Church of Ireland 5
Lent 187
Lent veil 94
Leper's window 32, 43
Lesene 32, 34, 44
Lesser Tithes 7
Libraries 11, 37, 175, 176
Lierne vaulting 48, 49, 53
Lincoln 1
Line-impressed tile 131
Little Ice Age 1
Liturgical seasons 85, 186
Liturgy 1, 137
London 1, 13, 113, 125, 142
London Blitz 129
Lorraine 113
Lucarne 32, 43
Lunette box 137
Lutheran 136
Lychgate, lichgate 150, 154, 156, 160
Lych stone 150, 156

M

Magdalen College, Oxford 69, 161
Majolica tiles 132
Manse 4, 52, 73, 78
Manual 165, 166
Marlborough Almshouses, St Albans, Herts 181
Martyrs' Memorial, Oxford 75
Mason's mark 32, 34
Mass 43, 137

Mass bell 136, 137
Mass dial 139
'Master and slave' 147
Mausolea and Monuments Trust 156
Mausoleum 73, 156
Mediaeval Warm Period 1
Memento mori 103, 107
Menai Suspension Bridge 79
Mercers' Company 77
Merlon 32
Methodist 5, 10, 67, 136
Methodist Conference 10
Midland Grand Hotel, St Pancras, London 74, 75
Million Act churches 4
Minor canon 8
Minster 37
Misericord 66, 87, 94, 96, 189
Monastery 1, 2, 3, 32, 37, 50, 52, 94, 155, 161, 179
Monstrance 137
Morthouse 156
Mortsafe 156, 158
Mosaic tile 131
Moveable feast 187
Mullion 37
Musicians 32, 93, 161, 162, 163, 164

N

Narthex 37
National Portrait Gallery, London 59
National Trust for Scotland 67
Nave 12, 25, 26, 28, 31, 37, 38, 44, 53, 55, 57, 59, 61, 69, 72, 76, 79, 80, 82, 84, 85, 87, 99, 100, 122, 193
Needle spire 43
Neo-Byzantine 54
Neo-classical 54, 58, 60, 61, 63, 64, 66, 73, 74, 76, 77, 79, 80, 81, 82, 83
Neo-Gothic 53, 54, 57, 58, 59, 60, 61, 62, 63, 64, 65, 66, 67, 68, 69, 70, 71, 72, 73, 74, 76, 77, 78, 79, 80, 81, 82, 83, 114, 118
Neo-Jacobean 64
Neo-Norman 58, 64, 70
Neo-Romanesque 76
Neo-Tudor 64, 73, 76, 80

Netherlands 113
Newcastle Central Station 60
New Churches in London and Westminster Act, 1711 3
New College, Oxford 83, 118, 126, 127
Newfoundland 75
New Zealand 75, 115, 167
Nonconformism 3, 4
Nonconformist 5, 78, 162
Norman 20, 22, 46, 49, 73, 92, 190
Northern Ireland 5, 8, 9, 13, 17, 19, 50, 94, 179, 180
Nunnery 52

O

Obedientary priory 52
Octagonal tower 37, 44
Oculus 37, 38
Ogee 20, 22, 37, 68
Oratory 37
Ordinary time 186, 187
Organ 3, 32, 62, 93, 161, 162, 165, 166, 167, 168, 169, 170, 171, 172, 173, 174
Organ pipe 165
Ossuary 26, 37
Ostensorium 137
Oxford Movement 162

P

Painted roof 37, 38
Pakistan 123
Pall 93, 99, 156
Pallet 165
Parapet spire 43
Parclose screen 96, 99
Pargetting 37, 60
Parish chest 97, 99
Parish Clerk 12, 99, 161
Parliamentary Churches 4, 79
Parlour pew 88, 99
Parochial Church Council 7, 11, 12
Parsonage 52
Parvis 35, 37, 176
Paten 137
Patron 7
Pectoral cross 137
Pedestal tomb 159, 160

Pedilavium 35, 37
Pendulum 142
Permanent deacon 9
Perpendicular 20, 37, 59, 67, 72, 73, 77, 78, 83
Perpetual Curate 8
Personal Ordinariate of Our Lady of Walsingham 8
Pew 87, 99
Phoedelia 137
Pilaster 25, 32, 37
Pinnacle 37
Piscina 35, 37, 88, 105
Plainchant 161
Plainsong 161
Plate tracery 37, 44
Polyphonic music 161
Pome 137
Pontcysyllte aqueduct 79
Poor box 85, 98, 99
Poor Clares 52
Porch 36, 37, 189
Portable altar 85, 99
Pot-metal glass 112, 113, 130
Prebendary 8
Precentor 8, 162
Predella 99
Pre-Raphaelite 115, 123, 124
Presbyterianism 9, 10
Presbytery 9, 10, 38, 52, 67, 72, 79, 82
Priest in charge 6, 7, 8
Priest's door 38, 39
Prior's Early English glass 113
Priory 52
Processional cross 137
Provost 8
Pulpit 62, 94, 98, 99, 105, 195
Pulpitum 25, 32, 38, 54, 55, 67, 68, 69, 72, 79
Puritanism 3, 85, 87, 94, 99, 100, 106, 111, 112, 166
Pyx 137, 141
Pyx cloth 137

Q

Quakers 9
Quarries 113

Quire 37, 56

R
Rector 6, 7
Rectorial benefice 11
Rectory 52
Reformation 85, 87, 88, 100, 105, 111, 112, 136, 137, 150, 155, 161, 175, 176, 179, 193
Regional dean 7
Relief tile 131
Reliquary 137
Representative Body, Church in Wales 5
Reredos 30, 62, 72, 79, 82, 93, 99, 100, 101
Respond 38
Restoration, The (1660) 3, 137, 161, 165, 179
Retable 100
Retrochoir 38, 67, 79, 81
Rheims 72
Rhenish helm 38, 39, 44
Ribs 38
Rib tracery 38, 44
Richmond Bridge, Dublin 74
Riddel 98, 100
Ridge rib 31, 49
Ringing chamber 180
Rolled glass 113
Roman Catholic 5, 8, 9, 11, 13, 18, 25, 38, 52, 54, 57, 60, 62, 63, 64, 66, 67, 70, 71, 73, 74, 75, 78, 94, 105, 129, 136, 137, 150, 161, 179, 186
Roman Catholic Relief Act, 1829 4
Romanesque 20, 58, 76, 80
Rome 1, 62
Rome Protestant Cemetery 94
Rood 3, 100
Rood beam 100
Rood loft 23, 85, 100, 101, 112
Rood screen 3, 25, 38, 100, 102, 189
Roof 38
Roof coverings 38
Rose window 38, 49, 72, 117
Rouen 75
Round churches 26, 38
Roundel 38
Round tower 38, 46

Royal Academy, London 77
Royal Albert Memorial Museum, Exeter 65
Royal Arms 93, 100
Royal College of Art, London 128
Royal College of Music, London 54
Royal Exchange, London 3
Royal Observatory, Edinburgh 147
Royal Observatory, Greenwich, London 145, 148
Royal Peculiar, Peculier 51, 52
Rural Dean 6
Russia 190

S
Sacristy 12, 38, 40
Saddleback roof 38, 40, 44
Saddle bars 112
Saints' bell 136, 137
Sanctuary 26, 38, 85, 105
Sanctuary chair 105
Sanctuary ring, sanctuary knocker 38, 102, 105
Sanctus bell 136, 137, 179
Saxon 1, 20, 44, 139
Sciapod 189, 190, 191
Science Museum, London 142
Scissors arch 38, 44
Scotland 1, 3, 4, 5, 8, 9, 10, 13, 17, 19, 50, 52, 64, 75, 79, 94, 112, 115, 116, 129, 155, 156, 160, 179, 180
Scottish Episcopal Church 6, 7, 8, 17
Scottish Redundant Churches Trust 5
Scratchdial 37, 139, 140
Second Council of Nicaea 105
Second World War 3, 61, 83, 116, 132, 142, 166, 172
Sedilia 23, 43, 79, 84
Sermon timer 94, 103, 105
Setback buttress 25
Seven sacraments font 88, 91, 105
Sheela na gig 190, 191
Sheffield plate 136
Shingles 38
Shrine 88, 93, 99, 105, 111
Shroud 105, 111, 150
Side gallery 93, 105

Sidesmen 12
Sidesperson 12
Silver-gilt 136
Silver plate 136
Single-cell churches 26, 43
Single framed roof 38, 43, 44
Slab glass 113, 128
Slype 43
Society for the Protection of Ancient Buildings 124
Soundboard 165
Sound hole 43
Sounding board 105, 106
South Africa 75, 130, 167
Spandrel 43
Spire 31, 37, 38, 44, 59, 61, 64, 72, 75, 76, 79, 193, 195
Spirelet 31
Spire light 32, 43
Splay-foot spire 43
Sprinkler 136, 137
Squinch 43
Squint 32, 41, 43
SS collar 87, 89
Stained glass 3, 57, 59, 85, 106, 112, 113, 115, 117, 190
Stair turret 41, 43, 49
Stations of the Cross 102, 105
Steeple 44
St John's College, Cambridge 73
St John's College, Oxford 68, 69
St Katherine's College, Tottenham, London 171
St Katherine's Dock, London 79
St Mary's Hall, Coventry, W Mid 128
Stoup 104, 105
Stove 104, 106
Strainer arch 38, 42, 44, 67
Straining spoon 137, 138
Stripwork 32, 44
Sub-dean 8
Succentor 8
Suffragan Bishop 6, 7
Sundial 37, 139, 141, 142
Super-frontal 85, 106

Swastika 188
Swell pedal, swell box 165
Switzerland 94, 190
Synod 6, 7, 10, 12

T
Tabernacle cross 150, 160
Table tomb 150, 156, 158, 160
Tapsel gate 160
Tea-caddy tomb 154, 160
Terra cotta 76
Tester 105, 106
Thatch 38, 39
Three-cell churches 26, 44
Three Choirs Festival 162
Three-decker pulpit 98, 99, 100
Three Hares 189, 191
Thurible 136, 137, 138
Thurifer 136
Tides 139
Tie beam roof 38, 44, 45
Tierceron vaulting 44, 49
Tiles 38, 43, 115, 131, 132, 133, 135
Tithe barn 52
Tithes 7, 11, 12, 52
Tomb 87, 103, 104, 106, 107, 159
Tombstone 155, 160
Tower 3, 20, 31, 32, 37, 38, 39, 40, 43, 44, 45, 53, 54, 57, 59, 61, 63, 65, 68, 72, 73, 75, 76, 77, 78, 82, 83, 193
Tower Captain 180
Tower clock 142, 145, 146
Tower of London 52, 67, 74, 80, 84, 173
Tracery 20, 22, 25, 37, 38, 44, 106
Tractarian Movement 162
Transept 26, 31, 44, 68, 72, 85, 195
Transitional deacon 9
Transom 44
Treasury 78, 136, 137, 138, 175
Tree of Jesse 32, 94, 106
Triangular tower 44
Triforium 25, 44, 46
Trussed rafter roof 43, 44
Tunnel vault 49
Turret clock 142, 145, 146, 147
Two-cell churches 26, 28, 44

Tympanum 37, 46, 49
U
Undercroft 49
Union of Benefices Act, 1860 3
United Reformed Church 10, 78, 166, 167, 174
United States 71, 115, 116, 123, 127, 130, 179, 180
Usher 12
V
Vault 31, 32, 38, 44, 49
Verger 12
Versicle 161
Vestry 12, 38, 49, 78
Vestry clerk 12
Viaticum 138
Vicar 6, 7, 25
Vicarage 52
Vicar forane 9
Vicar-general 9
Vice 43, 49
Victorian 93, 100, 126, 131, 135, 145, 168
Viking 1, 156
W
Wafer box 138
Wagon roof 25, 31, 49
Wagon vault 49
Wales 1, 2, 4, 5, 9, 10, 13, 17, 19, 50, 74, 94, 149, 155, 162, 180, 193
Wall monument 94, 106, 109
Wall painting 3, 110, 111, 112
Watch-box 155, 160
Watching loft 111
Waterloo churches 4
Webbing 31, 49
Weepers 106, 110, 111
Welsh Religious Buildings Trust 5
West Country 49, 70, 99, 120, 181
West gallery 92, 93, 111, 163
West Gallery music 162
Westminster College, Fulton, Missouri 3
Westminster Hall, London 65
Westminster Palace, London 84
Wheel window 38, 49
Whitechapel Bell Foundry 181, 182, 184

White Friars 52
Whitefriars Glass Company 126
Whitehall Palace, London 72
Whitstable Harbour 79
Winchester College, Hants 83
Wind braces 48, 49
Winding sheet 111
Windows 20, 22, 25, 26, 32, 37, 44, 49, 106, 126
Windsor Castle, Berks 50, 52, 57, 60, 67, 70, 72, 74, 78, 80, 83, 84, 94, 130, 168, 174
Wodehouse 189
Wodewose 189, 191
Wren Library, Lincoln Cathedral 175
Y
Yew 160
York 1, 16, 17, 53, 118, 125
York Abbey 2, 175
York Castle 72
Yorkist collar 87
York Place, London 72

INDEX OF PERSONAL NAMES

A
Abbott, George Lewslie 61
Alan of Walsingham 14, 53, 81
Alexander the Mason 14, 53
Allan, George 114
Almquist, Carl 113, 127
Archer, Thomas 4, 13, 53
Aristophanes 190
Arnold, Edward 181, 182
Arnold, Hugh 113
Arnold, John Roger 145
Arthur, Prince 94
Ashlin, G C 19
Atkinson, Peter 53
Austin, Hubert 54, 69
Aveline of Lancaster 68

B
Bagley family 181
Baillie, Alexander Benjamin 113
Baillie, Edward 113
Baillie, Thomas 114
Baird, Thomas 19
Ballantine, Alexander 114
Ballantine, James 114
Ballantine, James II 61, 62, 114
Bardolph, Lord 87, 89
Barraud, Francis Philip 124
Barrington, Sir Charles 176
Barry, Sir Charles 16, 54, 65, 71
Bartlett family 181
Bayne, Basil Richard 118
Bayne, Richard Cato 118
Bayne, Robert Turnill 118
Beard, George Wales 172
Beauchamp, Richard 93, 95, 111

Beckynton, Bishop Thomas 107
Beke, Richard 14, 54, 55
Bell, Alfred 115, 120, 121
Bell, John Clement 115
Bell, Reginald Otto 115
Benson, Alfred 145
Benson, Arthur 145
Benson, James 145
Benson, Samuel Suckley 145
Bentley, J F 18
Bentley, John Francis 54
Betton, Sir John 114, 117, 122
Bilbie family 181
Binns, J J 166, 169
Bird, Richard 97
Bishop, Charles 114, 166
Bishop, Charles Kenwrick Kenelm 166
Bishop, George 166
Bishop, James Chapman 166
Bland, Charles 146, 182
Blomfield, Sir Arthur 16, 54
Blore, Edward 54, 57
Bodley, George Frederick 57, 62, 123
Bonomi, Ignatius 57, 70, 74
Bonomi, Joseph 57, 74
Bossanyi, Ervin 114
Brandon, Raphael 13, 14
Braunche, Robert 87
Bray, Sir Reginald 57
Briant, John 181
Bridge, Richard 166
Brindley, Charles 167
Brindley, Charles Frederick 167
Brocas, Bernard 87

211

Brown, Ford Madox 124
Bruce, Robert 94
Bucknall, Benjamin 57
Bucknall, William 59
Bulliston, Thomas 195
Burges, William 57, 124
Burlison, John 114, 120
Burne-Jones, Sir Edward 115, 123, 124, 126, 130
Burn, William 57
Butler, James 118
Butler, Samuel 162
Butterfield, William 17, 58, 65, 81, 82, 117, 125, 128
Byfield, John 165, 167, 168
Byfield, John II 166, 167, 168
Byrd, William 161

C

Calvin, John 137
Campbell, Colin Minton 132
Caroe, A D R 17, 58
Caroe, Martin 58
Caröe, W D 17, 58, 59
Carver, Richard 58
Casson, Sir Lewis 172
Casson, Thomas 170, 172
Chalmers, James 17, 58
Chamberlain, Robert 181
Chamberlain, Walter 132
Chambers, Sir William 64
Chantrell, Robert Dennis 59
Chapman, William 181
Charles II 3, 62
Charles IV of Lorraine 113
Chilton, Margaret 115
Christian, Ewan 16, 17, 59, 63
Clarke, Geoffrey 113, 124
Clarke, Harry 113
Clayton, John Richard 115, 120, 121
Clerk, Simon 59
Clutterbuck, Charles Edmund junior 115
Clutterbuck, Charles Edmund senior 115
Clyve, John 16, 59
Cobham, Joan de 87
Coke, John 109

Cole, John 59, 76
Collins, Peter 167
Colvin, Sir Howard 57, 58, 62, 65, 72, 82
Comper, Sir Ninian 59, 100, 116, 129
Compton, Bishop Henry 176
Compton, John 167
Coombes, Cecil 146
Coombes, Doris 146
Coombes, Stephen 146
Cope, David 145
Cope, Francis 145
Cope, George 130, 145
Cope, Richard 145
Cope, William 145
Cope, William II 145
Cory, John Augustus 57
Cottier, Daniel 116
Cottingham, Lewis Nockalls 14, 16, 17, 59
Cowper, John 59
Cragg, John 73
Craven, James 135
Cromwell, Oliver 161
Crossland, W H 63
Crowther, J S 16, 60
Curtis, Thomas Figgis 129

D

Dance, George, the Younger 76
Darwin, Charles 145
Davis, Louis 116, 118, 130
Davison, Frederick 168, 169
De la Mare, Abbot Thomas 87
Dempster, James 19
Dent, Edward John 145
Dent, Frederick Rippon 145
Dent, Richard Rippon 145
Dobson, John 60, 63
Douglas, John 60, 67
Dowsing, William 85
Dreaper (Christian names not known) 173
Drew, Sir Thomas 17, 18, 60
Drury, Alfred J 116, 124
Duff, Thomas 19
Dunn, Archibald M 60
Dunnill, Henry Powell 135
Durward, Joseph 147

Dykes Bower, Stephen 13, 14, 61

E
Easton, Hugh 116
Eastwood, John Henry 18
Eayre family 181
Eayre, Thomas 181, 182
Edmund Crouchback 68
Edward II 105
Edward III 66, 83
Edward, Lord Despenser 49
Edwards, Carl 116, 126, 130
Edward, the Black Prince 83, 189
Edward the Confessor 105
Edward VI 85, 100
Egremont, Lord 173
Eleanor of Castile 93
Elias of Dereham 16
Elizabeth I 87, 100
Elliot, Thomas 167, 168
Elliott, Thomas 18
Ellis, Alexander 19, 130
Ely, Reginald (or Reynold) 61
Erasmus, Desiderius 175
Evans, Charles 114, 166
Evans, David 114, 117
Evans, William 68, 114
Evelyn, John 3, 62
Everard, Robert 14, 61

F
Farrar-Bell, Michael 115
Farrell, William 18
Ferrey, Benjamin 61
Fisher, Joseph 127
Fitzherbert, Ralph 111
Fitzherbert, Sir Nicholas 87
Fleming, Richard 103, 106
Flockton, Thomas James 61
Flockton, William 16, 61
Flower, Barnard 117, 123
Forsyth, Moira 117, 118
Foster, Albert Healey 167
Foster, James 61
Foster, James II 61, 62, 114
Foster, Thomas 61
Fowler, C Hodgson 61

G
Gabriel, S B 62
Gardiner, Herbert 114
Garner, Thomas 57, 62
Gauld, David 117, 118
Geddes, Wilhelmina 113, 117, 118
George I 62
George IV 130
Gibberd, Sir Frederick 18
Gibbons, Grinling 62
Gibbons, Orlando 161
Gibbs, Alexander 117
Gibbs, Charles Alexander 117
Gibbs, Edward Mitchel 16, 61
Gibbs, Isaac Alexander 117
Gibbs, Isaac Alexander jnr 117
Gibbs, James 4, 14, 61, 62, 77
Gillett, William 145, 182
Glazier, Thomas 118, 128
Godwin, Henry 133, 135
Godwin, William 133, 135
Goetze, Martin 166, 167
Goldie, George 62, 63
Goodwin, Francis 62
Gower, Bishop Henry 137, 176
Gower, John 111
Graham, James Gillespie 19, 62
Graham, Margaret 62
Gray, Benjamin 148
Gray, John 168, 169
Gray, Robert 168
Gray, William 168
Green, Benjamin 63
Green, John 63
Green, Samuel 167, 168
Gregory I, Pope 149
Grimthorpe, Lord 16, 63, 146
Grylls, T H 114
Grylls, Thomas 114, 120
Gurney, Sir Goldsworthy 104, 106
Guthrie, John 118
Guthrie, John senior 118
Guthrie, William 118
Gwilt, George 16, 63
Gwilt, George, the Elder 63

Gwynn, Dominic 166, 167
Gyles, Henry 118, 127

H

Habershon, E 17, 63
Habershon, Matthew 59, 63
Habershon, W G 17, 63
Hackett, Maria 162
Hadfield, M E 19, 63
Hague, William 17
Hamilton, David 64
Hamilton, Thomas 64
Hamilton, Walter Kerr 162
Handley, George 146
Hansom, C F 19, 57, 60, 64
Hansom, E J 60, 64
Hansom, J A 19, 64, 81
Hardman, John 118, 120, 127
Hardwick, Philip 64, 70
Hardwick, Thomas 64
Hardy, Thomas 54, 162
Hargreaves, James 135
Harris, John 166
Harrison, Arthur 168
Harrison, Harry 168
Harrison, James 64
Harrison, Thomas 168
Harris, Renatus 165, 166, 168, 173
Harvey, John 53
Hawksmoor, Nicholas 4, 65, 67, 184
Haycock, Edward 65
Haynes, John 97
Hayward, John 65
Heaton, Clement 118
Hedgeland, George 123
Henry III 72, 174
Henry IV 68, 87, 174
Henry VII 57, 67, 73, 80, 87
Henry VIII 2, 4, 100, 145, 175
Herland, Hugh 65
Herod, King 186
Hewitt, William 135
Hicks, S J 62
Hill, William 168, 169, 170, 172
Holiday, Henry 123, 124, 126, 130
Holland, Mildred 37

Hollins, Michael Daintry 132
Hone, Evie 113, 123
Hone, Gaylon 123
Honeyman, John 65, 66
Honywood, Michael 175, 176
Hopkins, William 66
Howard, Richard 87
Hugall, John West 66
Hughes family 181
Hughes, Henry 129
Hunt, Arthur 127
Hurley, William 14, 53, 66
Hurst, William 66, 68, 82
Hussey, R C 66
Huygens, Christian 142

I

Inwood, Henry William 66
Inwood, William 66

J

Jackson, Sir Thomas 16, 66
James I 105
James II 62
James, John 4, 65, 67
James VI of Scotland 3
Janyns, Henry 67
Janyns, Robert 67
Janyns, Robert II 67
Jenkins, William 67
Jewitt, Edward Holmes 123, 127
John, King 93
John of Eltham 111
John of Gaunt 87
Johnson, John 13, 14
Johnston, Arthur 146, 182
Johnston, Cyril 146
Jordan, Abraham 166
Joyce, Norman 146
Joyce, Thomas 146
Joyce, William 146
Joy, William 14, 16, 67

K

Kedermister, Sir John 176
Kempe, C E 115, 121, 123
Kemp, Marjorie 115
Keppie, John 66

Ketelbarn, Robert 124
Kibblewhite, Edith 129
Kirby, Edmund 67
Kitchener, Field Marshall Lord 106
Knox, John 3
L
Lamplugh, Archbishop 62
Laud, William, Archbishop of Canterbury 85, 161
Lavers, Nathaniel Wood 124
Lee, Lawrence 124, 128
Leofric, Bishop 176
Leo XIII 5
Lester, Thomas 181, 182
Lethaby, William 38
Lewis, Thomas Christopher 172
Lilly, Charles 17
Lindley, William 81
Lindsay, Ian G 17, 67
Livingstone, David 145
Llewellin, Peter 182
Lock, Adam 13, 16, 55, 67, 69
Lote, Stephen 56, 67
Louis XIII 113
Lowndes, Mary 116, 118, 124, 126
Luther, Martin 2
Lutwyche, William 114
M
Mackintosh, Charles Rennie 66, 118
Mander, Noel 172
Mangey, John 176
Manners, George Phillips 68
Mapilton, Thomas 13, 14, 16, 68
Mathewson, George 19
Maufe, Sir Edward 14, 16, 68
Maw, George 133, 135
Maw, John Hornby 135
Mayer, George 114
May, Hugh 83
McAuley, Fr Jeremiah 19
McCarthy, James Joseph 17, 19
McGivern, Dr Thomas 19
Mears family 181
Mears, Thomas 181, 182, 183
Medlock, Dr 113, 130

Michael of Canterbury 14, 58, 68
Milton, John 161
Minton, Herbert 132, 133
Moffat (or Moffatt), William Lambie 66, 68
Moore, George 146
Moore, Henry James 146
Moore, John 146
Moore, Temple 68, 75
Morley, Thomas 161
Morris, William 71, 78, 115, 124
Mosse, Dr Miles 176
Mot, Robert 181
Musson, J F 167
N
Nash, John 74, 77
Newall, Walter 68
New, Keith 124
Nicholson, John 172
Nicholson, Sir Charles 16, 17, 68
Nixon, James 129
Norman, E W 170, 172
Norman, Herbert 170
Norreys, Thomas 16, 69
Norris family 182
Nuttgens, Eddie 118, 125, 126
Nuttgens, Joseph Ambrose 125
O
Oates, John 69
O'Connor, Arthur 125
O'Connor, Michael 125, 128
O'Connor, W H 125, 128
Okeley, William Ignatius 61
O'Neill, John 19
Orchard, William 14, 69
Osborn, Thomas 182
Osborn, William 182
Oswald, Arthur 53
Owen, T E 69
P
Pace, George 16, 17, 69, 70, 76
Paley, E G 18, 54, 69, 76
Palmer, John 16, 70
Pannell, Charles T 181
Pannell, William 181
Paris, Nicholas 144

Parrot(t), William 17
Parsons, Karl 116, 118, 125, 130
Payne, Henry 122, 125
Pearson, Frank 16, 17, 70
Pearson, James 125
Pearson, J L 13, 14, 16, 17, 58, 70, 128
Peckham, Archbishop 68
Peckitt, William 125
Percy Thomas Partnership 18
Pevsner, Sir Nikolaus 63
Phelps, Richard 181, 183
Pickersgill, Thomas 69
Pinch, John, the elder 70
Pinch, John, the younger 70
Piper, John 126, 127
Pius IX 5
Ponting, Charles 70
Portway, Charles 106
Potts, Anthony 147
Potts, Charles 147
Potts, James 147
Potts, Joseph 147
Potts, Robert 147
Potts, Tom 147
Potts, William 147
Potts, William II 147
Powell, Anne 118
Powell, Arthur 126
Powell, Harry 126
Powell, James 122, 126
Powell, John 126
Powell, John Hardman 118
Powell, Nathanael 126
Pratt, Sir Roger 83
Price, Joshua 127
Price, William, the elder 127
Price, William, the younger 127
Prichard, John 17, 70
Prior, Edward 70
Prior, E S 113
Pritchett, J P 70, 81
Prudde, John 127
Pugin, A C 61
Pugin, A W N 5, 18, 19, 61, 63, 71, 82, 118, 125, 128, 129, 130

Pugin, E W 18, 71
Pugin, Peter Paul 19, 71
Purser, Sarah 113

R
Raghton, Ivo de 14, 16, 17, 72
Raglan, Lady 189
Railton, William 72
Ramsey, William (de) 72
Rawstorne, Walker 72
Redman, Henry 72
Reed, George Jeremiah 148
Renn, Samuel 173
Reyns, Henry de 72
Reyntiens, Patrick 126, 127
Richard II 65, 83
Richard of Farleigh 14, 16, 72
Rickman, Thomas 16, 66, 72, 195
Rigby, Alexander 182
Rippon, Richard 145
Ritchie, Frederick James 147
Ritchie, James 147
Ritchie, James II 147
Ritchie, Leone 147
Robert Curthose 93, 106
Roberts, Henry 73
Robertson, William 73
Robert the Mason 16, 73
Roger de Caen 50
Ross, Alexander 17, 73
Rossetti, Dante Gabriel 115, 124
Ross, James 73
Rouault, Georges 123
Rudhall family 182
Rushworth, William 167, 173, 174
Ruskin, John 71
Russell, Richard 73

S
Salisbury, Marquis of 106
Salvin, Anthony 14, 16, 74
Savage, James 74
Scoles, Joseph John 74
Scott, Adrian 75
Scott, George Gilbert Jnr 18, 68
Scott, Oldrid 14, 16, 17, 75
Scott, Sir Gilbert 13, 14, 16, 17, 18, 19, 26, 57,

61, 66, 68, 74, 75, 78, 81, 87
Scott, Sir Giles Gilbert 75
Scune, Christopher 16, 76, 79
Sharpe, Edmund 54, 69, 76
Sharp, R H 53
Shaw, Norman 70, 76
Shelley, Percy Bysshe 94
Shovell, Sir Cloudesley 62
Simon of Cyrene 105
Simon the Mason 17, 76
Simpson, Archibald 17, 76, 77
Sims, Ronald 76
Smirke, Sir Robert 14, 57, 73, 76, 80
Smith, Alan 147
Smith, Bernard 173
Smith, Francis 77
Smith, Frank 147
Smith, George 77
Smith, Howard 147
Smith, John (architect) 77
Smith, John II 147
Smith, John, of Derby 144, 147, 148
Smith, Joseph 182
Smith, Nicholas 147
Smith, S Pountney 77
Smith, William 77
Smyth, William 16, 77
Snetzler, John 167, 170, 173
Soane, Sir Robert 59, 77
Spence, Sir Basil 14, 78
Sponlee, John de 78
Stainburn Taylor Architects 58
St Alban 16, 74, 105
Stanley, Sir Henry 145
St Aubyn, J P 74
St Augustine 1, 149, 161
St Cuthbert 149
St Denys 105
Stedman, Fabian 179
Stephenson, Robert 87
Stirling, William 78
St Magnus 105
St Melangell 105
Stow, Richard de 78
St Patrick 1

Strafford, Thomas Wentworth, Earl of 161
Strang, Thomas Rankine 128
Street, G E 13, 14, 69, 76, 77, 78, 81, 87
St Veronica 105
St Wite 105
Suggate, Edward Hadlow 166
Swainston, Frank 18
Swarbrick, Thomas 171, 173
Sweetland, William 171, 174
Symondes, Symon 123
Symonds, John 87

T
Tallis, Thomas 161
Tapsel, John 160
Tarring, John 78
Taylor, John 180
Taylor, Robert Minton 132
Taylor, Thomas 78
Taylor, W G 121, 125, 128
Telford, Thomas 4, 79
Tempas, John 79
Terry, Quinlan 18
Tertullian 1
Teulon, S S 79
Thamar, Thomas 171, 174
Thomas a Becket 105
Thomas de Cambridge 14, 79
Thomas of Witney 14, 16, 79, 82
Thomson, David 17, 79, 82
Thornhill, Sir James 127
Thornton, John 128
Thwaites, Aynsworth (or Ainsworth) 148
Thwaites, John 148
Tomkins, Thomas 161
Tower, Walter 123
Traherne, Margaret 128
Tresk, Simon de 80
Trigge, Francis 175
Trubshaw, James 80
Trubshaw, Thomas 80
Tuckney, Anthony 176
Tunstall, John 172
Turner, J M W 64

U
Underwood, Henry Jones 80

V
Vanbrugh, Sir John 65
Van Gogh, Vincent 116
Van Linge, Abraham 127
Vertue, Robert 80
Vertue, Robert II 80
Vertue, William 80
Victoria, Queen 130
Vulliamy, Benjamin 80, 148
Vulliamy, Benjamin Lewis 80, 148
Vulliamy, Justin 148
Vulliamy, Lewis 80

W
Wailes, William 128
Wailes, William Thomas 128
Walker, John James 174
Walker, J W 174
Walker, Leonard 126, 128
Walker, Reginald 174
Walsoken, Adam de 87
Ward, Thomas 121, 129
Warner, John 182
Warrington, William 129, 130
Wastell, John 13, 14, 16, 59, 80, 81, 84
Watson, Charles 71, 81
Watts family 183
Webb, Christopher 129
Webb, Geoffrey 129
Webb, Philip 78
Webb, Sir Aston 129
Webster, George 81
Weelkes, Thomas 161
Welch, Edward 64, 81
Welch, John 81
Wesley, John 10
Wesley, Samuel Sebastian 162
Westlake, Nathaniel 124
Whall, Christopher 113, 115, 116, 118, 125, 126, 129
Whall, Veronica 129
White, Bishop Thomas 176
Whitehurst, John I 148
Whitehurst, John II 148
Whitehurst, John III 147, 148
White, William 81
Whittacker, John 172
Whittingham, Sir Robert 189
Wightwick, George 82
Willement, Thomas 125, 129, 130
William de Ramsey 14, 78
William III 62
William of Louth, Bishop 68
William of Sens 14, 56, 76, 82
Williamson, Francis 123
William the Englishman 14, 61, 82
Willis, Henry 171, 174
Willis, Henry II 174
Willis, Henry III 174
Willis, Henry IV 174
Willson, Edward James 82
Wilson, Charles 17, 79, 82
Wilson, R G 19
Winston, Charles 113, 126, 130
Wodehirst, Robert (de) 82
Wolryche, Mary 107
Woodhead, John 66, 82
Woodyer, Henry 82
Wooldridge, Harry 126, 130
Wren, Sir Christopher 3, 14, 16, 62, 65, 67, 73, 83
Wright, Samuel 132
Wyatt, James 14, 16, 83
Wyatt, Matthew 57
Wyatt, Samuel 79
Wyatville, Sir Jeffrey 58, 65
Wynford, William 14, 16, 83

Y
Yevele, Henry 14, 16, 35, 55, 67, 68, 83, 84
Younger, Alan 130

INDEX OF CHURCHES

A
Aberdeen Cathedral 172
Abingdon Abbey, Oxon 83
Abingdon School chapel, Oxon 116
Aboyne Church, Aberdeenshire 77
Acomb Church, W Yorks 81
Addiewell Parish Church, Motherwell, North Lanarkshire 80
Addington Methodist Church, W Yorkshire 156
Airth Parish Church, Stirling 78
All Hallows, Greenford, London 117
All Hallows, Southwark, London 75
All Hallows, Twickenham, London 168
Alloa St John's Episcopal Church, Clackmannanshire 115
All Saints', Bingley, W Yorks 139
All Saints', Bourton, Oxon 147
All Saints', Brixworth, Northants 1, 44, 115
All Saints', Brockhampton, Herefs 130
All Saints', Camden, London 66
All Saints', Carleton Rode, Norfolk 31, 172
All Saints', Challoch, Dumfries and Galloway 63
All Saints', Claverley, Salop 110, 151
All Saints', Croxley Green, Herts 129
All Saints', Daresbury, Ches 189
All Saints', Deganwy, Conwy 60
All Saints', Derby 62, 77
All Saints', Dogmersfield, Hants 61
All Saints', Driffield, E Yorks 139
All Saints', Durrington, Wilts 66
All Saints', East Budleigh, Devon 99, 189
All Saints', East Huntspill, Som 68
All Saints', East Pennard, Som 184
All Saints', East Tuddenham, Norfolk 129
All Saints', Ebbw Vale, Glam 125
All Saints', Elm, Cambs 32
All Saints', Ennismore Gardens, London 81
All Saints' Episcopal Church, Inverary, Argyll and Bute 183
All Saints', Evesham, Worcs 80, 180
All Saints', Farnborough, Berks 126
All Saints', Fleet, Hants 57
All Saints', Freethorpe, Norfolk 173
All Saints', Gainsborough, Lincs 77
All Saints', Glasbury, Powys 130
All Saints', Glossop, Derbys 63
All Saints', Great Chesterford, Essex 59
All Saints', Gresford, Wrexham 115
All Saints', Handley, Ches 65
All Saints', Hereford 88, 90, 94, 96, 135
All Saints', Herstmonceux, Sussex 38
All Saints', Highbrook, Sussex 115
All Saints', Higher Walton, Lancs 69, 124
All Saints', High Wycombe, Bucks 168
All Saints', Hillingdon, London 69
All Saints', Hinton Ampner, Hants 127
All Saints', Hockerill, Herts 61, 116
All Saints', Hollesley, Suffolk 190
All Saints', Hough on the Hill, Lincs 44
All Saints', Hove, Sussex 70, 115
All Saints', Hovingham, N Yorks 128
All Saints', Huntingdon, Cambs 172
All Saints', Hursley, Hants 128
All Saints', Hutton Rudby, N Yorks 125
All Saints', Icklingham, Suffolk 38
All Saints', Ilkley, W Yorks 146, 147
All Saints', Jesus Lane, Cambridge 115
All Saints', Jordanhill, Glasgow 59

All Saints', Kettesworth, Norfolk 44
All Saints', Kettlestone, Norfolk 170, 173
All Saints', Ladbroke, Warwicks 118
All Saints', Laleham, Surrey 117
All Saints', Leek, Staffs 76
All Saints', Leighton Buzzard, Beds 20
All Saints', Lindfield, Sussex 130
All Saints', Longstanton, Cambs 116
All Saints', Maidenhead, Berks 78, 174
All Saints', Maidstone, Kent 68
All Saints', Maldon, Essex 44
All Saints', Margaret Street, London 58, 117
All Saints', Marlow, Bucks 114, 172
All Saints', Milton Ernest, Beds 88
All Saints', Milton Keynes, Bucks 147
All Saints', Murston, Kent 57
All Saints', Necton, Norfolk 20, 160
All Saints', Newcastle upon Tyne, Tyne & W 26
All Saints', North Cerney, Glos 93
All Saints', North Street, York 20, 128
All Saints', Notting Hill, London 82
All Saints', Okehampton, Devon 65
All Saints', Old Byland, N Yorks 139
All Saints', Orton, Cumbria 123
All Saints', Oving, Bucks 115
All Saints', Patcham, Sussex 31, 43
All Saints Pavement, York 32, 34
All Saints', Porthcawl, Glam 125
All Saints', Ramsholt, Suffolk 44
All Saints', Richard's Castle, Salop 76
All Saints', Roos, E Yorks 59
All Saints', Runcorn, Ches 74
All Saints', Selsey, Glos 57, 125
All Saints', Shipdham, Norfolk 31
All Saints', Southill, Beds 116
All Saints', Stretton-on-Dunsmore, Warwicks 73
All Saints', Sudbourne, Suffolk 43
All Saints', Swanton Morley, Norfolk 82
All Saints', Theddlethorpe, Lincs 100
All Saints', Thorpe Acre, Loughborough, Leics 72
All Saints', Thorpe Basset, N Yorks 135
All Saints', Thurcaston, Leics 128
All Saints', Westbury, Wilts 183
All Saints', Weston, Som 70
All Saints', Weston-super-Mare, Som 167
All Saints', Whitefield, Manchester 54
All Saints', Wickhambrook, Suffolk 146
All Saints', Wilby, Norfolk 93
All Saints', Wilden, Worcs 66
All Saints', Windsor, Berks 54
All Saints', Wingerworth, Derbys 173
All Saints', Winterton, Lincs 162
All Saints', Wokingham, Berks 148
All Saints', Woodchurch, Kent 38
All Souls, Blackman Lane, Leeds, W Yorks 75
All Souls College chapel, Oxford 127
Ampleforth Abbey, N Yorks 127, 183
Annunciation, Bryanston Street, London 166
Annunciation to the Blessed Virgin Mary, Souldern, Oxon 64
Anwoth Church, Dumfries and Galloway 68
Armagh Cathedral 19
Armagh Protestant Cathedral 17, 59, 60
Arundel Cathedral, Sussex 19
Ashridge chapel, Berkhamsted, Herts 167
Askham Church, Cumbria 77
Avoch Parish Church, Highland 73
Aylesford Priory, Kent 117
Ayr Cathedral, South Ayrshire 19
Ayr New Church 64

B

Balfron Chapel, Stirling 79
Balliol College chapel, Oxford 58, 148
Bangor Cathedral, Gwynedd 17, 114, 115, 126, 135, 168
Bath Abbey, Som 47, 72, 80, 96, 109, 111, 120, 121
Bath Central United Reformed Church, Som 174
Bellahouston Parish Church, Glasgow 117
Beverley Minster, E Yorks 30, 38, 72, 92, 94, 120, 144, 147, 163, 164, 172, 173, 183, 184, 195
Birmingham Cathedral, W Mid 13, 53, 115,

173
Bishop St chapel, Leicester 67
Blackburn Cathedral, Lancs 16, 70
Blackfriars Priory, London 94
Bondgate chapel, Darlington, Co Durham 67
Bothwell Church, Lanarkshire 64
Bradford Cathedral, W Yorks 16
Bramhope Chapel, W Yorks 3
Brasenose College chapel, Oxford 125
Brechin Cathedral, Angus 66
Brecon Cathedral, Powys 17, 58, 69, 75, 88, 90, 115, 121, 127, 128
Bremilham Church, Foxley-cum-Bremilham, Malmesbury, Wilts 193
Brentwood Cathedral, Essex 18
Bridgeyate Methodist Church, Bristol 174
Bridlington Priory, E Yorks 172
Bristol Cathedral 2, 13, 31, 67, 70, 78, 130, 168, 174
Brompton Oratory, London 174
Buckfast Abbey, Devon 183
Buildwas Abbey, Salop 175
Buittle Church, Dumfries and Galloway 68
Burford Church, Oxon 67
Bury St Edmunds Abbey, Suffolk 59, 68
Byland Abbey, N Yorks 132
C
Campsie High Church, Lennoxtown, Stirling 64
Canongate Church, Edinburgh 67
Canterbury Cathedral, Kent 8, 14, 35, 38, 54, 55, 56, 58, 62, 67, 68, 75, 81, 82, 83, 84, 105, 106, 113, 114, 119, 130, 174, 189, 195
Carlisle Cathedral, Cumbria 16, 59, 69, 72, 135
Carmelite Church, Kensington, London 75
Carver Street Chapel, Sheffield, S Yorks 67
Cathcart Free Church, Glasgow 65
Cathedral of St Michael and St George, Aldershot, Hants 18
Cathedral of St Michael and St George, Grahamstown, South Africa 75
Cathedral of the Annunciation and St Nathy, Ballaghaderreen, Co

Roscommon 63
Cathedral of the Isles, Millport, Cumbrae, Argyll and Bute 17, 58, 115, 193
Chalmers Memorial Church, Port Seton, East Lothian 115
Chapel of St Etheldreda, Ely Place, London 68
Chapel of St John the Evangelist, Tower of London 52
Chapel Royal, Hampton Court, London 52
Chapel Royal, Holyrood Palace, Edinburgh 52
Chapel Royal, St James's Palace, London 52, 167
Chapel Royal, St Peter's ad Vincula, Tower of London 52, 173
Charles Church, Plymouth, Devon 3
Charterhouse Chapel, Godalming, Surrey 115
Chelmsford Cathedral, Essex 13, 14, 68, 172
Cheltenham College chapel, Glos 116
Chester Cathedral, Ches 2, 10, 11, 16, 69, 75, 94, 95, 106, 123, 125, 130, 135, 150, 157, 177, 180, 190
Chichester Cathedral, Sussex 14, 70, 75, 82, 128, 129, 135, 167, 172, 180, 195
Chiddingly Parish Church, Sussex 155
Christ Church, Adlington, Lancs 81
Christ Church, Ashford, Kent 54
Christ Church, Bradford-on-Avon, Wilts 68
Christ Church, Brampton Bierlow, W Yorks 71
Christ Church, Bryn-y-Maen, Conwy 60
Christ Church Cathedral, Dublin 60, 78, 168, 180
Christ Church Cathedral, New Zealand 75
Christ Church Cathedral, Oxford 2, 14, 69, 75, 115, 127, 173, 193
Christ Church, Catshill, Worcs 125
Christ Church, Chester, Ches 167
Christ Church, Colbury, Hants 61
Christ Church, Cressage, Salop 65, 114
Christ Church, Croft, Lancs 57
Christ Church, Doncaster, S Yorks 132
Christ Church, Downside, Som 70

Christ Church, Flackwell Heath, Bucks 126
Christ Church, Freemantle, Hants 82
Christ Church, Hanham, Glos 61
Christ Church, Hartlepool, Durham 147
Christ Church, Heald Green, Stockport, Manchester 125
Christ Church, Hilderstone, Staffs 80
Christ Church, Kilndown, Kent 74
Christ Church, Knightley, Staffs 80
Christ Church, Lanner, Cornwall 82
Christ Church, Lewisham, London 59
Christ Church, Little Drayton, Salop 77
Christ Church, Little Heath, Herts 129
Christ Church, Liversedge, W Yorks 78
Christ Church, Pitsmoor Road, Sheffield, S Yorks 61
Christ Church, Port Sunlight, Mersey 174
Christchurch Priory, Dorset 100, 172
Christ Church, Shaw, Wilts 70
Christ Church, Skipton, W Yorks 59
Christ Church, Spitalfields, London 3, 65, 166
Christ Church, Theale, Som 58
Christ Church, Tintwistle, Derbys 145
Christ Church, Tunstall, Staffs 135
Christ Church United Reformed Church, Enfield, London 78
Christ Church, Walmsley, Manchester 114
Christ Church, Watford, Herts 166
Christ Church, Worthing, Sussex 123
Christ's College chapel, Cambridge 173
Christ's Hospital chapel, Horsham, Sussex 173
Christ the Consoler, Skelton-on-Ure, N Yorks 57
Christ the King, Gordon Square, London 168
Chryston Parish Church, North Lanarkshire 80
Churchill College chapel, Cambridge 126
Church of Christ the King, Plymouth, Devon 75
Church of Our Lady, Llandovery, Carms 125
Church of the Annunciation, Bournemouth, Dorset 75
Church of the Ascension, Littleworth, Oxon 80
Church of the Assumption, Ufford, Suffolk 93, 99, 100
Church of the Epiphany, Gipton, Leeds, W Yorks 129
Church of the Holy Name of Jesus, Manchester 64
Church of the Holy Rood, Watford, Herts 54
Church of the Transfiguration, Pyecombe, Sussex 160
Clackmannan Church, Clackmannanshire 63
Cleeve Abbey, Washford, Som 132
Clifton Cathedral, Bristol 18
Clumber Park chapel, Worksop, Notts 168
Cock Road Methodist Church, Bristol 174
Congregational Memorial Hall, Farringdon Street, London 78
Coombes Church, Sussex 160
Corpus Christi Priory, Manchester 25
Corpus Christi, Tremeirchion, Den 114
Corstorphine Old Parish Church, Edinburgh 114
Cotehele Chapel, Calstock, Cornwall 190
Cotham Church, Bristol 58
Courthill Chapel, Lochcarron, Highland 73
Coventry Cathedral, W Mid 1, 14, 31, 78, 124, 126, 127, 128, 168
Cow Honeybourne Church, Worcs 66
Craigmillar Park Church, Edinburgh 67
Cranleigh School chapel, Surrey 126
Crimond Church, Aberdeenshire 146
Croxton Abbey, Lincs 93
Culbone Church, Porlock Weir, Som 193

D

Dalserf Church, South Lanarkshire 156
Dennistoun Church, Glasgow 79
Derby Cathedral 14, 62, 77, 167, 193
Dirleton Parish Kirk, East Lothian 115
Dorchester Abbey, Dorchester, Oxon 106
Dore Abbey, Abbeydore, Herefs 93
Dowanhill Parish Church, Glasgow 116
Down Cathedral, Downpatrick, Co Down

17
Downside Abbey, Stratton-on-the-Fosse, Som 25, 167
Dromore Cathedral, Armagh 18
Dron Parish Church, Perth and Kinross 78
Drumbeg Parish Church, Co Down 60
Dunblane Abbey, Perthshire 116
Dunfermline Abbey, Fife 94
Dunino Church, Fife 63
Dunipace (Old) Parish Church, Stirling 78
Durham Cathedral 8, 16, 26, 31, 38, 49, 58, 61, 68, 74, 75, 76, 84, 116, 130, 136, 168, 173, 174, 175

E
Eastwood Parish Church, Pollokshaws, Glasgow 79, 82
Ebenezer Chapel, Little Stonegate, York 71
Ely Cathedral, Cambs 14, 26, 32, 53, 66, 68, 75, 82, 106, 129, 132, 168, 172, 179
Emanuel School chapel, Battersea, London 117
Emmanuel Church, Buckley, Flint 114
Emmanuel Church, Lockwood, W Yorks 59
Emmanuel College chapel, Cambridge 173
Emmanuel United Reformed Church, Worthing, Sussex 167
Episcopal Mission Church, Inverness, Highland 73
Errol Church, Perth and Kinross 63
Eton College chapel, Berks 80, 123, 172, 173
Evesham Abbey, Worcs 80, 195
Ewenny Priory Church, Bridgend, Glam 174
Exeter Cathedral, Devon 14, 43, 49, 67, 70, 72, 75, 79, 94, 106, 135, 142, 166, 168, 176, 183

F
Falkirk Old and St Modan's, Falkirk 114, 130
Ferryhill Parish Church, Aberdeen 115
Fintray Church, Aberdeenshire 77
Fountains Abbey, N Yorks 57, 76, 132
Free Church, Dunbar, East Lothian 64
Free West Church, Greenock, Renfrewshire 65

Free West Church, Perth, Perth and Kinross 65
Freuchie Parish Church, Fife 114
Friends' Meeting House, Friargate, York 81

G
Giggleswick School chapel, N Yorks 66
Gillingham Methodist Church, Dorset 174
Glasgow Cathedral 17, 168
Gloucester Cathedral 2, 14, 25, 26, 32, 43, 49, 75, 79, 88, 93, 105, 106, 112, 115, 118, 124, 127, 128, 130, 132, 135, 136, 162, 172, 174
Gold St Chapel, Northampton 67
Good Shepherd's, Hook Common, Worcs 125
Good Shepherd's, Lake, IoW 174
Good Shepherd's, Tatham, Lancs 54
Gordon Chapel, Fochabers, Moray 76
Grantshouse Free Church, Borders 58
Gray's Inn chapel, London 172
Greatham Parish Church, Sussex 99
Great Malvern Priory, Worcs 128, 132, 172
Great St Mary's, Cambridge 59, 81, 172, 173
Greyfriars Kirkyard, Edinburgh 156
Grosvenor Chapel, Chapel St, London 77
Guildford Cathedral, Surrey 14, 68, 117, 124, 173

H
Halifax Minster, W Yorks 123
Heath Chapel, Heath, Salop 26, 28
Helensburgh Parish Church, Argyll and Bute 82
Hereford Cathedral 14, 35, 59, 75, 76, 79, 135, 168, 174, 175
Hinde Street Methodist Church, London 166
Holy Angels, Hoar Cross, Staffs 57, 168, 183
Holy Ascension, Upton, Ches 65
Holy Cross, Binstead, IoW 124
Holy Cross, Hucknall, Nottingham 125
Holy Cross, Owlpen, Glos 135
Holy Cross, Sherston, Wilts 160
Holy Cross, St Helens, Lancs 74
Holy Family and St Ninian's, Kirkintilloch, East Dunbartonshire 71

Holy Family, Broxwood, Herefs 64
Holy Family, Farnham, Surrey 117
Holy Family, Mossend, North Lanarkshire 71
Holy Ghost, Crowcombe, Som 189
Holy Innocents', Highnam, Glos 83
Holy Innocents', Orpington, Kent 128
Holy Innocents', Tuck Hill, Salop 74
Holy Jesus's, Lydbrook, Glos 83
Holy Redeemer, Clydebank, East Dunbartonshire 71
Holy Rood, Ampney Crucis, Glos 150
Holy Rood, Daglingworth, Glos 139
Holy Saviour, Sugley, Northumb 63
Holy Sepulchre, Cambridge 26, 130
Holy Spirit, Southsea, Hants 61
Holy Trinity, Aberaeron, Cered 124
Holy Trinity and St Mary's, Berwick upon Tweed, Northumb 3
Holy Trinity, Ashton-in-Makerfield, Lancs 70
Holy Trinity, Balsham, Cambs 93
Holy Trinity, Bardsea, Cumbria 81, 117
Holy Trinity, Barkingside, Essex 57
Holy Trinity, Barnstaple, Devon 82
Holy Trinity, Berwick-on-Tweed, Northumb 167
Holy Trinity, Bingley, W Yorks 76
Holy Trinity, Blackburn, Lancs 76
Holy Trinity, Blackford, near Wedmore, Som 58
Holy Trinity, Blackpool, Lancs 127
Holy Trinity, Blythburgh, Suffolk 20, 88
Holy Trinity, Bolton, Lancs 64
Holy Trinity, Bordesley, Birmingham, W Mid 62
Holy Trinity, Bosbury, Herefs 44
Holy Trinity, Bothenhampton, Dorset 70
Holy Trinity, Bottisham, Cambs 100
Holy Trinity, Bracknell, Berks 130
Holy Trinity, Bradford-on-Avon, Wilts 43
Holy Trinity, Brimscombe, Glos 61
Holy Trinity, Burdrop, Oxon 80
Holy Trinity, Cambo, Northumb 63
Holy Trinity, Capenhurst, Ches 65

Holy Trinity Cathedral, Waterford 60
Holy Trinity, Chelsea, London 130
Holy Trinity, Chester, Ches 65
Holy Trinity, Cleeve, Som 68
Holy Trinity, Colemans Hatch, Sussex 127
Holy Trinity, Coventry, W Mid 116, 173
Holy Trinity, Dalton, Northumb 63
Holy Trinity, Darlington, Durham 74
Holy Trinity, Deanshanger, Northants 61
Holy Trinity, Ebernoe, Sussex 63
Holy Trinity, Eccleshall, Staffs 58
Holy Trinity, Elgin, Moray 73
Holy Trinity, Ely, Cambs 53
Holy Trinity, Fareham, Hants 69
Holy Trinity, Formby, Lancs 172
Holy Trinity, Goodramgate, York 43, 85, 99
Holy Trinity, Hadley, Salop 69
Holy Trinity, Hanley, Staffs 80
Holy Trinity, Hastings, Sussex 79
Holy Trinity, Holdgate, Salop 151, 190
Holy Trinity, Horsley, Northumb 63
Holy Trinity, Huddersfield, W Yorks 79
Holy Trinity, Hull, E Yorks 135, 173, 193
Holy Trinity, Hurstpierpoint, Sussex 54
Holy Trinity, Idle, W Yorks 69
Holy Trinity, Kendal, Cumbria 60, 81
Holy Trinity, Kensington, London 126
Holy Trinity, Kingwood, Bristol 174
Holy Trinity, Lawrence Hill, Bristol 73
Holy Trinity, Leaton, Salop 77
Holy Trinity, Lenton, Nottingham 145, 167
Holy Trinity, Leven, E Yorks 59
Holy Trinity, Lezayre, IoM 81
Holy Trinity, Llanegwad, Carms 57
Holy Trinity, Long Itchington, Warwicks 31
Holy Trinity, Long Melford, Suffolk 190
Holy Trinity, Lower Beeding, Sussex 63, 128
Holy Trinity, Meanwood, Leeds, W Yorks 145, 146
Holy Trinity, Melbecks, N Yorks 173
Holy Trinity, Messingham, Lincs 82
Holy Trinity, Millom, Cumbria 113
Holy Trinity, Minchinhampton, Glos 106
Holy Trinity, Nailsea, Som 174
Holy Trinity, Paulton, Som 70

Holy Trinity, Queensbury, W Yorks 147
Holy Trinity, Radford, Oxon 71
Holy Trinity, Ripon, N Yorks 79
Holy Trinity, Rothwell, Northants 26
Holy Trinity, Rusholme, Manchester 76
Holy Trinity, Seathwaite, Cumbria 54
Holy Trinity, Seghill, Northumb 63
Holy Trinity, Sheffield, S Yorks 61
Holy Trinity, Sibford Gower, Oxon 80
Holy Trinity, Sissinghurst, Kent 125
Holy Trinity, Skipton, N Yorks 132
Holy Trinity, Sloane Street, London 174
Holy Trinity, South Kensington, London 57
Holy Trinity, Staunton Harold, Leics 3
Holy Trinity, Stirling 115, 124
Holy Trinity, Stratford-on-Avon, Warwicks 172
Holy Trinity, Sunk Island, E Yorks 59
Holy Trinity, Tattershall, Lincs 100
Holy Trinity, Taunton, Som 58
Holy Trinity, Tottenham Green, London 74
Holy Trinity, Uffington, Salop 77
Holy Trinity, Waltham Cross, Herts 57
Holy Trinity, Wensley, N Yorks 87, 88, 147
Holy Trinity, Wood Green, Witney, Oxon 61
Hospital Chapel, Kirkleatham, N Yorks 62

I

Ibrox Parish Church, Glasgow 117
Immaculate Conception, Farm Street, London 166
Independent Chapel, Sunderland, Durham 60
Inverness Cathedral, Highland 17, 73
Iona Abbey, Argyll and Bute 66, 67
Iona Cathedral, Argyll and Bute 66

J

Jesmond Parish Church, Newcastle on Tyne, Tyne & W 60, 166
Jesus College chapel, Oxford 123

K

Keble College chapel, Oxford 58, 117
Keele University Chapel, Newcastle-under-Lyme, Staffs 69
Keir Church, Dumfries and Galloway 58
Kensington Palace chapel, London 168

Kilmadock Church, Perth and Kinross 63
Kilmore Church, Crossgar, Co Down 60
Kilmuir Free Church, Skye, Highland 73
Kincardine O'Neil Church, Aberdeenshire 77
King Charles the Martyr, Tunbridge Wells, Kent 124
King's College Chapel, Cambridge 49, 59, 61, 73, 80, 81, 94, 113, 115, 117, 123, 168, 172
King's Lynn Minster, Norfolk 87
Kintore Parish Church, Aberdeenshire 76
Kirk Christ Lezayre, IoM 116
Kirkcudbright Free Church, Dumfries and Galloway 66
Kirkmahoe Church, Dumfries and Galloway 68
Kirkpatrick Durham Church, Dumfries and Galloway 68
Kirriemuir Baptist Church, Angus 58

L

Lancaster Cathedral 18, 54, 69
Lansdowne United Presbyterian Church, Glasgow 65
Larbert Old Church, Stirling 64
Leicester Cathedral 13, 14, 69, 130, 168
Leighton Buzzard RC Church, Beds 167
Lendal Independent Chapel, York 71, 81
Lesmahagow Old Parish Church, South Lanarkshire 167
Letheringsett Church, Norfolk 129
Lichfield Cathedral, Staffs 14, 35, 37, 43, 68, 72, 75, 83, 114, 124, 132, 146, 168, 172
Lincoln Cathedral 2, 14, 15, 24, 26, 32, 38, 53, 61, 68, 70, 72, 78, 80, 94, 102, 103, 105, 106, 123, 126, 129, 130, 132, 138, 146, 147, 152, 168, 174, 175, 181, 183, 195
Lisburn Cathedral 18
Liverpool Anglican Cathedral, Mersey 16, 75, 116, 126, 148, 166, 174, 181, 183, 193, 195
Liverpool Metropolitan Cathedral, Mersey 18, 126, 127, 128, 174, 193
Llandaff Cathedral, Cardiff, Glam 17, 68, 69, 70, 115, 172

Llanrhychwyn Church, Trefriw, Conwy 1
Logie Parish Church, Stirling 78
Logierait Church, Perth and Kinross 156
Longside Parish Church, Aberdeenshire 77
Ludlow Castle chapel, Salop 26
Lugwardine Chapel, Herefs 135
Luton Hoo Park Chapel, Beds 77
Lyle Community Kirk, Greenock, Inverclyde 116

M
Magdalen College chapel, Oxford 127
Malmesbury Abbey, Wilts 111
Manchester Cathedral 16, 60, 75, 99, 128
Maryhill Free Church, Glasgow 82
Melrose Abbey, Borders 94, 132
Melrose Free Church, Borders 82
Mereworth Castle chapel, Kent 127
Merton College chapel, Oxford 67, 79, 118, 127
Methodist Chapel, Lady Margaret Road, Kentish Town, London 78
Methodist Church, Ealing Broadway, London 78
Middlesbrough Cathedral, N Yorks 18
Milton Abbey, Dorset 78
Milton Mausoleum, Markham Clinton, Notts 77
Motherwell Cathedral, North Lanarkshire 19, 71
Mount St Mary's Church, Leeds, W Yorks 64
Much Wenlock Priory, Salop 34, 195

N
National Cathedral, Washington DC, USA 127
New Abbey Church, Dumfries and Galloway 68
New Abbey Church, Dunfermline, Fife 58
Newcastle Cathedral, Tyne & W 43, 67, 75, 147, 172
New College chapel, Oxford 83, 118, 126, 127
New North Free Church, Forrest Road, Edinburgh 64
Newport Cathedral, Glam 17, 32, 58, 118
Newry Cathedral 19
New Testament Church of God, Sheffield, S Yorks 61
Northampton Cathedral 9, 18
North Church, Aberdeen 77
North Leith Parish Church, Edinburgh 58
Norton Priory, Runcorn, Ches 139
Norwich Cathedral, Norfolk 14, 26, 28, 32, 61, 72, 74, 82, 91, 115, 117, 129, 136, 172, 179, 193
Nottingham Cathedral 18, 71

O
Oban Cathedral (St John's), Argyll and Bute 17, 59, 67, 79, 82
Old Independent Church, Haverhill, Suffolk 166
Oriel College chapel, Oxford 126
Oundle School chapel, Northants 116, 126
Our Lady and All Saints', Parbold, Lancs 67
Our Lady and St Alphege's, Bath, Som 75
Our Lady and St Alphonsus's, Hanley Swan, Worcs 64
Our Lady and St Cuthbert's, Prudhoe, Northumb 116
Our Lady and St Michael's, Abergavenny, Mon 57
Our Lady and St Michael's, Workington, Cumbria 71
Our Lady and St Neot's, Liskeard, Cornwall 64
Our Lady and St Paulinus's, Dewsbury, W Yorks 71
Our Lady and St Thomas of Canterbury's, Harrow, London 125
Our Lady and St Wilfred's, Warwick Bridge, Cumbria 71
Our Lady and St Wilfrid's, Blyth, Northumb 60
Our Lady Help of Christians, Kentish Town, London 78
Our Lady of Good Aid, Motherwell, North Lanarkshire 71
Our Lady of the Snows, Prior Park College, Bath, Som 74
Our Lady of Victories, Kensington, London 62
Our Lady of Walsingham, Norfolk 117

Our Lady's, Lydiate, Lancs 74
Our Lady Star of the Sea and St Maughold Church, Ramsey, IoM 75
Oxford Oratory, Oxford 64

P

Paisley Abbey, Renfrewshire 116
Park Free Church, Helensborough, Argyll and Bute 65
Parton Church, Dumfries and Galloway 68
Peel Cathedral, IoM 16
Pembroke College chapel, Cambridge 83, 171, 174
Pershore Abbey, Worcs 32, 72, 146, 195
Perth Cathedral 17, 58
Peterborough Cathedral, Cambs 2, 14, 37, 70, 75, 81, 106, 115, 118, 168, 172
Peterhouse chapel, Cambridge 173
Plaxtol Parish Church, Kent 3
Pleasington Priory, Lancs 70
Pluscarden Abbey, Elgin, Moray 67
Plymouth Cathedral, Devon 19, 64
Portpatrick Church, Dumfries and Galloway 58
Portsmouth Cathedral, Hants 14, 68, 117, 129, 172
Pudsey Parish Church, Leeds, W Yorks 147

Q

Queen's Chapel of the Savoy, London 52
Queen's Chapel, St James's Palace, London 52
Queen's College chapel, Oxford 127

R

Radley College chapel, Berks 66
Rattray Parish Church, Perth and Kinross 78
Reading Abbey, Berks 72
Reading Minster, Berks 115, 129
Rhos-y-Medre Church, Den 81
Rievaulx Abbey, N Yorks 132
Ripon Cathedral, N Yorks 4, 16, 75, 76, 99, 195
Roath Park Presbyterian Chapel, Cardiff, Glam 63
Robinson College chapel, Cambridge 126
Rochester Cathedral, Kent 14, 59, 61, 75, 127, 189
Romsey Abbey, Hants 126, 139, 174
Rosslyn Chapel, Roslin, Midlothian 189
Rotherham Minster, S Yorks 173
Rothesay Free Church, Argyll and Bute 76
Royal Chapel of All Saints, Windsor, Berks 52
Royal Memorial Chapel, Sandhurst, Berks 173
Royal Naval College chapel, Greenwich, London 168
Rugby School chapel, Warwicks 58
Rutherglen Free Church, South Lanarkshire 82

S

Sacred Heart, Henley, Oxon 167
Saintfield C of I Church, Co Down 156
Salford Cathedral, Manchester 1, 19, 63
Salisbury Cathedral, Wilts 16, 26, 72, 75, 88, 93, 94, 106, 125, 126, 129, 132, 142, 162, 168, 174, 179, 193, 194, 195
Saltaire Congregational Church, W Yorks 147
Sandyford Henderson Church, Glasgow 114, 128
Scargill House chapel, Kettlewell, N Yorks 69
Schlosskirche, Wittenberg, Saxony-Anhalt, Germany 2
Scotstoun Parish Church, Whiteinch, Glasgow 58
Scottish Presbyterian Church, North Shields, Tyne & W 60
Seafield Church, Portnockie, Moray 73
Selby Abbey, N Yorks 34, 46, 72, 84, 106, 169, 172, 190
Sheffield Cathedral, S Yorks 16, 68, 129
Sherborne Abbey, Dorset 78, 129, 166, 183
Shipbourne Church, Kent 62
Shrewsbury Abbey, Salop 132
Shrewsbury Cathedral, Salop 18, 71, 135
Sir William Turner's almshouses chapel, Kirkleatham, Redcar, N Yorks 127
Skelmorlie Parish Church, Ayrshire 117
Skene Parish Church, Aberdeenshire 156

Sorbie Parish Church, Dumfries and Galloway 79
Southwark Cathedral, London 54, 63, 76, 111, 118, 123, 124, 130, 172
Southwell Minster, Notts 17, 31, 58, 59, 72, 127, 146, 172
St Adoenus's, Mounton, Mon 115
St Aelhaiarn's, Guilsfield, Powys 160
St Agnes's, Cawston, Norfolk 21, 32, 93, 98, 100
St Agnes's, Kennington, London 75
St Agnes's, Lambhill, Glasgow 71
St Agnes, Toxteth Park, Liverpool, Mersey 70
St Aidan's, Carlton, N Yorks 68
St Aidan's, Llawhaden, Pembs 190
St Aidan's, Skelmanthorpe, W Yorks 57
St Alban and St Michael's, Golders Green, London 75
St Albans Abbey, Herts 73
St Alban's Anglican Church, Muswellbrook, NSW 74
St Alban's, Bordesley, Birmingham, W Mid 125
St Albans Cathedral, Herts 16, 59, 63, 73, 75, 76, 84, 87, 105, 111, 129, 130, 132, 168
St Alban's Copnor, Portsmouth, Hants 61
St Alban's, Hindhead, Surrey 125
St Alban's, Macclesfield, Ches 71
St Alban's, Pontypool, Mon 74
St Alban's, Westcliffe-on-Sea, Essex 69
St Aldhelm's, Sandleheath, Hants 70
St Alfege's, Greenwich, London 3, 25, 62, 65, 147
St Alkmund's, Whitchurch, Salop 93, 146
St Andrew and St John's, Kemberton, Salop 135
St Andrew and St Mary's, Condover, Salop 154
St Andrew's, Abbots Ripton, Cambs 145
St Andrew's, Aysgarth, N Yorks 147
St Andrew's, Barnwell, Northants 41
St Andrew's, Bayvil, Pembs 100
St Andrew's, Bedingham, Norfolk 44
St Andrew's, Biggleswade, Beds 117

St Andrew's, Bishopstone, Sussex 139
St Andrew's, Bishopthorpe, York 62
St Andrew's, Boynton, E Yorks 126
St Andrew's, Bramfield, Suffolk 44, 102
St Andrew's, Brigstock, Northants 44
St Andrew's, Bromley, London 69
St Andrew's, Broughton, Northants 43
St Andrew's, Burton Overy, Leics 32
St Andrew's, Bywell, Northumb 44
St Andrew-by-the-Wardrobe, Victoria Street, London 127
St Andrew's Cathedral, Aberdeen 17, 172
St Andrew's Cathedral, Dundee 19
St Andrew's Cathedral, Glasgow 19, 71, 168
St Andrew's, Chesterton, Cambs 88
St Andrew's, Churcham, Glos 38
St Andrew's, Cleeve Prior, Worcs 139
St Andrew's, Clifton, Bristol 61
St Andrew's, Congresbury, Som 183
St Andrew's, Cotton, Suffolk 32
St Andrew's, Covehithe, Suffolk 38
St Andrew's, Eastleach Turville, Glos 38
St Andrew's, Enfield, London 166
St Andrew's, Exwick, Devon 65
St Andrew's, Feniton, Devon 106
St Andrew's, Gatton, Surrey 88
St Andrew's, Great Ryburgh, Norfolk 26
St Andrew's, Hampstead, London 115
St Andrew's, Heckington, Lincs 31
St Andrew's, Helion Bumstead, Essex 146
St Andrew's, Hempstead, Essex 25
St Andrew's, Holborn, London 172
St Andrew's, Hope Bowdler, Salop 77, 146, 152
St Andrew's, Hove, Sussex 54
St Andrew's, Jevington, Sussex 160
St Andrew's, Kettleburgh, Suffolk 189
St Andrew's, Kingswood, Surrey 125, 146
St Andrew's, Leytonstone, London 115
St Andrew's, Little Snoring, Norfolk 44, 46
St Andrew's, Livesey, Blackburn, Lancs 69
St Andrew's, Luton, Beds 75
St Andrew's, Maghull, Sefton, Mersey 145
St Andrew's, Marks Tey, Essex 88
St Andrew's, Meonstoke, Hants 124

St Andrew's, Much Hadham, Herts 127
St Andrew's new church, Upleatham, N Yorks 57
St Andrew's, Ombersley, Worcs 73, 156
St Andrew's, Oving, Sussex 114
St Andrew's, Pickworth, Lincs 88, 100
St Andrew's, Plymouth, Devon 173
St Andrew's, Quatt, Salop 92, 107
St Andrew's, Roker, Tyne & W 70, 125
St Andrew's, Rushmere St Andrew, Ipswich, Suffolk 69
St Andrew's, Sherborne St John, Hants 87
St Andrew's, Shifnal, Salop 24, 33
St Andrew's, Soham, Cambs 81
St Andrew's, Southburgh, Norfolk 129
St Andrew's, Surbiton, London 54
St Andrew's, Tain, Highland 114
St Andrew's, Thringstone, Leics 74
St Andrew's, Thursford, Norfolk 130
St Andrew's old church, Upleatham, N Yorks 193
St Andrew's, West Tarring, Sussex 114
St Andrew's, Winterborne Tomson, Dorset 26, 49
St Andrew's, Worcester 43
St Andrew's, Worthing, Sussex 54, 124
St Andrew's, Wraysbury, Bucks 124
St Anne's Cathedral, Belfast 17, 43, 60, 68
St Anne's Cathedral, Leeds, W Yorks 18
St Anne's, East Wittering, Sussex 174
St Anne's, Ellerker, E Yorkshire 70
St Anne's, Lewes, Sussex 128
St Anne's, Limehouse, London 3, 65, 146
St Anne's, Moseley, Birmingham, W Mid 129
St Anne's, Singleton, Lancs 69
St Anne's, Soho, London 146
St Anne's, Wandsworth, London 77
St Anne's, Warrington, Ches 60
St Anselm's, Hatch End, London 116
St Anthony of Padua's, Walker, Newcastle, Tyne & W 60
St Anthony's, Glasgow 66
St Anthony's, Preston, Lancs 75
St Asaph Cathedral, Den 17, 75, 135, 193

St Augustine's Abbey, Bristol 67
St Augustine's, Brookland, Kent 43, 44, 88, 154, 155, 178
St Augustine's, Darlington, Durham 57
St Augustine's, Edgbaston, Birmingham, W Mid 118
St Augustine's, Gillingham, Kent 68
St Augustine's, Kenilworth, Warwicks 71
St Augustine's, Kilburn, London 70
St Augustine's, Langloan, Coatbridge, North Lanarkshire 71
St Augustine's of Canterbury, East Hendred, Oxon 142
St Augustine's, Pendlebury, Lancs 57
St Augustine's, Ramsgate, Kent 71
St Augustine's, Scaynes Hill, Sussex 63
St Barnabas's, Bexhill, Sussex 123
St Barnabas's, Brampton Bryan, Herefs 3
St Barnabas's, Bromborough, Mersey 173
St Barnabas's, Burnmoor, Durham 168
St Barnabas's Cathedral, Nottingham 71
St Barnabas's, Great Strickland, Cumbria 127
St Barnabas's, Great Tey, Essex 156
St Barnabas's, Highfield Place, Sheffield, S Yorks 61
St Barnabas's, Horton-cum-Studley, Oxon 58
St Barnabas's, Jericho, Oxford 54
St Barnabas's, King Square, Finsbury, London 64
St Barnabas's, Queen Camel, Som 183
St Barnabas's, Swanmore, Hants 61
St Barnabas's, Tunbridge Wells, Kent 172
St Barnabas's, Walthamstow, London 58
St Bartholomew's, Binley, Coventry, W Mid 126
St Bartholomew's, Crewkerne, Som 78
St Bartholomew's, Great Gransden, Beds 166
St Bartholomew's, Hognaston, Derbys 147
St Bartholomew's, Nettlebed, Oxon 126
St Bartholomew's, Orford, Suffolk 189
St Bartholomew's, Sydenham, London 81
St Bartholomew's, Tong, Salop 59, 104, 121

St Bartholomew's, Wednesbury, W Mid 146
St Bartholomew the Great's, West Smithfield, London 195
St Bede's, Clapham Road, London 68
St Bede's, Rotherham, S Yorks 63
St Bees Priory Church, Cumbria 88, 174
St Benedict's, Manchester 60
St Benet's, Paul's Wharf, London 83
St Beuno's, Aberffraw, Anglesey 117
St Beuno's Theologate, St Asaph, Den 64
St Birinus's, Redlynch, Wilts 70
St Blane's, Bute, Argyll and Bute 156
St Bledrws's, Betws Bledrws, Cered 127
St Boniface's, Bunbury, Ches 129
St Botolph's, Aldersgate, London 125
St Botolph's, Aldgate, London 165, 168
St Botolph's, Apsley Guise, Beds 114
St Botolph's, Boston, Lincs 32, 61, 79, 94, 176, 193, 195
St Botolph's, Carleton-in-Cleveland, N Yorks 125
St Botolph's, Chevening, Kent 117
St Botolph's, Hadstock, Essex 195
St Botolph's, Trunch, Norfolk 93, 168
St Botolph-without-Bishopsgate, London 167
St Brannock's, Braunton, Devon 99
St Brendan's Cathedral, Clonfert, South Galway 1
St Bride's, Douglas, South Lanarkshire 142
St Bride's Episcopal Church, Glasgow 125
St Bride's, London 167
St Bridget's, Dyserth, Den 106
St Bridget's, Liverpool, Mersey 117
St Buryan's, St Buryan, Cornwall 183
St Candida and Holy Cross, Whitchurch Canonicorum, Dorset 105
St Catharine's College chapel, Cambridge 118
St Catherine's, Baglan, Glam 70
St Catherine's, Kingsdown, Kent 71
St Catherine's, Littlehampton, Sussex 63
St Catherine's, Norwich, Norfolk 58
St Catherine's, Tugford, Salop 190
St Cattwg's, Llanspyddid, Powys 117
St Cenydd's, Llangennith, Glam 38
St Chad's Cathedral, Birmingham, W Mid 5, 25, 71, 118, 129, 174
St Chad's, Coventry, W Mid 78
St Chad's, Far Headingly, Leeds, W Yorks 63, 147
St Chad's, Patchway, Bristol 128
St Chad's, Poulton-le-Fylde, Lancs 60
St Chad's, Shrewsbury, Salop 26, 93, 114, 172
St Chad's, Wybunbury, Ches 80
St Christopher's, Warden Hill, Cheltenham, Glos 183, 184
St Clement Danes, Strand, London 83, 117
St Clement's, Ashamptead, Berks 111
St Clement's, Eastcheap, London 83
St Clement's, Footdee, Aberdeenshire 77
St Clement's, Kensington, London 74
St Clement's, Sandwich, Kent 172
St Clement's, Spotland, Lancs 81
St Columba's Cathedral, Oban, Argyll and Bute 19, 75
St Columba's, Gruline, Isle of Mull, Argyll and Bute 156
St Columba's, Knightbridge, London 68
St Columba's Presbyterian Church, North Shields, Tyne & W 60
St Columba's, Warcop, Cumbria 127
St Columb's Cathedral, Derry 60
St Cross, Appleton Thorn, Ches 67
St Cross, Clayton, Manchester 58
St Cuthbert's, Amble, Northumb 147
St Cuthbert's, Bewcastle, Cumbria 139
St Cuthbert's, Cowpen, Northumb 60
St Cuthbert's, Darwen, Lancs 135
St Cuthbert's, Holme Lacy, Herefs 150
St Cuthbert's, Philbeach Gardens, Kensington, London 116
St Cuthbert's, Wells, Som 20, 37, 106, 174
St Cuthbert's, Wigton, Cumbria 57
St Cuthburga's, Wimborne Minster, Dorset 44
St Cybi's, Holyhead, Anglesey 116
St Cynllo, Nantmell, Powys 114

St Cynon, Tregynon, Powys 128
St Cyprian's, Clarence Gate, London 59, 116
St Cyprian's, Hay Mills, Birmingham, W Mid 118
St David and St Cyfelach's, Llangefelach, Swansea, Glam 115
St David's, Ashprington, Devon 150
St David's, Carmarthen, Carms 65
St David's Cathedral, Cardiff, Glam 19, 71
St Davids Cathedral, Pembs 15, 17, 31, 51, 58, 75, 86, 117, 118, 126, 132, 134, 135, 136, 137, 168, 176, 177, 180, 190
St David's, Glasgow 73
St David's, Swansea, Glam 118
St David's, Upper Largo, Fife 117
St Deiniol's, Hawarden, Flint 115, 123, 128
St Deiniol's, Worthenbury, Wrexham 114
St Denys's, Stanford-in-the-Vale, Berks 105
St Digain's, Llangernyw, Conwy 116
St Dingad's, Llandovery, Carms 128
St Dionis Backchurch, Lombard Street, London 168
St Dionis's, Fulham, London 59
St Dominic's, Newcastle, Tyne & W 60
St Donard's, Dundrum, Co Down 60
St Dubricius's, Porlock, Som 38
St Dunstan-in-the-East, London 43
St Dunstan's, Ashhurst Wood, Sussex 63
St Dunstan's, Canterbury, Kent 179, 195
St Editha's, Tamworth, Staffs 128, 130
St Edith's, Coates-by-Stow, Lincs 100
St Edith's, Eaton-under-Heywood, Salop 44, 45, 100
St Edmund's Abbey, Bury St Edmunds, Suffolk 81
St Edmund's, Acle, Norfolk 38
St Edmundsbury Cathedral, Bury St Edmunds, Suffolk 13, 61, 75, 81
St Edmund's, Crickhowell, Powys 117
St Edmund's, Emneth, Norfolk 128
St Edmund's, South Burlingham, Norfolk 105
St Edmund's, Southwold, Suffolk 88
St Edmund's, Thurne, Norfolk 38
St Edward King and Confessor, Clifford, W Yorks 64

St Edward's, Cambridge 51, 52
St Edward's, Dorrington, Salop 65
St Edward's, Knighton, Powys 132
St Edward's, Rusholme, Manchester 71
St Edwin's, Coniscliffe, Durham 43
St Elidyr's, Crunwere, Pembs 128
St Elisabeth's, Dagenham, London 69
St Elphin's, Warrington, Ches 116, 195
St Endelienta's, Endellion, Cornwall 50, 167
St Etheldreda's, Guilsborough, Northants 115
St Ethedreda's, Hatfield, Herts 106
St Ethelbert's, Hessett, Suffolk 137
St Ethelburga's, Bishopsgate, London 124, 128
St Etheldreda's, Holborn, London 125
St Eugene's Cathedral, Derry, Co Londonderry 167
St Eurgain and St Peter's, Northop, Flint 114, 118, 125
St Eustachius's, Tavistock, Devon 190
St Faith's, Havant, Hants 126
St Faith's, Overbury, Worcs 155
St Ffinan's, Llanffinan, Anglesey 81
St Ffraid's, Llansanffraid Glan Conwy, Conwy 115
St Finbarre's Cathedral, Cork 57
St Finnbarr's, Dornoch, Highland 73
St Finnian's, Lochgelly, Fife 115
St Francis Xavier's, Carfin, North Lanarkshire 71
St Gabriel's, Cricklewood, London 126
St Gabriel's, Govan, Glasgow 58
St George and St Martin of Tours, Caernarfon, Gwynnedd 130
St George's, Altrincham, Ches 124
St George's, Barnsley, S Yorks 166
St George's, Beckenham, London 154, 156
St George's, Bells Close, Lemington, Tyne & W 60
St George's, Bicknolter, Som 173
St George's, Birmingham, W Mid 73
St George's, Bloomsbury, London 3, 65
St George's, Brailes, Warwicks 183
St George's, Brandon Hill, Bristol 77

St George's Cathedral, Southwark, London 19
St George's Chapel, Windsor Castle, Berks 52, 57, 60, 67, 70, 78, 80, 94, 130, 168
St George's, Doncaster, S Yorks 75
St George's, Dunster, Som 155
St George's, Everton, Mersey 73, 195
St George's, Frankwell, Shrewbury, Salop 65
St George's, Gravesend, Kent 4
St George's, Hanover Square, London 4, 67
St George's, Hanworth, London 83
St George's, Hinton St George, Som 25
St George's, Hulme, Manchester 60
St George's in the East, London 3
St George's, Ivychurch, Kent 146
St George's, Kendal, Cumbria 81
St George's, Nailsworth, Glos 173
St George's, New Mills, Derbys 59, 173
St George's, Perry Hill, London 123
St George's, Portobello, Sheffield, S Yorks 66
St George's, Quarry Hill, Sowerbury, W Yorks 81
St George's, Taunton, Som 57
St George's, Toddington, Beds 146
St George's, Tyldesley, Lancs 77
St George's, Walthamstow, London 167
St George's Wesleyan Chapel, Stepney, London 77
St George's, Wolverton, Bucks 126
St George's, Woodsetts, W Yorks 66
St George's, Peel St, York 64
St George the Martyr, Holborn, London 4
St George the Martyr, Southwark, London 4
St German's, Roath, Cardiff, Glam 57
St Giles and St Peter's, Sidbury, Devon 93
St Giles in the Fields, London 4
St Giles's, Bredon, Worcs 93
St Giles's, Camberwell, London 75
St Giles's Cathedral, Edinburgh 43, 116, 142, 147, 179
St Giles's, Chalfont St Giles, Bucks 129
St Giles's, Cheadle, Staffs 71, 132
St Giles's, Codicote, Herts 155
St Giles's, Cripplegate, London 166
St Giles's, Dallington, Sussex 63, 125
St Giles's, Downton, Herefs 135
St Giles's, Horstead Keynes, Sussex 93
St Giles's, Pipe Aston, Herefs 26, 46, 111
St Giles's, Shipbourne, Kent 172
St Giles's, Shrewsbury, Salop 77
St Giles's, Skelton, N Yorks 59
St Giles's, Stoke Poges, Bucks 116
St Giles's, Wendlebury, Oxon 76
St Giles's, Wimborne St Giles, Dorset 25
St Giles's, Wrexham 114, 127
St Giles without Cripplegate, London 172
St Gobban's, Portbradden, Co Antrim 193
St Gregory's, Cheltenham, Glos 64
St Gregory's, Heckingham, Norfolk 29, 151
St Gregory's Minster, Kirkdale, N Yorks 139
St Gregory's, Norwich, Norfolk 82
St Gwendoline's, Llyswen, Powys 117
St Gwyrthwl's, Llanwyrthwyl, Powys 129
St Helen and St Mary's, Bourn, Cambs 32
St Helen's, Abingdon, Oxon 58, 106, 146
St Helen's, Benson, Oxon 148
St Helen's, Berrick Salome, Oxon 93
St Helen's, Bishopsgate, London 43, 167
St Helen's, Clifford Chambers, Warwicks 139
St Helen's, Denton, W Yorks 118
St Helen's, Etwall, Derbys 94
St Helen's, Grove, Notts 61
St Helen's, Hangleton, Sussex 31
St Helen's, Norwich, Norfolk 189
St Helen's, Trowell, Notts 145
St Helen's, Wheathampstead, Herts 129
St Helen Witton's, Northwich, Ches 128
St Hilary's, Spridlington, Lincs 172
St Hilda's, Crofton Park, London 123
St Hilda's, Whitby, N Yorks 63, 124
St Hubert's, Corfe Mullen, Dorset 49, 190
St Ia's, St Ives, Cornwall 20, 49
St Idloes's, Llanidloes, Powys 115
St Illogan's, Illogan, Cornwall 74
St James Garlickhythe, London 83, 184
St James's, Bermondsey, London 74, 166
St James's, Bourton, Oxon 66

St James's, Bury St Edmunds, Suffolk 81
St James's, Chedington, Dorset 58
St James's, Chipping Campden, Glos 125
St James's, Clerkenwell, London 172
St James's, Colchester, Essex 74
St James's, Congleton, Ches 80
St James's, Fulmer, Bucks 114
St James's, Gerrards Cross, Bucks 128
St James's, Goldenacre, Edinburgh 125
St James's, Grimsby, Lincs 116
St James's, Hampton Hill, London 166
St James's, Hereford 135
St James's, Hunstansworth, Durham 168
St James's, Idlicote, Warwicks 99
St James's, Kidbrooke, London 117
St James's, Kinnersley, Herefs 38, 40
St James's, Leckhampstead, Berks 79
St James's, Lissett, E Yorks 179
St James's, Longton, Stoke-on-Trent, Staffs 80
St James's, Louth, Lincs 59, 76, 79, 97, 99, 132, 193
St James's, Milton Abbas, Dorset 83
St James's, Nayland, Suffolk 81, 114
St James's, Norton, Worcs 94, 195
St James's, Piccadilly. London 62, 83, 129
St James's, Pyle, Glam 125
St James's, Salt, Staffs 80
St James's, Shipton, Salop 24
St James's, Somerton, Oxon 130
St James's, Spanish Place, London 166
St James's, Staveley, Cumbria 60, 125
St James's, Stretham, Cambs 174
St James's, Swimbridge, Devon 93
St James's, Tebay, Cumbria 129
St James's, Warter, E Yorks 63
St James's, Welland, Worcs 66
St James's, West Derby, Lancs 81
St James's, Westminster, London 115
St James's, Wigmore, Herefs 132
St James's, Wrightington Bar, Lancs 69
St James the Less, Iron Acton, Glos 150
St James the Less, Pimlico, London 78
St James the Less, Plymouth, Devon 74
St James the Less, Rawtenstall, Lancs 71

St John and All Saints', Easingwold, N Yorks 150
St John Baptist Cathedral, Norwich, Norfolk 118
St John Baptist's, Burford, Oxon 124
St John Baptist's, Garboldisham, Diss, Norfolk 126
St John Evangelist's, Higham, Kent 117
St John Horsleydown, Bermondsey, London 4, 65
St John of Beverley's, Harpham, E Yorks 126
St John's, Adel, Leeds, W Yorks 118
St John's, Aldbury, Herts 189
St John's, Axbridge, Som 109
St John's, Barmouth, Gwynnedd 60
St John's, Barnack, Cambs 44
St John's, Bath, Som 64
St John's, Beachley, Glos 61
St John's, Bethnal Green, London 146
St John's, Boldre, Hants 130
St John's, Bollington, Ches 173
St John's, Brearton, N Yorks 71
St John's, Brownston, Devon 82
St John's, Buckhurst Hill, Essex 117
St John's, Burford, Oxon 37
St John's, Burslem, Staffs 135
St John's, Cardiff, Glam 135
St John's Cathedral, Newfoundland, Canada 75
St John's Cathedral, Portsmouth, Hants 19
St John's Cathedral, Salford, Manchester 63
St John's, Chester, Ches 106
St John's, Cinderford, Glos 57
St John's, Cirencester, Glos 37, 135
St John's, Clayton, Sussex 88
St John's, Clayton, W Yorks 147
St John's, Cleckheaton, W Yorks 54
St John's, Clerkenwell, London 4
St John's College chapel, Cambridge 115, 174
St John's College chapel, Oxford 114
St John's, Copthorne, Sussex 63
St John's, Corby Glen, Lincs 156

St John's, Crosscanonby, Cumbria 93
St John's, Crowle, Worcs 94
St John's, Derby 62
St John's, Dewsbury Moor, W Yorks 79
St John's, Edinburgh 58
St John's, Elkestone, Glos 125, 155
St John's, Escomb, Durham 1, 139
St John's, Farnworth, Lancs 64
St John's, Felbridge, East Grinstead, Sussex 82
St John's Free Church, Johnston Terrace, Edinburgh 64
St John's, Friern Barnet, London 70
St John's, Gamrie, Moray 73
St John's, Glastonbury, Som 93, 99
St John's, Hazlewood, Derbys 117
St John's, High Legh, Macclesfield, Ches 67
St John's, Hildenborough, Kent 59
St John's, Hove, Sussex 63
St John's, Hoxton, London 146
St John's, Hughley, Salop 146
St John's, Hutton Roof, Cumbria 54
St John's, Keswick, Cumbria 74, 123
St John's, Kingsley, Ches 43
St John's, Kinlet, Salop 122
St John's, Lacey Green, Bucks 168
St John's, Lemsford, Herts 129
St John's, Leytonstone, London 57
St John's, Lichfield, Staffs 126
St John's, Llandenny, Mon 70
St John's, Locks Heath, Hants 59
St John's, Norwich, Norfolk 61
St John's, Paignton, Devon 31
St John's, Perlethorpe, Notts 74
St John's, Pewsey, Wilts 149
St John's, Ranmoor, Sheffield, S Yorks 61, 167
St John's, Redhill, Surrey 132
St John's Renfield, Glasgow 115
St John's, Ridgeway, Derbys 66
St John's, Ruyton XI Towns, Salop 77
St John's, Slebech, Pembs 132
St John's, Smith Square, London 4, 53
St John's, Staveley, Derbys 118
St John's, Stratford, London 148

St John's, Thorpe End, Melton Mowbray, Leics 82
St John's, Toxteth Park, Liverpool, Mersey 81
St John's, Treslothan, Cornwall 82
St John's, Upper Hopton, W Yorks 57
St John's, Wakefield, W Yorks 81
St John's, Weston, Bath, Som 68
St John's, Weston, Ches 60
St John's, Wittersham, Kent 124
St John's, Wolverhampton, W Mid 129, 168
St John's, Workington, Cumbria 64
St John's, Worksop, Notts 167
St John the Baptist Cathedral, Norwich, Norfolk 18, 75, 118
St John the Baptist's, Armitage, Staffs 168
St John the Baptist's, Aston Cantlow, Warwicks 125
St John the Baptist's, Crowle, Worcs 195
St John the Baptist's, Farrington Gurney, Som 70
St John the Baptist's, Fladbury, Worcs 172
St John the Baptist's, Flitton, Beds 156
St John the Baptist's, Godolphin Cross, Cornwall 74
St John the Baptist's, Hafod, Swansea, Glam 83
St John the Baptist's, Huntley, Glos 79
St John the Baptist's, Little Maplestead, Essex 26
St John the Baptist's, Liverpool, Mersey 57
St John the Baptist's, Marldon, Devon 167
St John the Baptist's, Meols, Mersey 67
St John the Baptist's, Meopham, Kent 84
St John the Baptist's, Midsomer Norton, Som 70
St John the Baptist's, Needham Market, Suffolk 32
St John the Baptist's, Norwich, Norfolk 75
St John the Baptist's, Old Colwyn, Conwy 60
St John the Baptist's, Pinner, London 116
St John the Baptist's, Stokesay, Salop 3, 91, 99, 122, 163
St John the Baptist's, Thaxted, Essex 25, 26
St John the Divine's, Coventry, W Mid 78

St John the Divine's, Penrhyn-coch, Cered 118
St John the Evangelist's, Cheetham Hill, Manchester 54
St John the Evangelist's, Clifton, Bristol 62
St John the Evangelist's, Edinburgh 114
St John the Evangelist's, Ford, Wilts 70
St John the Evangelist's, Grantham, Lincs 74
St John the Evangelist's, Hook, Hants 68
St John the Evangelist's, Kirkham, Lancs 71
St John the Evangelist's, Knypersley, Staffs 66
St John the Evangelist's, Newbury, Berks 61
St John the Evangelist's, Palmers Green, London 76
St John the Evangelist's, Stoke Row, Oxon 66
St John the Evangelist's, Tipton St John, Devon 65
St John the Evangelist's, Upper Norwood, London 172
St John the Evangelist's, Warrington, Ches 54
St John the Evangelist's, West Hendon, London 68
St Joseph's, Avon Dassett, Warwicks 118
St Joseph's Cathedral, Swansea, Glam 71
St Joseph's, Gateshead, Tyne & W 60
St Joseph's, Tranmere, Birkenhead, Mersey 67
St Jude's, Ormeau Road, Belfast 60
St Jude's, Southsea, Hants 69
St Jude the Apostle with St Matthias-on-the-Weir, Old Market, Bristol 62
St Julian's, Shrewsbury, Salop 114
St Katharine and St Peter's, Milford Haven, Pembs 146
St Katharine's by the Tower, Limehouse, London 52
St Katherine's, Loversall, W Yorks 160
St Katherine's, Regent's Park, London 168
St Kenneth's, Kennoway, Fife 64
St Kentigern's, Crosthwaite, Cumbria 31
St Kyneburgha's, Castor, Cambs 20, 150
St Laurence's, Bradford-on-Avon, Wilts 1, 85
St Laurence's, Church Stretton, Salop 190
St Laurence's, Corringham, Lincs 130
St Laurence's, Ludlow, Salop 94, 101, 106, 116, 130, 146, 170, 173, 178, 179, 189
St Laurence's, South Weston, Oxon 66
St Laurence's, Stanwick, Northants 139
St Laurence's, Upton, Slough, Berks 126
St Lawence's, Evesham, Worcs 80
St Lawrence Jewry, London 129
St Lawrence's, Alton, Hants 139, 145
St Lawrence's, Ansley, Warwicks 125
St Lawrence's, Biddulph, Staffs 80
St Lawrence's, Broughton, Milton Keynes, Bucks 111
St Lawrence's, Chapel Chorlton, Staffs 80
St Lawrence's, Crosby Ravensworth, Cumbria 127
St Lawrence's, Eastcote, London 69
St Lawrence's, Heanor, Derbys 147
St Lawrence's, Ingworth, Norfolk 103, 105, 140
St Lawrence's, Ipswich, Suffolk 195
St Lawrence's, Little Stanmore, London 67
St Lawrence's, Pudsey, W Yorks 79
St Lawrence's, South Cove, Suffolk 35, 38
St Lawrence's, Swindon Village, Glos 44
St Lawrence's, Tubney, Oxon 71
St Lawrence's, West Woodhay, Berks 126
St Lawrence Whitchurch, Edgeware, London 167
St Leodegar's, Hunston, Sussex 126
St Leonard's, Bilston, W Mid 156
St Leonard's, Cleator, Cumbria 81
St Leonard's, Hythe, Kent 26
St Leonard's, Leverington, Cambs 106
St Leonard's, Malinslee, Salop 79
St Leonard's, Rodney Stoke, Som 106
St Leonard's, South Stoke, Sussex 26
St Leonard's, St Andrew's, Fife 115
St Leonard's, St Leonards-on-Sea, Sussex 75
St Leonard's, Swithland, Leics 173

St Leonard's, Waterstock, Oxon 69
St Llonio's, Llandinam, Powys 115
St Lucius's, Farnley Tyas, W Yorks 59
St Luke Old Street, London 65
St Luke's, Battersea, London 126, 172
St Luke's, Bromley, London 126
St Luke's, Camden, London 123
St Luke's, Chelsea, London 74, 116, 167
St Luke's, Downham, Lewisham, London 69
St Luke's, Dunham on the Hill, Ches 65
St Luke's, Eccleshill, W Yorks 72
St Luke's, Hodnet, Salop 44
St Luke's, Ironbridge, Salop 114
St Luke's, Kew, London 126
St Luke's, Maidenhead, Berks 115
St Luke's, Milland, Sussex 130
St Luke's, Old Street, London 4, 166
St Luke's, Sambrook, Salop 117
St Luke's, Wallsend, Tyne & W 117
St Luke's, West Norwood, London 148
St Macartan's Cathedral, Clogher, Co Tyrone 17
St Macartin's Cathedral, Enniskillen, Co Fermanagh 18
St Machar's Cathedral, Aberdeen 116
St Magnus's Cathedral, Kirkwall, Orkney 105, 135
St Magnus the Martyr, London Bridge, London 124
St Mahew's Church, Cardross, Argyll and Bute 67
St Malangell's, Pennant Melangell, Powys 160
St Margaret and St Peter's, Pett, Sussex 117
St Margaret of Antioch, Leeds, W Yorks 68
St Margaret Pattens, Eastcheap, London 83
St Margaret's, Angmering, Sussex 117, 124, 129
St Margaret's, Bodelwyddan, Den 125, 129
St Margaret's, Bowers Gifford, Essex 124
St Margaret's, Burnham Norton, Norfolk 44
St Margaret's, Buxted, Sussex 114
St Margaret's Chapel, Edinburgh Castle 1
St Margaret's, Cley, Norfolk 87, 88

St Margaret's, Crick, Northants 167
St Margaret's, Dalry, N Ayrshire 79
St Margaret's, Darenth, Kent 153, 155
St Margaret's, Hales, Norfolk 38
St Margaret's, Hardley, Norfolk 61
St Margaret's, Herringfleet, Suffolk 38
St Margaret's, Ilkley, W Yorks 76
St Margaret's, King's Lynn, Norfolk 94
St Margaret's Lothbury, London 83
St Margaret's, Margaretting, Essex 127
St Margaret's, Mountain Ash, Glam 124
St Margaret's, Paston, Norfolk 172
St Margaret's, Roath, Cardiff, Glam 70
St Margaret's, Spaxton, Som 99
St Margaret's, St Margarets, Herefs 23, 100, 101
St Margaret's, West Hoathly, Sussex 156
St Margaret's, Westminster, London 73, 139
St Margaret's, Whaddon, Glos 173
St Marie's, Brewood, Staffs 71
St Marie's Cathedral, Sheffield, S Yorks 19, 63
St Mark's, Bilton, Rugby, Warwicks 174
St Mark's, Binfield, Berks 54
St Mark's, Blackburn, Lancs 76
St Mark's, Chadderton, Manchester 69
St Mark's, Easton, Bristol 62
St Mark's, Kennington, London 146
St Mark's, Leicester 59
St Mark's, Mansfield, Notts 68, 167
St Mark's, Shelton, Staffs 69
St Mark's, Staplefield, Sussex 125
St Martin-cum-Gregory, York 126
St Martin-in-the-Fields, London 62
St Martin Ludgate, London 126
St Martin's, Brampton, Cumbria 115
St Martin's, Brasted, Kent 124
St Martin's, Brighton, Sussex 1
St Martin's, Canterbury, Kent 1
St Martin's, Dorking, Surrey 83, 126
St Martin's, Epsom, Surrey 130
St Martin's, Haverfordwest, Pembs 123
St Martin's, Kensal Rise, London 125
St Martin's, Lewannick, Cornwall 88
St Martin's, Ludgate, London 83

St Martin's, Oswestry Ferry, Lincs 129
St Martin's, Roath, Cardiff, Glam 116
St Martin's, Ruislip, London 88
St Martin's, Scarborough, N Yorks 57
St Martin's, South Willingham, Lincs 145
St Martin's, The Bullring, Birmingham, W Mid 180
St Martin's, Yapham, E Yorks 128
St Mary Abbots, Kensington, London 75, 195
St Mary Abchurch, London 62
St Mary and All Saints', Fotheringhay, Northants 68
St Mary and All Saints', Great Budworth, Ches 173
St Mary and All Saints', Whalley, Lancs 70, 99
St Mary and St Augustine's, Stamford, Lincs 62
St Mary and St Barlock's, Norbury, Derbys 87, 111
St Mary and St Blaise's, Boxgrove, Sussex 124
St Mary and St David's, Kilpeck, Herefs 26, 29, 93, 105, 189, 190, 191, 192
St Mary and St Finnan's, Glenfinnan, Highland 71
St Mary and St John's, Oxford 114
St Mary and St John's, Pleasington, Lancs 70
St Mary and St Lambert's, Stonham Aspall, Suffolk 159
St Mary and St Michael's, Bonds, Lancs 69
St Mary and St Nicholas's, Beaumaris, Anglesey 128
St Mary and St Nicholas's, Littlemore, Oxon 80, 116
St Mary and St Nicholas's, Spalding, Lincs 20, 32
St Mary Brookfield, Camden, London 58
St Mary de Crypt, Gloucester 132
St Mary de Haura, Shoreham, Sussex 128
St Mary Immaculate, Falmouth, Cornwall 64
St Mary in the Marsh, Kent 145, 155

St Mary-le-Bow, Cheapside, London 63
St Mary-le-Strand, London 4, 62
St Mary Magdalene's, Bolney, Sussex 150
St Mary Magdalene's, Bridgnorth, Salop 1, 79
St Mary Magdalene's, Caldecote, Herts 105
St Mary Magdalene's, East Moors, N Yorks 75
St Mary Magdalene's, Enfield, London 123
St Mary Magdalene's, Flaunden, Herts 75
St Mary Magdalene's, Great Alne, Warwicks 118
St Mary Magdalene's, Great Hamden, Bucks 129
St Mary Magdalene's, Helmsley, N Yorks 49
St Mary Magdalene's, Himbleton, Worcs 100
St Mary Magdalene's, Lanercost Priory, Cumbria 123
St Mary Magdalene's, Lockleaze, Bristol 128
St Mary Magdalene's, Newark, Notts 53, 176
St Mary Magdalene's, Paddington, London 78, 123, 167
St Mary Magdalene's, Taunton, Som 57, 117
St Mary Magdalene's, Torquay, Devon 74
St Mary Magdalene's, Westerfield, Suffolk 100
St Mary Magdalene's, Woolwich, London 4
St Mary Magdalene's, Yarm, Stockton-on-Tees, Durham 126
St Mary Major's, Ilchester, Som 44
St Mary of Furness, Barrow-in-Furness, Lancs 71
St Mary Redcliffe's, Bristol 193
St Mary's, Abbey-cym-hir, Powys 123
St Mary's, Abbeydore, Herefs 104
St Mary's, Abbots Ann, Andover, Hants 145
St Mary's, Acocks Green, Birmingham, W Mid 26
St Mary's, Acton Burnell, Salop 132
St Mary's, Amersham, Bucks 128
St Mary's, Amport, Hants 126

St Mary's, Arnold, Notts 31, 167
St Mary's, Ashby, Suffolk 39, 44
St Mary's, Ashford, Kent 87
St Mary's, Ashwell, Herts 32, 43
St Mary's, Atherington, Devon 100
St Mary's, Avington, Hants 93
St Mary's, Bagillt, Flint 81
St Mary's, Baldock, Herts 100
St Mary's, Barnsley, S Yorks 173
St Mary's, Bathwick, Som 70
St Mary's, Battlefield, Salop 77, 132, 135
St Mary's, Battle, Sussex 117
St Mary's, Beaumaris, Anglesey 155
St Mary's, Bepton, Sussex 114
St Mary's, Berkeley, Glos 44, 100, 139, 160
St Mary's, Betws-y-Coed, Conwy 54
St Mary's, Bexley, London 38, 41, 43, 140
St Mary's, Bibury, Glos 125
St Mary's, Bickleigh, Devon 65
St Mary's, Bicton, Devon 65
St Mary's, Billingsley, Salop 30
St Mary's, Bilston, W Mid 62, 156
St Mary's, Bishop's Lydeard, Som 99
St Mary's, Blackburn, Lancs 70
St Mary's, Blackhill, Durham 60
St Mary's, Bletchingley, Surrey 32
St Mary's, Blundeston, Suffolk 105
St Mary's, Bodney, Norfolk 173
St Mary's, Boston Spa, W Yorks 147
St Mary's, Bournemouth, Hants 69
St Mary's, Bourne Street, London 124, 172
St Mary's, Brabourne, Kent 93
St Mary's, Bradford Abbas, Dorset 99
St Mary's, Bramford, Suffolk 93, 100
St Mary's, Bramshott, Hants 123
St Mary's, Brecon, Powys 31
St Mary's, Bromfield, Salop 37
St Mary's, Broughton, Hants 155
St Mary's, Broughton, Lincs 44
St Mary's, Brownsea Island, Dorset 114
St Mary's, Bryanston Square, London 77
St Mary's, Bucklebury, Berks 155
St Mary's, Bures, Suffolk 106
St Mary's, Burghfield, Berks 127
St Mary's, Burley in Wharfedale, W Yorks 72

St Mary's, Burnham on Crouch, Essex 139
St Mary's, Burpham, Sussex 128
St Mary's, Burton Bradstock, Dorset 70
St Mary's, Burwell, Cambs 61, 116, 189
St Mary's, Bury St Edmunds, Suffolk 20, 59
St Mary's-by-the-sea, Wemyss, Fife 67
St Mary's, Cadogan Street, London 115
St Mary's, Caernarfon, Gwynedd 124
St Mary's Cathedral, Aberdeen 19
St Mary's Cathedral, Edinburgh 75, 124, 193
St Mary's Cathedral, Newcastle on Tyne, Tyne & W 128
St Mary's, Chalgrove, Oxon 106
St Mary's Chapel, Alnwick, Northumb 63
St Mary's, Chelsea, London 116
St Mary's, Chiddingfold, Surrey 150
St Mary's, Chilham, Kent 128
St Mary's, Chilton Foliat, Wilts 130
St Mary's, Chippenham, Wilts 130
St Mary's, South Leith, Edinburgh 64
St Mary's, Claverton, Som 156
St Mary's, Cleator, Cumbria 71
St Mary's, Cleland, North Lanarkshire 71
St Mary's, Cleobury Mortimer, Salop 85, 190
St Mary's, Clifton, Bristol 76
St Mary's, Climping, Sussex 156
St Mary's, Clumber, Notts 57
St Mary's, Cobham, Kent 87
St Mary's, Colkirk, Norfolk 32
St Mary's College chapel, Oscott, Birmingham, W Mid 129
St Mary's, Crich, Derbys 94
St Mary's, Cratfield, Suffolk 191
St Mary's, Cricklade, Wilts 150
St Mary's, Cropredy, Oxon 146
St Mary's, Croscombe, Som 49
St Mary's, Dedham, Essex 81
St Mary's, Deerhurst, Glos 20
St Mary's, Denham, Bucks 117
St Mary's, Dennington, Suffolk 22, 39, 40, 87, 89, 98, 108, 119, 137, 141, 171, 190, 191
St Mary's, Derby 71, 129

St Mary's, Derwen, Den 130, 150
St Mary's, Devizes, Wilts 174
St Mary's, Devonport, Devon 74
St Mary's, Disley, Ches 173
St Mary's, Diss, Norfolk 31
St Mary's, Dodington, Glos 83
St Mary's, Dymock, Glos 139, 172
St Mary's, Ealing, London 79
St Mary's, East Barnet, Herts 155
St Mary's, East Bergholt, Suffolk 180, 184
St Mary's, East Stoke, Dorset 69
St Mary's, Edith Weston, Rut 113, 168
St Mary's, Elsing, Norfolk 93
St Mary's, Ewelme, Oxon 20
St Mary's, Fairfield, Worcs 61
St Mary's, Fairford, Glos 113, 158
St Mary's, Fawley, Bucks 126
St Mary's, Fawsley, Northants 111
St Mary's, Feltwell, Norfolk 99
St Mary's, Fen Ditton, Cambs 99
St Mary's, Fishguard, Pembs 115
St Mary's, Fordwich, Kent 43
St Mary's, Fountains Abbey, Ripon, N Yorks 57
St Mary's, Frampton on Severn, Glos 135
St Mary's, Friston, Sussex 117, 160
St Mary's, Frittenden, Kent 66
St Mary's, Gamlingay, Beds 145
St Mary's, Garthorpe, Leics 93
St Mary's, Gillingham, Dorset 31, 58
St Mary's, Gislingham, Suffolk 32
St Mary's, Gladestry, Powys 43
St Mary's, Glasgow 79
St Mary's, Glynde, Sussex 125
St Mary's, Gosforth, Cumbria 156
St Mary's, Grantham, Lincs 82
St Mary's, Greasbrough, W Yorks 81
St Mary's, Great Milton, Oxon 85
St Mary's, Great Ouseburn, N Yorks 127
St Mary's, Grendon, Northants 150
St Mary's, Haddiscoe, Norfolk 22, 44
St Mary's, Hale, Hants 53
St Mary's, Hampden Park, Eastbourne, Sussex 117
St Mary's, Hampton, London 123, 166
St Mary's, Hanley Castle, Worcs 115
St Mary's, Harley, Salop 77
St Mary's, Hatfield Broad Oak, Essex 176
St Mary's, Henham, Essex 160
St Mary's, Hickling, Norfolk 184
St Mary's, Higham Ferrers, Northants 128
St Mary's, Highley, Salop 77
St Mary's, Holystone, Nothumb 160
St Mary's, Houghton-on-the-Hill, Norfolk 99
St Mary's, Hulme, Manchester 60
St Mary's, Huntingfield, Suffolk 37
St Mary's, Ilford, Essex 74
St Mary's, Ilminster, Som 147
St Mary's, Inverness, Highland 73
St Mary's, Iwerne Minster, Dorset 130
St Mary's, Jackfield, Salop 135
St Mary's, Kempley, Glos 99
St Mary's, Knowsley, Mersey 173
St Mary's, Lakenheath, Suffolk 111
St Mary's, Lamberhurst, Kent 126
St Mary's, Langley Marish, Berks 88, 176
St Mary's, Lasborough, Glos 81
St Mary's, Laverstoke, Hants 70
St Mary's, Leighton Bromswold, Cambs 184
St Mary's, Liss, Hants 54
St Mary's, Longnor, Salop 141, 163
St Mary's, Louth, Lincs 82
St Mary's, Lower Dicker, Sussex 155
St Mary's, Lydiard Tregoze, Wilts 25
St Mary's, Lytchett Maltravers, Dorset 43
St Mary's, Madresfield, Worcs 125
St Mary's, Marston Moretaine, Beds 44
St Mary's, Martham, Norfolk 61
St Mary's, Marylebone Road, London 64
St Mary's, Middleton, W Yorks 59
St Mary's, Mildenhall, Suffolk 26
St Mary's, Molesey, Manchester 43
St Mary's, Molland, Devon 99
St Mary's, Monmouth 77, 124, 132
St Mary's (RC), Monmouth 57
St Mary's, Moreton, Staffs 80
St Mary's, Mulberry Street, Manchester 38
St Mary's, Myton-on-Swale, N Yorks 147

St Mary's, Nantwich, Ches 37
St Mary's, New Mills, Derbys 43
St Mary's, Newport, Mon 74
St Mary's, New Radnor, Powys 132
St Mary's, North Creake, Norfolk 20
St Mary's, North Stifford, Essex 128
St Mary's, North Stoke, Oxon 139
St Mary's, Nun Monkton, N Yorks 127
St Mary's, Oakley, Bucks 116
St Mary's, Offton, Suffolk 106
St Mary's, Osterley, London 123, 168
St Mary's, Ottery St Mary, Devon 37, 67, 94, 109, 129, 131
St Mary's, Oxenhope, W Yorks 57
St Mary's, Oxford 57
St Mary's, Paddington Green, London 167
St Mary's, Painswick, Glos 145, 160
St Mary's, Patshull, Staffs 62
St Mary's, Pembridge, Herefs 180
St Mary's, Plympton, Devon 150, 172
St Mary's, Portreath, Cornwall 82
St Mary's, Powerstock, Devon 88
St Mary's, Prescot, Lancs 99
St Mary's, Preston-on-Stour, Warwicks 127
St Mary's, Princes Risborough, Bucks 135
St Mary's Priory, Fulham Road, London 64
St Mary's, Pulford, Ches 60
St Mary's, Pulham St Mary, Norfolk 37
St Mary's, Putney, London 130
St Mary's RC Cathedral, Newcastle, Tyne & W 172
St Mary's, Redbourne, Herts 129
St Mary's, Rhuddlan, Den 129
St Mary's, Rockbeare, Devon 116
St Mary's, Rotherhithe, London 67, 167
St Mary's, Roughton, Norfolk 44
St Mary's, Ruabon, Wrexham 117, 129
St Mary's, Rydal, Cumbria 81
St Mary's, Rye, Sussex 142
St Mary's, Saffron Walden, Essex 81
St Mary's, Saxlingham Nethergate, Norfolk 113
St Mary's, Scarborough, N Yorks 59
St Mary's, Shrewsbury, Salop 22, 23, 29, 106, 108, 119, 130, 132, 133, 146, 166, 169

St Mary's, Silverton, Devon 155
St Mary's, Somers Town, London 66
St Mary's, Sompting, Sussex 31, 38, 39, 44
St Mary's, South Creake, Norfolk 20
St Mary's, South Hylton, Sunderland, Tyne & W 61, 76
St Mary's, Staindrop, Durham 100, 147
St Mary's, Stamford, Lincs 130
St Mary's, Stapleford Abbots, Essex 168
St Mary's, Staverton, Northants 123, 129
St Mary's, St Mary in the Marsh, Kent 145
St Mary's, St Neots, Cambs 20
St Mary's, Stockton-on-Tees, Durham 71
St Mary's, Stoke-sub-Hamdon, Som 155
St Mary's, Strata Florida, Cered 127
St Mary's, Sturminster Newton, Dorset 124
St Mary's, Sunderland, Durham 57
St Mary's, Swansea, Glam 54, 126, 129
St Mary's, Tadcaster, N Yorks 147
St Mary's, Tenby, Pembs 125, 146
St Mary Steps, Exeter, Devon 142
St Mary's, Thame, Oxon 139
St Mary's, Thenford, Northants 118
St Mary, St Katherine and All Saints', Edington, Wilts 31
St Mary's, Totnes, Devon 100
St Mary's, Truro, Cornwall 167
St Mary's, Twickenham, London 67
St Mary's, Twyford, Hants 117
St Mary's, Tyndalls Park, Bristol 74
St Mary's, Uffculme, Devon 65
St Mary's, Walberton, Sussex 117
St Mary's, Walmer, Kent 54
St Mary's, Wanstead, Essex 64
St Mary's, Wargrave, Berks 146
St Mary's, Warwick 26, 30, 31, 88, 93, 95, 97, 111, 127, 144, 171, 173
St Mary's, Wavendon, Bucks 114
St Mary's, Weeford, Staffs 83
St Mary's, Wellingborough, Northants 59, 116
St Mary's, Welwyn, Herts 129
St Mary's, West Chiltington, Sussex 43
St Mary's, Westerham, Kent 100
St Mary's, West Fordington, Dorchester,

Dorset 70
St Mary's, West Walton, Norfolk 44
St Mary's, Whitby, N Yorks 88
St Mary's, Wiggenhall, Norfolk 99
St Mary's, Wirksworth, Derbys 149
St Mary's, Wisbech, Cambs 139
St Mary's, Wiveton, Norfolk 86
St Mary's, Wollaton Park, Nottingham 174
St Mary's, Wombwell, S Yorks 166
St Mary's, Woolpit, Suffolk 32, 99
St Mary's, Wroxham, Norfolk 190
St Mary's, Wymeswold, Leics 118
St Mary's, Yarmouth, Norfolk 74
St Mary's, Yealand Conyers, Lancs 69
St Mary the Virgin's, Halkyn, Flint 60
St Mary the Virgin's, Plumtree, Notts 114
St Mary the Virgin's, Turville, Bucks 126
St Mary Undercroft, Palace of Westminster, London 52
St Mary Woolnoth, London 65
St Mathias and St George's, Astwood Bank, Worcs 66
St Matthew and St James's, Liverpool, Mersey 117
St Matthew's, Bristol 73
St Matthew's, Buckley, Flint 69, 123, 166
St Matthew's, Campfield, Manchester 54
St Matthew's, Chelston, Torquay, Devon 69
St Matthew's, Landscove, Devon 70
St Matthew's, Oxhey, Herts 125
St Matthew's, Sheffield, S Yorks 61, 167
St Matthew's, Torquay, Devon 74
St Matthew's, Westminster, London 116
St Matthias Old Church, Tower Hamlets, London 3
St Matthias's, Richmond, London 128
St Maxentius's, Bradshaw, Manchester 54
St Melangell's, Pennant Melangell, Powys 105
St Mellanus's, Mullion, Cornwall 31
St Meubred's, Cardinham, Cornwall 99
St Michael and All Angels, Alphington, Exeter 65
St Michael and All Angels, Atherton, Manchester 54
St Michael and All Angels, Averham, Notts 145
St Michael and All Angels, Bassett, Southampton, Hants 173
St Michael and All Angels, Bedford Park, London 76
St Michael and All Angels, Brighton, Sussex 57, 125
St Michael and All Angels, Brownsover, Warwicks 174
St Michael and All Angels, Bude, Cornwall 82
St Michael and All Angels Chapel, Blackheath, London 77
St Michael and All Angels, Croydon, London 70
St Michael and All Angels, Galleywood Common, Essex 74
St Michael and All Angels, Great Houghton, S Yorks 3
St Michael and All Angels, Great Witley, Worcs 172
St Michael and All Angels, Hafod, Cered 83
St Michael and All Angels, Inverness, Highland 59, 116
St Michael and All Angels, Ledbury, Herefs 180
St Michael and All Angels, Little Leigh, Ches 67
St Michael and All Angels, Little Marcle, Herefs 66
St Michael and All Angels, Lowfield Heath, Sussex 57
St Michael and All Angels, Lyndhurst, Hants 82
St Michael and All Angels, Lyneham, Wilts 174
St Michael and All Angels, Mitcheldean, Glos 26
St Michael and All Angels, South Shields, Tyne & W 167
St Michael and All Angels, Thornton, Bucks 78
St Michael and All Angels, Waterford, Herts 115, 125

St Michael and All Angels, Winwick, Northants 149
St Michael and All Angels, Withyham, Sussex 25
St Michael and St Mary's, Melbourne, Derbys 26
St Michael's, Aigburth, Mersey 73
St Michael's, Alberbury, Salop 24
St Michael's, Altcar, Lancs 60
St Michael's, Aughton, Lancs 148
St Michael's, Aylsham, Norfolk 35, 41, 87, 116, 156, 158
St Michael's, Baldhu, Cornwall 82
St Michael's, Basingstoke, Hants 148
St Michael's, Bath, Som 1, 68, 171, 174
St Michael's, Bettws yn Rhos, Conwy 81
St Michael's, Bishops Stortford, Herts 129
St Michael's, Boulge, Suffolk 63
St Michael's, Brantham, Suffolk 166
St Michael's, Brereton, Staffs 80
St Michael's, Bulley, Glos 26
St Michael's, Burrowbridge, Som 58
St Michael's, Castle Frome, Herefs 93
St Michael's, Chagford, Devon 190
St Michael's, Chester, Ches 65
St Michael's, Compton Martin, Som 155
St Michael's, Cornhill, London 4
St Michael's, Coxwold, N Yorks 44, 126
St Michael's, Croft, Herefs 132
St Michael's, Cwmystwyth, Cered 123
St Michael's, Dowdeswell, Glos 26
St Michael's, Dufftown, Moray 73
St Michael's, Ewenny, Glam 130
St Michael's, Framlingham, Suffolk 22, 70, 171, 174
St Michael's, Great Witley, Worcs 127
St Michael's, Great Wolford, Warwicks 80, 150
St Michael's, Grimsargh, Lancs 54
St Michael's, Haselbech, Northants 130
St Michael's, Highgate, London 123
St Michael's, Hughenden, Bucks 54
St Michael's, Kirk Langley, Derbys 100
St Michael's, Kirk Michael, IoM 81
St Michael's, Lambourn, Berks 130
St Michael's, Ledbury, Worcs 167
St Michael's, Llanyblodwel, Salop 37
St Michael's, Madeley, Salop 79, 154, 156, 157, 159
St Michael's, Munslow, Salop 77, 114
St Michael's, Newhaven, Sussex 63
St Michael's, Northchapel, Sussex 117
St Michael's, North Waltham, Hants 114
St Michael's, Partridge Green, Sussex 63
St Michael's, Peasenhall, Suffolk 189
St Michael's, Silverstone, Northants 74
St Michael's, Sowton, Devon 65
St Michael's, Spreyton, Devon 190
St Michael's, St Albans, Herts 63
St Michael's, Stanton Harcourt, Oxon 69
St Michael's, Stewkley, Bucks 26
St Michael's, Stinsford, Dorset 94, 162
St Michael's, St Michael's on Wyre, Lancs 128
St Michael's, West Overton, Wilts 70
St Michael's, Winterbourne Earls, Wilts 124
St Michael's, Winterbourne, Glos 130
St Michael's, Wood Green, London 129, 147
St Michael the Archangel's, Two-Mile-Hill, Bristol 62
St Mildred's, Lee, London 117
St Mirin's Cathedral, Paisley, Renfrewshire 19
St Modwen's, Burton-on-Trent, Staffs 77
St Mor and St Deiniol's, Llanfor, Gwynedd 124
St Morwenna and St John's, Morwenstow, Cornwall 99
St Mungo's Cathedral, Glasgow 62
St Nevet's, Lanivet, Cornwall 156
St Nicholas and St Cyriac's, South Pool, Devon 41, 86, 192
St Nicholas Buccleuch, Dalkeith, Midlothian 166
St Nicholas's, Addlethorpe, Lincs 20
St Nicholas's, Arundel, Sussex 117
St Nicholas's, Baulking, Oxon 100
St Nicholas's, Blakeney, Norfolk 32, 122, 170, 172

St Nicholas's, Brighton, Sussex 124
St Nicholas's, Buckenham, Norfolk 44, 155
St Nicholas's, Castle Hedingham, Essex 32
St Nicholas's, Denston, Suffolk 100
St Nicholas's, East Grafton, Wilts 132
St Nicholas's, Fyfield, Oxon 106
St Nicholas's, Grafton, Wilts 130
St Nicholas's, Great Yarmouth, Norfolk 61, 166, 193
St Nicholas's, Harpenden, Herts 129
St Nicholas's, Heythrop, Oxon 54
St Nicholas's, Newport, Salop 125
St Nicholas's, Nicholaston, Swansea, Glam 115
St Nicholas's, North Walsham, Norfolk 93
St Nicholas's, Ozleworth, Glos 44
St Nicholas's, Rushbrooke, Suffolk 100
St Nicholas's, Saltdean, Sussex 68
St Nicholas's, Stanford on Avon, Northants 174
St Nicholas's, Stevenage, Herts 32
St Nicholas's, Studland, Dorset 190
St Nicholas's, Warwick 116
St Nicholas's West, Aberdeen 62
St Nicholas's, West Itchenor, Sussex 125
St Nicholas's, Willoughby, Warwicks 115
St Nicholas's, Winterborne Clenston, Dorset 81
St Nicholas's, Worth, Sussex 31
St Nicolas's, Kings Norton, Birmingham, W Mid 118
St Nicolas's, Newbury, Berks 118, 167
St Nicolas's, Oddington, Glos 111
St Nicolas's, South Kilworth, Leics 168
St Nicolas's, Taplow, Bucks 123
St Nidan's, Llanidan, Anglesey 81
St Nikolaus's, Hamburg, Germany 75
St Ninian's Cathedral, Perth and Kinross 58
St Ninian's, Kilmartin, Glenurquhart, Highland 73
St Ninian's, Nairn, Highland 172
St Ninian's, Ninekirks, Cumbria 3
St Olave's, Stoke Newington, London 126
St Olave's, York 127
St Osmund's, Evershot, Dorset 145

St Oswald's, Collingham, W Yorks 88
St Oswald's, Coventry, W Mid 78
St Oswald's, Durham 167
St Oswald's, Flamborough, E Yorks 100
St Oswald's, Preesall, Lancs 128
St Oswald's, Sowerby, N Yorks 43
St Oswald's, Warton, Lancs 129
St Oswald's, Winwick, Ches 173
St Padarn's, Llanbadarn Fawr, Cered 113
St Pancras's, Alton Pancras, Dorset 88
St Pancras's, Ipswich, Suffolk 62
St Pancras's, Kingston, Sussex 160
St Pancras's New Church, London 66
St Pancras's, Widecombe-in-the-Moor, Devon 121, 190, 191
St Patrick's, Anderston, Glasgow 118
St Patrick's, Bampton, Cumbria 127
St Patrick's Cathedral, Armagh 17
St Patrick's Cathedral, Dublin 60
St Patrick's, Kilrea, Co Londonderry 77
St Patrick's RC Cathedral, Armagh 19
St Paul and St John's, Monklands, Airdrie, North Lanarkshire 167
St Paul's, Addlestone, Surrey 74
St Paul's, Alnwick, Northumb 74
St Paul's, Alverthorpe, W Yorks 53
St Paul's, Arbourthorne, S Yorks 173
St Paul's, Bledlow Ridge, Bucks 126
St Paul's, Buttershaw, W Yorks 72
St Paul's Cathedral, Dundee 75
St Paul's Cathedral, London 3, 8, 62, 67, 72, 83, 85, 106, 146, 147, 162, 166, 172, 173, 174, 176, 180, 183, 184, 193
St Paul's Cathedral, Melbourne, Victoria, Australia 58
St Paul's Church for Seamen, Whitechapel, London 73
St Paul's, Colwyn Bay, Conwy 60
St Paul's, Covent Garden, London 62
St Paul's, Deptford, London 4, 53, 130
St Paul's, Farington, Lancs 76
St Paul's, Hendon, Durham 60
St Paul's, Herne Hill, London 172
St Paul's, Jarrow, Tyne & W 126
St Paul's, Lindale, Cumbria 81

St Paul's, Mautby, Norfolk 38
St Paul's, Meadowside, Dundee 82
St Paul's, Pilrig, Leith, Edinburgh 116
St Paul's, Pishill, Oxon 126
St Paul's, Preston, Lancs 73
St Paul's, Scotforth, Lancaster 76
St Paul's, Sheffield, S Yorks 78, 173
St Paul's, Sketty, Glam 83
St Paul's, Slough, Bucks 123
St Paul's, Stoneycroft, Liverpool, Mersey 75
St Paul's, Walton Street, Oxford 80
St Paul's, Witherslack, Cumbria 118
St Paul's, Yelverton, Devon 69
St Peblig's, Caernarfon, Gwynedd 124
St Peter ad Vincula, Hampton Lucy, Warwicks 73
St Peter ad Vincula, Tibberton, Worcs 66
St Peter ad Vincula, Tower of London 52, 80
St Peter and St Francis's, Prestatyn, Den 67
St Peter and St Paul's, Aldeburgh, Suffolk 126
St Peter and St Paul's, Appleford, Oxon 168
St Peter and St Paul's, Bardwell, Suffolk 166
St Peter and St Paul's, Broadhempston, Devon 31
St Peter and St Paul's, Buckingham 115
St Peter and St Paul's, Chingford, Essex 81
St Peter and St Paul's, Coleshill, Warwicks 77
St Peter and St Paul's, Great Missenden, Bucks 128
St Peter and St Paul's, Hawkley, Hants 38
St Peter and St Paul's, Knapton, Norfolk 32
St Peter and St Paul's, Lavenham, Suffolk 59, 81, 139
St Peter and St Paul's, Leominster, Herefs 132
St Peter and St Paul's, Leybourne, Kent 93
St Peter and St Paul's, Little Gaddesden, Herts 99, 155
St Peter and St Paul's, Mappowder, Dorset 93
St Peter and St Paul's, Mitcham, Surrey 77
St Peter and St Paul's, Newport, Salop 71
St Peter and St Paul's, Peasmarsh, Sussex 155
St Peter and St Paul's, Pickering, N Yorks 111
St Peter and St Paul's, Sheinton, Salop 77
St Peter and St Paul's, Shropham, Norfolk 124
St Peter and St Paul's, Skendlesby, Lincs 145
St Peter and St Paul's, South Petherton, Som 44
St Peter and St Paul's, Swaffham, Norfolk 20, 31, 32
St Peter and St Paul's, Thruxton, Hants 130
St Peter and St Paul's, Weobley, Herefs 139
St Peter and St Paul's, Westbury on Severn, Glos 44
St Peter and St Paul's, West Newton, Norfolk 123
St Peter and St Paul's, Weston in Gordano, Som 160
St Peter Mancroft, Norwich, Norfolk 20, 88, 93, 167
St-Peter-on-the-Wall, Bradwell-on-Sea, Essex 1
St Peter's, Aberdeen 125
St Peter's, Anlaby, E Yorks 135
St Peter's, Babraham, Cambs 126
St Peter's, Bardon, Leics 125
St Peter's, Barton-upon-Humber, Lincs 20
St Peter's, Bocking, Essex 129
St Peter's, Bournemouth, Hants 94
St Peter's, Brighton, Sussex 54
St Peter's, Britford, Wilts 126
St Peter's, Bushey Heath, Herts 80, 123
St Peter's, Bushley, Worcs 148
St Peter's Cathedral, Belfast 19
St Peter's, Church Lawford, Warwicks 145
St Peter's, Cleethorpes, Lincs 145
St Peter's College chapel, Oxford 114
St Peter's, Cornhill, London 83
St Peter's, Cound, Salop 102
St Peter's, Creeting St Peter, Suffolk 31
St Peter's, Cretingham, Suffolk 99
St Peter's, Croft-on-Tees, N Yorks 88
St Peter's, Daylesford, Glos 70
St Peter's, Diddlebury, Salop 190

St Peter's, Dowanhill, Glasgow 72
St Peter's, Duddon, Ches 72
St Peter's, Dunstable, Beds 129
St Peter's, Duntisbourne Abbotts, Glos 38
St Peter's, Ealing, London 166
St Peter's, Eaton Square, London 166
St Peter's, Elerch, Cered 117
St Peter's, Englishcombe, Som 139
St Peter's, Eype, Dorset 123
St Peter's, Finsthwaite, Cumbria 127
St Peter's, Firle, Sussex 126
St Peter's, Frimley, Surrey 126
St Peter's, Gorleston-on-Sea, Norfolk 125
St Peter's, Great Cheverell, Wilts 124
St Peter's, Great Livermere, Suffolk 31
St Peter's, Hampton Lucy, Warwicks 130
St Peter's, Hanwell, Banbury, Oxon 139
St Peter's, Hascombe, Surrey 58
St Peter's, Hereford 100, 135
St Peter's, Heswall, Mersey 124, 173
St Peter's, Heversham, Cumbria 129
St Peter's, Heysham, Lancs 156
St Peter's, Huddersfield, W Yorks 116
St Peter's, Kensington, London 124
St Peter's, Ketteringham, Norfolk 139
St Peter's, Lampeter, Cered 117
St Peter's, Leeds, W Yorks 59
St Peter's, Limpsfield, Surrey 32
St Peter's, London Colney, Herts 77
St Peter's, Machynlleth, Powys 65
St Peter's, Mancetter, Warwicks 184
St Peter's, Marlow, Bucks 71
St Peter's, Maxey, Cambs 149
St Peter's, Melverley, Salop 92, 93
St Peter's, Mithian, Cornwall 82
St Peter's, Nether Hoyland, W Yorks 71, 81
St Peter's, North Tawton, Devon 38
St Peter's, Noss Mayo, Devon 74
St Peter's, Nottingham 128, 145
St Peter's, Onchan, IoM 81
St Peter's, Peebles, Borders 58
St Peter's, Preston, Lancs 73
St Peter's, Quernmore, Lancs 69
St Peter's, Racton, Sussex 130
St Peter's, Rock Ferry, Ches 66

St Peter's, Sandy, Beds 63
St Peter's, Scremerston, Northumb 57
St Peter's, Shelley, Essex 63
St Peter's, Sheringham, Norfolk 166
St Peter's, Southsea, Hants 174
St Peter's, St Albans, Herts 172
St Peter's, Stanton Lacy, Salop 34
St Peter's, Stanton Long, Salop 169
St Peter's, St Peters St, Canterbury, Kent 67
St Peter's, Stockport, Manchester 148
St Peter's, Stourton, Wilts 156
St Peter's, Stepney, London 57
St Peter's, Theberton, Suffolk 38
St Peter, St Paul and St Thomas of
    Canterbury's, Bovey Tracey, Devon 100
St Peter's, Twineham, Sussex 155
St Peter's, Vauxhall, London 70
St Peter's, Vere Street, London 62
St Peter's, Walsingham, Norfolk 30
St Peter's, Wenhaston, Suffolk 91
St Peter's, Willerby, N Yorks 135
St Peter's, Wolvercote, Oxon 126
St Peter's, Wolverhampton, W Mid 59
St Peter's, Wootton Wawen, Warwicks 128,
    176
St Peter's, Wrestlingworth, Beds 145
St Peter's, Yarmouth, Norfolk 74
St Peter's, Yaxley, Cambs 93
St Philip and St James's, Ilfracombe, Devon
    65
St Philip and St James's, Escot, Devon 73
St Philip and St James's, Groby, Leics 72
St Philip and St James's, Oxford 78
St Philip and St James's, Rock, Northumb
    168
St Philip's, Alderley Edge, Manchester 60
St Philip's, Birmingham, W Mid 53
St Philip's, Cosham, Portsmouth, Hants 59
St Philip's, Hove, Sussex 76
St Philip's, Liverpool, Mersey 73
St Philip's, Salford, Manchester 77, 173
Strand Church, Dawlish, Devon 78
Strata Florida Abbey, Cered 132
St Salvator's Chapel, St Andrew's, Fife 123
St Saviour's, Aughton, Lancs 69

St Saviour's Church for the Deaf, Acton, London 68
St Saviour's, East Retford, Notts 82
St Saviour's, Foremark, Derbys 99
St Saviour's, Ringley, Manchester 54
St Saviour's, Southwark, London 63
St Saviour's, Walcot, Bath, Som 70
St Seiriol's, Penmaenmawr, Conwy 130
St Seiriol's, Penmon, Anglesey 114, 190
St Sepulchre's, Northampton 26
St Serf's, Dunning, Perth and Kinross 114
St Silas's, Kentish Town, London 116
St Silas's, Pentonville, London 167
St Simon and St Jude's, East Dean, Sussex 160
St Simon and St Jude's, Milton under Wychwood, Oxon 78
St Simon the Apostle's, Baptist Mills, Bristol 62
St Sophia Greek Orthodox Cathedral, Bayswater, London 76
St Stephen and All Martyrs, Bolton, Manchester 76
St Stephen's, Bournemouth, Dorset 70
St Stephen's Chapel, Westminster, London 68, 72, 79, 82
St Stephen's Greek Orthodox Chapel, West Norwood Cemetery, London 76
St Stephen's, Inverness, Highland 114
St Stephen's, Islington, London 66
St Stephen's, Kingston Lacy, Dorset 70
St Stephen's, Lewisham, London 125
St Stephen's, New Hutton, Cumbria 81
St Stephen's, Norwich, Norfolk 111
St Stephen's, Old Radnor, Powys 31, 100, 102, 132, 133, 135, 149
St Stephen's, Rosslyn Hill, Hampstead, London 79
St Stephen's, Sheffield, S Yorks 61
St Stephen's, Sneinton, Notts 73
St Stephen's, Tonbridge, Kent 59
St Stephen Walbrook, London 68, 83
St Swithin's, Ganarew, Herefs 70
St Swithun's, Cheswardine, Salop 115
St Swithun's, East Grinstead, Sussex 83

St Thomas of Canterbury's, Fulham, London 71
St Thomas of Canterbury's, Salisbury, Wilts 88
St Thomas's, Brightside, Sheffield, S Yorks 61
St Thomas's, Brompton, N Yorks 156
St Thomas's, Garstang, Lancs 127
St Thomas's, Hanwell, London 117
St Thomas's, Heptonstall, W Yorks 156
St Thomas's, Keith, Moray 73
St Thomas's, Kendal, Cumbria 81
St Thomas's, Mellor, Manchester 195
St Thomas's, Monmouth 70
St Thomas's, New Brampton, Derbys 66
St Thomas's, Newman Road, Sheffield, S Yorks 61
St Thomas's, Noak Hill, Essex 77
St Thomas's, Regent Street, London 167
St Thomas's, Salisbury, Wilts 142
St Thomas's, Southwick, Wilts 70
St Thomas's, Winchelsea, Sussex 32
St Thomas the Apostle's, Hanwell, London 68
St Thomas the Martyr's, Barras Bridge, Newcastle, Tyne & W 60
St Trillo's Chapel, Rhos on Sea, Conwy 193
St Tudius's, St Tudys, Cornwall 149
St Tysilio and St Mary's, Meifod, Powys 114
St Tysilio's, Llandysilio, Powys 149
St Tysul's, Llandysul, Cered 156
St Vincent's, Sheffield, S Yorks 62, 63
St Walburge's, Preston, Lancs 64, 193
St Wedreda's, March, Cambs 20
St Werburgh's, Chester, Ches 67
St Wilfred's, Hulme, Manchester 71
St Wilfrid's, Church Norton, Sussex 117
St Wilfrid's, Harrogate, N Yorks 68
St Wilfrid's, Northenden, Manchester 60
St Wilfrid's, York 62
St Winifrede's, Holywell, Flint 118
St Winifred's, Branscombe, Devon 100
St Wulfram's, Grantham, Lincs 43, 53, 175, 195
St Wulfstan's, Malvern, Worcs 57

St Yeghiches, Kensington, London 124
Swedish Church, Liverpool, Mersey 58
T
Temple Church, London 26, 74, 117, 130, 132
Tewkesbury Abbey, Glos 49, 88, 106, 118, 123, 135, 161, 189
Thornliebank Church, Renfrewshire 80
Tillicoultry Parish Church, Clackmannanshire 78
Tolbooth St John's Church, Edinburgh 63
Trier Cathedral, Rheinland-Pfalz, Germany 190
Trinity Church, Hawick, Borders 166
Trinity College chapel, Cambridge 118, 173
Truro Cathedral, Cornwall 16, 70, 115, 167, 174, 195
Tunstall Chapel, Durham Castle 173
U
Unitarian Chapel, Manchester 54
United Reformed Church, Caterham, Surrey 166
United Reformed Church, Dawlish, Devon 78
United Secession Meeting House, Clavering Place, Newcastle, Tyne & W 63
Urquhart Parish Church, Drumnadrochit, Highland 73
W
Wadham College chapel, Oxford 118
Wakefield Cathedral, W Yorks 17, 68, 75, 167
Walcot Chapel, Bath, Som 67
Walkerburn Parish Church, Innerleithen, Borders 114
Wearmouth Monastery, Jarrow, Tyne & W 112
Wellington College chapel, Crowthorne, Berks 116
Wells Cathedral, Som 16, 26, 27, 42, 44, 48, 55, 58, 67, 68, 69, 74, 78, 79, 83, 88, 89, 98, 106, 107, 132, 142, 143, 153, 168, 175, 177, 183, 189
West Calder Parish Church, Midlothian 79
West Church, Dalkeith, Midlothian 166

West Church of Scotland, Rothesay, Argyll and Bute 82
West End Synagogue, Bayswater, London 114
Westminster Abbey, London 2, 50, 52, 57, 61, 62, 65, 67, 68, 70, 72, 73, 80, 82, 83, 84, 87, 93, 94, 100, 105, 106, 111, 115, 116, 117, 123, 127, 130, 132, 150, 168, 172, 184
Westminster Cathedral, London 18, 54, 172, 174, 193
Weybridge United Reformed Church, Surrey 78
Wigtown Parish Church, Dumfries and Galloway 73
William Temple Memorial Church, Wythenshawe, Manchester 69
Wimborne Minster, Dorset 44, 118, 132, 142, 174, 175
Winchester Cathedral, Hants 16, 43, 60, 69, 75, 79, 83, 106, 114, 115, 116, 117, 124, 126, 130, 132, 168, 174, 180, 195
Winchester College chapel, Hants 114, 118
Wishaw Church, East Lanarkshire 43
Withcote Chapel, Oakham, Rut 123
Woodside Church, Aberdeen 76
Worcester Cathedral 16, 59, 75, 93, 94, 111, 118, 124, 135, 146, 175, 195
Wythburn Church, Cumbria 113
Y
York Abbey 2
York Minster 15, 17, 26, 38, 62, 69, 72, 76, 112, 113, 124, 126, 128, 130, 132, 142, 175, 183, 193
Ysgeiviog Church, Flint 81

www.ingramcontent.com/pod-product-compliance
Lightning Source LLC
Chambersburg PA
CBHW071707160426
43195CB00012B/1602